NEW EDITION
for the 2015 exam specifications

Cambridge English
Advanced
Practice Tests Plus 2 with Key

Nick Kenny
Jacky Newbrook

TEACHING NOT JUST TESTING

Pearson Education Limited
Edinburgh Gate
Harlow
Essex CM20 2JE
England
and Associated Companies throughout the world.

www.pearsonelt.com/exams

© Pearson Education Limited 2014

The right of Nick Kenny and Jacky Newbrook to be identified as authors of this Work has been asserted by them in accordance with the Copyright, Designs and Patents Act 1988.

All rights reserved; no part of this publication may be reproduced, stored in a retrieval system, or transmitted in any form or by any means, electronic, mechanical, photocopying, recording, or otherwise without the prior written permission of the Publishers.

First published 2014
Fifth impression 2018

ISBN: 978-1-4479-6620-3 (Cambridge English Advanced Practice Tests Plus New Edition Students' Book with Key)
ISBN: 978-1-4479-6621-0 (Cambridge English Advanced Practice Tests Plus New Edition Students' Book without Key)

Set in 10.5pt Arial Regular
Printed in China (CTPS/05)

Acknowledgements
We are grateful to the following for permission to reproduce copyright material:

Extract on page 8 adapted from Fragile I'île mystérieuse risks being trampled away, *The Guardian*, 12/08/2010, p.14 (Tearse, G.), Copyright Guardian News & Media Ltd 2010; Extract on page 12 adapted from How the internet is making us stupid, *Daily Telegraph*, 28/08/2010, p.27 (Carr, N.), © Telegraph Media Group Limited 2010; Extract on page 16 adapted from Watch out Daniel Craig, *Sunday Telegraph (Life)*, 19/10/2008, L21 (Benady, A.), © Telegraph Media Group Limited 2008; Extract on page 19 adapted from The way we worked, *Sunday Telegraph (Seven)*, 22/08/2010, pp.12-14 (Lyle, P.), © Telegraph Media Group Limited 2010; Extract on page 34 adapted from Net Assets, *Eastern Daily Press Norfolk Magazine*, pp.150-51 (Wedge, N.), August 2010, with permission from EDP Norfolk Magazine; Extract on page 35 adapted from Meat on the menu: bones with cut marks show stone tools in use 3.4m years ago, *The Guardian*, 12/08/2010, p.6 (Sample, I.), Copyright Guardian News & Media Ltd 2010; Extract on page 36 adapted from On the right track, *Eastern Daily Press Norfolk Magazine*, pp.21-23 (Cassells, S.), March 2010, with permission from EDP Norfolk Magazine; Extract on page 38 adapted from How a non-policy on holidays can be the break you need, *Sunday Telegraph (Business)*, 15/08/2010, B9 (Pink, D.H.), © Telegraph Media Group Limited 2010; Extract on page 42 adapted from Fluttering down to Mexico, *Sunday Telegraph (Travel)*, 15/08/2010, T9 (Evans, S.), © Telegraph Media Group Limited 2010; Extract on page 45 adapted from Seeing through the fakes, *Daily Telegraph*, 29/06/2010, p.25 (Dorment, R.), © Telegraph Media Group Limited 2010; Interview on page 50 adapted from adapted from What do you mean you don't buy clothes?, The Times, 21/10/2003, p.11 (Davies, E.), http://women.timesonline.co.uk/tol/life_and_style/women/fashion/article862454.ece, © Emily Davies, News Syndication, 21 October 2003; Interview on page 52 adapted from Slave labour gave us our big break, *Evening Standard*, 20/06/2005, p.5 (Williams, A.), esjobs, with permission from The Evening Standard; Interview on page 53 adapted from A CurtainUp Interview, Set Designer Derek McLane by Elyse Sommer, CurtainUp.com (c) Copyright Elyse Sommer, Curtainup.com, online since 1997 with theater features, news and reviews, www.curtainup.com; Extract on page 58 adapted from Caving, *The Guardian Guide to Adventure*, 01/09/2007, p.34, Copyright Guardian News & Media Ltd 2007; Extract on page 59 adapted from Why are sunglasses cool?, The Sceptical Shopper, *Intelligent Life Magazine*, Vol.3, Issue 4, Summer 2010, p.66, © The Economist Newspaper Limited, London, 1.5.2010; Extract on page 62 from *The Glass Room*, by Kate Holmquist (Penguin Ireland 2006) pp.14-16, Copyright (c) Kathryn Holmquist, 2006. Reproduced by permission of Penguin Books Ltd; Extract on page 66 adapted from Across Britain it's secateurs at dawn, *Sunday Telegraph*, 15/08/2010, p.16 (Langley, W.), © Telegraph Media Group Limited 2010; Extract on page 69 adapted from On the trail of Kit Man, *Sunday Telegraph*, 14/02/2010, p.20 (Langley, W.), copyright © Telegraph Media Group Limited 2010; Extract on page 78 adapted from Earthly Delights, *Living France*, May, p.14 (Beart-Albert, J. 2002), with permission from Living France; Extract on page 79 adapted from Cheating? Fine by me, *Intelligent Life Magazine*, Vol.3, Issue 4, Summer, p.47 (Standage, T. 2010), © The Economist Newspaper Limited, London, 1.5.2010; Extract on page 82 adapted from The impossible moment of delight, *Daily Telegraph*, 06/08/2010, p.25 (Hensher, P.), © Telegraph Media Group Limited 2010; Extract on page 86 adapted from Rise of publishing's natural phenomenon, *Daily Telegraph (Weekend)*, 17/10/2009, W17 (Marren, P.), © Telegraph Media Group Limited 2009; Extract on page 89 adapted from The intern's tale, *Sunday Telegraph Stella magazine*, 19/08/2010, pp.30-35 (Barnes, S.), © Telegraph Media Group Limited 2010; Extract on page 99 adapted from The History of Table Tennis, http://www.robbinstabletennis.com/history.htm, Copyright (c) 2010 Robbins Table Tennis Specialities, Inc., copyrighted material with permission of Dan Robbins; Extract on page 102 adapted from Say hello to your new management guru, *Sunday Telegraph (Business)*, 01/08/2010, B8 (Peacock, L.), © Telegraph Media Group Limited 2010; Extract on page 106 adapted from Is Kieron Britain's most exciting painter?, *Daily Telegraph*, 04/08/2010, p.21 (Stanford, P.), copyright © Telegraph Media Group Limited 2010; Extract on page 109 adapted from The unstoppable spirit of inquiry, *Daily Telegraph*, 09/02/2010, p.27 (Rees, M.), © Telegraph Media Group Limited 2010; Extract on page 112 adapted from Hanging a work of art, *Metro*, p.10 (Walsh, A.), 08/04/2010, with permission from Metro; Extract on page 115 adapted from Daily News: August 13/09 10:23 am - Interview: Daniel Martin - From Rower to Cyclist, http://www.canadiancyclist.com/dailynews.php?id=17281, with pemission from Amy Smolens; Extract on page 118 adapted from Mr Expresso taught the world how to drink coffee, *Financial Times Weekend*, 19/03/2010, p.11 (Boland, V.), © The Financial Times Limited 2010. All Rights Reserved. Pearson Education Ltd is responsible for providing this adaptation of the original article; Extract on page 119 adapted from Drift diving, *The Guardian Guide to Adventure*, 01/09/2007, p.28, Copyright Guardian News & Media Ltd 2007; Extract on page 122 adapted from Cooking shouldn't be child's play, *Daily Telegraph*, 22/09/2010, p.27 (Prince, R.), © Telegraph Media Group Limited 2010; Extract on page 126 adapted from The birth of Coronation Street, *Daily Telegraph (Review)*, 11/09/2010, R29 (Little, D.), copyright © Telegraph Media Group Limited 2010; Extract on page 129 adapted from Top 15 Activities, *Daily Telegraph supplement - Norway's Northern Lights*, 18/09/2010, pp.8-10 (Derrick, S.), © Telegraph Media Group Limited 2010; Interview on page 135 adapted from Dead Interesting, *Latest Homes Sussex*, December, pp.12-14 (Kay, A. 2007), Latest Homes Ltd; Extract on page 138 adapted from Wind, Wave and Tidal Energy, *Independent, Supplement*, 20/10/2009, p.1 (McCaffery, M.), with permission from The Evening Standard; Extract on page 139 adapted from You Take the Hire Road, *Financial Times Magazine*, 12 October 2007, p.16 (Tomkins, R.), © The Financial Times Limited 2007. All Rights Reserved. Pearson Education Ltd is responsible for providing this adaptation of the original article; Extract on page 140 adapted from Outside edge: Towards a theory of finite niceness, *Financial Times Weekend*, 19/03/2010, p.13 (Engel, M.), © The Financial Times Limited 2010. All Rights Reserved. Pearson Education Ltd is responsible for providing this adaptation of the original article; Extract on page 142 from *Waiting for an Angel*, Hamish Hamilton 2002, 2003 (Habila, H. 2002) pp.61-64, Copyright (c) Helon Habila, 2002, reproduced by permission of Penguin Books Ltd; Extract on page 146 adapted from Sky's the limit for a new high society, *Daily Telegraph (Weekend)*, 11/09/2010, W14 (Middleton, C.), © Telegraph Media Group Limited 2010; Extract on page 149 adapted from What lies beneath, *Daily Telegraph*, 04/08/2010, p.17 (Ecott, T.), © Telegraph Media Group Limited 2010; Extract on page 155 adapted from Interview with Lauren Burress, Amazing Young Kayaker by Brittany, Student Editor-in-Chief, http://www.amazing-kids.org/c9, with permission from Amazing Kids!; Extract on page 155 adapted from Ben Oakley - Interview - UK National Team - Kayaking, http://www.exelement.co.uk/blog/2010/03/ben-oakley-interview-uk-national-team-ka, with kind permission from Extreme Element - Experience Day Gift Vouchers & Bookings

In some instances we have been unable to trace the owners of copyright material, and we would appreciate any information that would enable us to do so.

Photo acknowledgements
The publisher would like to thank the following for their kind permission to reproduce their photographs:

(Key: b-bottom; c-centre; l-left; r-right; t-top)

Alamy Images: Ashley Cooper 189r, David J Green 185tl, David Lyons 186b, Rene Fluger 173tr, Graficart.net 186tr, Iain Masterton 183c, Image Source 179l, James Nesterwitz 176bl, Janine Wiedel 171br, Jeremy Sutton-Hibbert 173tl, MBI 182bl, 188tl, Photo Alto 180bl, Radius Images 176r, Redsnapper 170tl, Scott Hartop 171tr, Adrian Sherratt 170r, Stuart Forster 185r, Tetra Images 185bl, 189c, Transportimage Picture Library 177l; **Corbis:** Artiga Photo 186tl, Kelly-Mooney Photography 171l, Steve Hix / Somos Images 174c; **Getty Images:** 179tr, Andrew Hetherington 183r, DAJ 182tl, Don Farrell 179br, Image Bank 177tr, 188tr, Jamie Grill 174r, Marc Debnam 174l, Nick Clements 170bl, Tom Grill 182r, Tyler Edwards 176tl; **Pearson Education:** 159, 160-161, 162; **Rex Features:** 183l, Alex Segre 177br, George Sweeney 180r, Image Source 189l; **Shutterstock.com:** Aletia 173b, Goodluz 188b; **Thinkstock:** Jack Hollingsworth 180tl

All other images © Pearson Education

Every effort has been made to trace the copyright holders and we apologise in advance for any unintentional omissions. We would be pleased to insert the appropriate acknowledgement in any subsequent edition of this publication.

Contents

Exam Overview	4
Practice Test 1	**6**
Reading and Use of English	6
Writing	20
Listening	23
Speaking	29
Practice Test 2	**32**
Reading and Use of English	32
Writing	46
Listening	49
Speaking	55
Practice Test 3	**58**
Reading and Use of English	58
Writing	70
Listening	72
Speaking	77
Practice Test 4	**78**
Reading and Use of English	78
Writing	90
Listening	92
Speaking	97
Practice Test 5	**98**
Reading and Use of English	98
Writing	110
Listening	112
Speaking	117
Practice Test 6	**118**
Reading and Use of English	118
Writing	130
Listening	132
Speaking	137
Practice Test 7	**138**
Reading and Use of English	138
Writing	150
Listening	152
Speaking	157
Speaking and Writing File	**158**
Speaking File	158
Writing File	163
Visuals for Speaking	**170**
Test 1 Speaking	170
Test 2 Speaking	173
Test 3 Speaking	176
Test 4 Speaking	179
Test 5 Speaking	182
Test 6 Speaking	185
Test 7 Speaking	188
Answer Key	191
Top 20 Questions	208

Exam Overview

The **Certificate in Advanced English** (Cambridge Advanced) is an examination at Cambridge/ALTE level 4, set at C1 level on the Common European Framework of Reference scale. Cambridge Advanced offers a high-level qualification to people wanting to use their English for professional or study purposes. There are four papers: the Reading and Use of English paper carries 40 percent of the marks, and the other three papers each carry 20 percent of the marks.

Reading and Use of English	1 hour 30 minutes
Writing	1 hour 30 minutes
Listening	40 minutes (approximately)
Speaking	15 minutes

The examination questions are task-based and simulate real-life tasks. Rubrics (instructions) are important and should be read carefully. They set the context and give important information about the tasks. There is a separate answer sheet for recording answers for the Reading and Use of English and Listening papers.

Paper	Formats	Task focus
Reading and Use of English eight parts 56 questions	**Part 1:** short text with a multiple-choice cloze task	**Part 1:** use of vocabulary, e.g. idioms, collocations, fixed phrases, complementation, phrasal verbs
	Part 2: short text with an open cloze task	**Part 2:** sentence structure and accurate use of grammar
	Part 3: short text with a word formation cloze task	**Part 3:** use of the correct form of a given word in context
	Part 4: keyword transformations	**Part 4:** use of grammatical and lexical structures
	Part 5: one long text with six multiple-choice questions	**Part 5:** reading for detailed understanding of a text, including opinion, attitude, tone, purpose, main idea
	Part 6: four short texts with four multiple-matching questions	**Part 6:** comparing and contrasting opinions and attitudes across different texts
	Part 7: one long text with a gapped paragraphs task (choosing which paragraphs fit into gaps in a base text)	**Part 7:** reading to understand text structure, coherence and cohesion
	Part 8: one long text divided into sections, or a series of short texts, with a multiple-matching task	**Part 8:** reading to locate relevant ideas and information in a text or texts

Writing **Part 1:** one compulsory task	**Part 1:** input texts provide the context and content for an essay of 220–260 words	**Part 1:** producing an essay based on two points given in the input text. Candidates have to evaluate the points and express their own opinions, giving reasons.
Part 2: one task from a choice of three	**Part 2:** instructions give information about context, text type, target reader and purpose of a text of 220–260 words	**Part 2:** writing for a specific reader using appropriate layout and register. Possible genres are: letter, proposal, report and review.
Listening four parts 30 questions	**Part 1:** three short unrelated extracts with two multiple-choice questions on each	**Part 1:** understanding gist, feeling, attitude, opinion, speaker purpose, etc.
	Part 2: long text with a sentence-completion task	**Part 2:** locating and recording specific information
	Part 3: long text with multiple-choice questions	**Part 3:** understanding attitude and opinion
	Part 4: series of five monologues on a theme with a multiple-matching task	**Part 4:** understanding gist, attitude, main points, etc.
Speaking four parts	**Part 1:** general conversation	**Part 1:** general interactional and social language
	Part 2: individual long turn based on visual prompts	**Part 2:** comparing and speculating
	Part 3: two-way conversation between candidates based on a question and written prompts	**Part 3:** giving and eliciting opinions, negotiating, turn-taking, etc.
	Part 4: discussion on topics related to Part 3	**Part 4:** expressing and justifying opinions and ideas

TEST 1
READING AND USE OF ENGLISH

Guidance: Parts 1–4

About the paper

The Reading and Use of English paper lasts for one hour and thirty minutes. It contains eight parts, and has a total of fifty-six questions.

There are texts of varying lengths, with a range of text type and style of writing, for example extracts from newspapers, magazines, websites and novels, as well as other short texts.

Part 1
In Part 1, you read a short text and complete a multiple-choice cloze task. Eight words or phrases have been removed from the text. For each gap, you have to choose from four options the word or phrase which fits best.

Part 2
In Part 2, you read a short text and complete an open cloze. Eight words have been removed from the text. You have to complete the gaps.

Part 3
In Part 3, you read a short text and complete a word formation task. Eight words have been removed from the text. You are given the base form of each missing word and you have to create the correct form of the base word to fit the gap.

Part 4
In Part 4, you read six pairs of sentences and complete a key-word transformation task. The pairs of sentences have the same meaning, but are expressed in different ways. Three to six words have been removed from the second sentence, and one of these words, the key word, is given as a prompt. You have to complete the second sentence, using the key word.

How to do the paper

Part 1
- Read the text, ignoring the gaps, to get a general understanding.
- Only one of the options (A–D) fits the gap.
- Check the words before and after the gap, e.g. some words can only be followed by one preposition.
- Some questions focus on linking words and require an understanding of the whole passage.
- If you are not sure which word to choose, eliminate the options you know are wrong.
- When you have finished, read your completed text again and check that it makes sense.

Part 2
- Read the text, ignoring the gaps, to get a general understanding.
- Think about the missing words. Each gap only needs one word, usually a grammatical word, e.g. pronoun, linker or preposition, rather than topic vocabulary.
- Carefully read the text around each gap and think about what type of word is missing, e.g. dependent preposition or part of a fixed expression.
- When you have finished, read your completed text again and check that it makes sense.

Part 3
- Read the text, ignoring the gaps, to get a general understanding.
- Decide which type of word is needed in each gap, e.g. noun, adjective, adverb. Look at the whole sentence, not just at the line including the gap.
- Look at the word in capitals on the right of the gap. You may need to add a prefix or suffix, or make other changes. More than one change may be required.
- Check to see if nouns should be singular or plural.
- When you have finished, read your completed text again and check that it makes sense.

Part 4
- Look at the key word. What type of word is it? What usually follows it, e.g. an infinitive, a preposition, or could it be part of a phrasal verb?
- Think about the other words that need to change in the new word order, e.g. an adjective may become a noun or vice versa.
- Your answer may include words or expressions not used in the first sentence, but these must express exactly the same idea.
- Remember that contracted words count as two words, e.g. won't = will not.

**TEST 1
READING AND
USE OF ENGLISH**

Guidance: Parts 5–8

About the paper

Part 5
In Part 5, there is one long text to read. You have to answer six four-option, multiple-choice questions, which follow the order of the text.

Part 6
In Part 6, there is a set of four short texts on the same topic. There are four prompts which report the opinions and views of the writers of the four texts. You have to match each prompt to the correct text or writer.

Part 7
In Part 7, there is one long text from which six paragraphs have been removed. These are placed in jumbled order after the text, along with an extra paragraph that does not fit into any of the gaps. You have to use your knowledge of grammar, vocabulary, referencing and text structure in order to reconstruct the text.

Part 8
In Part 8, there is either one long text that has been divided into sections, or a series of short texts on the same topic. There are also ten prompts which report information and ideas from the text(s). You have to match each prompt to the correct text or section of text.

How to do the paper

Part 5
- Read the text quickly to get a general understanding of what it's about and how it's organised.
- Read through the questions or question stems without looking at the options (A–D), and underline keywords in the question stem.
- The questions follow the order of the text. Find the piece of text where a question is answered and read it carefully, underlining keywords and phrases.
- Try to answer the question. Then read the four options (A–D) and choose the one that is closest to your own answer. Look for the same meaning expressed in different ways.
- Check that the other options are all clearly wrong. If you're still unsure, see which of the options can be ruled out, and why.

Part 6
- Read the prompts (37–40) first, underlining key words and ideas. There are two main types of question. In most questions you are told which piece of text to read and which idea you are looking for. Do these questions first. In these questions:
  - Read through the section of text mentioned in the question prompt and find the relevant topic or idea. Read this carefully to make sure you understand what the writer thinks about it.
  - The question prompt then asks you to compare the writer's ideas on the topic with those of the other three writers. It may ask you who has the same ideas and opinions, or who expresses different ones.
  - Now read the other three texts quickly to locate references to the topic or idea. Then read these sections carefully to make sure you have found the writer who has the same or different ideas.
- In the other type of question, you are told the topic or idea and asked to find the writer who has a different opinion from the others on that topic. Do this question last. In this question:
  - Read all the texts quickly to locate references to the topic or idea mentioned in the question prompt.
  - Read these sections of text carefully to see which writer has different ideas on the topic to the other three.

Part 7
- Read the base text first, ignoring the gaps, to get a general understanding of what it's about and how it's organised.
- Next, carefully read the text around each gap and think about what type of information might be missing.
- Read paragraphs A–G. Check for topic and language links with the base text. Highlight words that relate to people, places, events and any time references. This will help you follow the development of the argument or narrative.
- Choose the best option to fit each gap. Make sure that all the pronouns and vocabulary references are clear.
- Once you've finished, re-read the completed text to be sure that it makes sense with the answers in the gaps.

Part 8
- In Part 8, you don't need to read the whole text or texts first. The text is long and contains information that you don't need to answer the questions.
- Read the prompts (47–56) first, underlining keywords and ideas.
- Read through the text(s) quickly and find information or ideas that are relevant to each question.
- For each question, when you find the relevant piece of text, read it very carefully to make sure it completely matches the meaning of the prompt.
- The ideas in each prompt are likely to occur in more than one section of the text, but only one text exactly matches the idea. You need to read all these sections carefully.

Tip Strip

Question 3: These words all have a similar meaning, but which one is used to refer to a precise location?

Question 5: These are all linking phrases, but only one of them tells you that another surprising thing will follow.

Question 8: Only one of these verbs is usually used together with the noun 'opportunity'.

Part 1

For questions **1–8**, read the text below and decide which answer (**A, B, C** or **D**) best fits each gap. There is an example at the beginning (**0**).

In the exam, mark your answers **on the separate answer sheet**.

Example:

0 A hit   **B** knocked   **C** banged   **D** beat

The Mysterious Isle

In the early morning of 23 January, 2009, the most powerful storm for a decade (**0**) …….. western France. With wind speeds in (**1**) …….. of 120 miles per hour, it flattened forests, (**2**) …….. down power lines and caused massive destruction to buildings and roads. But it also left behind an extraordinary creation. Seven miles out to sea at the (**3**) …….. where the Atlantic Ocean meets the estuary of the River Gironde, a small island had (**4**) …….. out of the water. Locals soon gave it the name The Mysterious Isle. What was so remarkable, (**5**) …….. its sudden apparition, was the fact that the island (**6**) …….. intact in what is often quite a hostile sea environment. It could well become a permanent (**7**) …….. .

Scientists quickly realised that the island's appearance (**8**) …….. a unique opportunity to study the creation and development of a new ecosystem. Within months, it had been colonised by seabirds, insects and vegetation.

1 **A** surplus   **B** advance   **C** excess   **D** put

2 **A** fetched   **B** brought   **C** carried   **D** sent

3 **A** scene   **B** mark   **C** stage   **D** point

4 **A** risen   **B** grown   **C** lifted   **D** surfaced

5 **A** in spite of   **B** instead of **C** apart from **D** on account of

6 **A** prolonged   **B** remained   **C** resided   **D** persevered

7 **A** item   **B** issue   **C** matter   **D** feature

8 **A** delivered   **B** awarded   **C** proposed   **D** offered

TEST 1: READING AND USE OF ENGLISH

Tip Strip

Question 9: Which preposition is used with the verb *to* 'invest'?

Question 11: Which word completes the common expression that tells you that another point is going to be made?

Question 12: You need a possessive pronoun here.

Part 2

For questions **9–16**, read the text below and think of the word which best fits each gap. Use only **one** word in each gap. There is an example at the beginning (**0**).

In the exam, write your answers **IN CAPITAL LETTERS on the separate answer sheet**.

Example: | 0 | G | R | E | A | T | | | | | | | | | |

Choosing Binoculars

For independent travellers, a good pair of binoculars often represents an essential piece of kit. Unless you're planning to do a (**0**) …….. deal of bird-watching or other specialist activities, however, there's no need to invest (**9**) …….. a full-size pair. Compact binoculars are fine when (**10**) …….. comes to general all-purpose viewing in good light. What's (**11**) …….., they are certainly easier to carry round.

Everyone has (**12**) …….. own idea of what makes a comfortable pair of binoculars. When you're considering (**13**) …….. of the many brands and models on the market you should choose, don't base your decision on price alone. A better idea (**14**) …….. to pop down to your local photographic store and (**15**) …….. those that fall within your price range a test run.

(**16**) …….. you might like the look of a particular pair, you may not find the handling and viewing position comfortable. Finally, make sure the binoculars come with a decent case and a comfortable neck strap. These details can make all the difference when you're out in the field.

Part 3

Tip Strip

Question 17: You need to add a prefix to create the opposite meaning of this word.

Question 19: Add another word to 'let' to form a compound word which completes a common collocation with 'retail'. Your answer needs to be plural.

Question 23: What noun can you make from this verb? It means 'use'.

Question 24: Add a suffix to make a noun. Which letter from the verb is dropped?

For questions **17–24**, read the text below. Use the word given in capitals at the end of some of the lines to form a word that fits in the gap **in the same line**. There is an example at the beginning (**0**).

In the exam, write your answers **IN CAPITAL LETTERS on the separate answer sheet**.

Example: **0** D A I L Y

The Inventor of the Bar Code

Although you may never have heard of Joe Woodland, you almost certainly use his invention on a (**0**) ………. basis. **DAY**
For Joe was the man who came up with the idea of the bar code – that little box containing parallel lines of (**17**) ………. **REGULAR**
width and (**18**) ………. that you find on the packaging **LONG**
of most products that are offered for sale at retail (**19**) ………. **LET**
world wide. Joe Woodland actually invented the bar code way back in 1949, when the manager of a supermarket in Philadelphia asked him to design an electronic (**20**) ………. **CHECK**
system which would be both simple and effective. The purpose of the bar code is to store (**21**) ………. information **CODED**
about the product, which (**22**) ………. speeds up the **POTENTIAL**
process of recording sales and restocking the shelves.
The idea was way ahead of its time however, and didn't find any immediate practical (**23**) ………. . It was the **APPLY**
(**24**) ………. of laser gun technology decades later which **ARRIVE**
allowed Joe's invention to come into everyday use.

Part 4

Tip Strip

Question 25: You need a phrase that talks about time. It also has a definite article.

Question 26: The key word is an adjective. Which verb usually comes before it?

Question 27: The key word comes first in the gap, and needs to be followed by an adjective and noun combination. Change two words from the input sentence to make this expression. You also need to add an article.

Question 29: Find the adjective in the input sentence. Use the noun of this word in the new phrase.

For questions **25–30**, complete the second sentence so that it has a similar meaning to the first sentence, using the word given. **Do not change the word given.** You must use between **three** and **six** words, including the word given. Here is an example (**0**).

Example:

0 Chloe would only eat a pizza if she could have a mushroom topping.

ON

Chloe .... a mushroom topping when she ate a pizza.

The gap can be filled with the words 'insisted on having', so you write:

| Example: | 0 | INSISTED ON HAVING |

In the exam, write **only** the missing words **IN CAPITAL LETTERS on the separate answer sheet**.

---

25 We were late arriving at the cinema and so missed the start of the film.

BY

The film had .... we arrived at the cinema.

26 Simon found the recipe book very hard to follow.

DIFFICULTY

Simon .... in following the recipe book.

27 The ice-skater performed faultlessly and received full marks.

GAVE

The ice-skater .... and received full marks.

28 I was just about to call you to see what time you were coming.

POINT

I .... you to see what time you were coming.

29 Harry was disappointed to hear the news that the match had been cancelled.

CAME

News of the cancellation of the match .... to Harry.

30 At this time of year, the area is often affected by violent storms.

FEELS

At this time of year, the area often .... violent storms.

TEST 1: READING AND USE OF ENGLISH

Part 5

You are going to read an article about the effects of digital media on people's minds. For questions **31–36**, choose the answer (**A**, **B**, **C** or **D**) which you think fits best according to the text.

In the exam, mark your answers **on the separate answer sheet**.

Is the internet making us stupid?

In an article in *Science*, Patricia Greenfield, a developmental psychologist who runs UCLA's Children's Digital Media Center, reviewed dozens of studies on how different media technologies influence our cognitive abilities. Some of the studies indicated that certain computer tasks, like playing video games, increase the speed at which people can shift their focus among icons and other images on screens. Other studies, however, found that such rapid shifts in focus, even if performed adeptly, result in less rigorous and 'more automatic' thinking.

In one experiment at an American university, half a class of students was allowed to use internet-connected laptops during a lecture, while the other half had to keep their computers shut. Those who browsed the web performed much worse on a subsequent test of how well they retained the lecture's content. Earlier experiments revealed that as the number of links in an online document goes up, reading comprehension falls, and as more types of information are placed on a screen, we remember less of what we see.

Greenfield concluded that 'every medium develops some cognitive skills at the expense of others'. Our growing use of screen-based media, she said, has strengthened visual-spatial intelligence, which can strengthen the ability to do jobs that involve keeping track of lots of rapidly changing signals, like piloting a plane or monitoring a patient during surgery. However, that has been accompanied by 'new weaknesses in higher-order cognitive processes', including 'abstract vocabulary, mindfulness, reflection, inductive problem-solving, critical thinking and imagination'. We're becoming, in a word, shallower.

Studies of our behaviour online support this conclusion. German researchers found that web browsers usually spend less than ten seconds looking at a page. Even people doing academic research online tend to 'bounce' rapidly between documents, rarely reading more than a page or two, according to a University College London study. Such mental juggling takes a big toll. In a recent experiment at Stanford University, researchers gave various cognitive tests to 49 people who do a lot of media multitasking and 52 people who multitask much less frequently. The heavy multitaskers performed poorly on all the tests. They were more easily distracted, had less control over their attention, and were much less able to distinguish important information from trivia. The researchers were surprised by the results. They expected the intensive multitaskers to have gained some mental advantages. That wasn't the case, though. In fact, the multitaskers weren't even good at multitasking. 'Everything distracts them,' said Clifford Nass, one of the researchers.

It would be one thing if the ill effects went away as soon as we turned off our computers and mobiles, but they don't. The cellular structure of the human brain, scientists have discovered, adapts readily to the tools we use to find, store and share information. By changing our habits of mind, each new technology strengthens certain neural pathways and weakens others. The alterations shape the way we think even when we're not using the technology. The pioneering neuroscientist Michael Merzenich believes our brains are being 'massively remodelled' by our ever-intensifying use of the web and related media. In 2009, he said that he was profoundly worried about the cognitive consequences of the constant distractions and interruptions the internet bombards us with. The long-term effect on the quality of our intellectual lives, he said, could be 'deadly'.

Not all distractions are bad. As most of us know, if we concentrate too intensively on a tough problem, we can get stuck in a mental rut. However, if we let the problem sit unattended for a time, we often return to it with a fresh perspective and a burst of creativity. Research by Dutch psychologist Ap Dijksterhuis indicates that such breaks in our attention give our unconscious mind time to grapple with a problem, bringing to bear information and cognitive processes unavailable to conscious deliberation. We usually make better decisions, his experiments reveal, if we shift our attention away from a mental challenge for a time.

But Dijksterhuis's work also shows that our unconscious thought processes don't engage with a problem until we've clearly and consciously defined what the problem is. If we don't have a particular goal in mind, he writes, 'unconscious thought does not occur'. The constant distractedness that the Net encourages is very different from the kind of temporary, purposeful diversion of our mind that refreshes our thinking. What we seem to be sacrificing in our surfing and searching is our capacity to engage in the quieter, attentive modes of thought that underpin contemplation, reflection and introspection.

Tip Strip

Question 31: Look for what Patricia's work actually involved.

Question 35: You need to read the whole paragraph to get this answer.

Question 36: Look before the name in the text to see what point his research supports.

31 What do we learn about Patricia Greenfield's research in the first paragraph?

  A It focused on problems resulting from use of media technologies.
  B It did not produce consistent patterns in connection with computer use.
  C It involved collating the results of work done by other people.
  D It highlighted differences between people when using computers.

32 Two of the experiments mentioned in the second paragraph concerned

  A the amount of attention people pay to what they see on computers.
  B the connection between computer use and memory.
  C the use and non-use of computers for studying.
  D changes that happen if people's computer use increases.

33 One of Greenfield's conclusions was that

  A certain claims about the advantages of computer use are false.
  B computer use has reduced a large number of mental abilities.
  C people do not care about the effects of computer use on their minds.
  D too much emphasis has been placed on the benefits of computer use.

34 One of the pieces of research mentioned in the fourth paragraph indicated that

  A some people are better at multitasking than others.
  B 'mental juggling' increases the mental abilities of only a few people.
  C beliefs about the effectiveness of multitasking are false.
  D people read online material less carefully than other material.

35 What is the writer's purpose in the fifth paragraph?

  A to advise on how to avoid the bad effects of new media technology
  B to present opposing views on the consequences of use of new media technology
  C to warn about the damage done by use of new media technology
  D to summarise the findings of the previously-mentioned research

36 The writer mentions Ap Dijksterhuis's research in order to make the point that

  A not all research supports beliefs about the dangers of computer use.
  B the mind functions in ways that computers cannot.
  C problem-solving can involve very complex mental processes.
  D uninterrupted concentration on something is not always a good thing.

TEST 1: READING AND USE OF ENGLISH

Part 6

You are going to read four extracts about a new high-rise building. For questions **37–40**, choose from the extracts **A–D**. The extracts may be chosen more than once.

The Pinnacle

Four writers give their opinions about the city's newest high-rise building.

A

Inhabitants of our capital city rarely get excited about modern architecture, only really sitting up and taking notice when new structures reach out above the neighbouring roofline and pierce the horizon. So it is with the Pinnacle – the country's tallest new office block which is nearing completion. It seems that, in the world of high-rise architecture, no sooner has a dizzying new height been achieved than work starts on the next contender for that particular crown. By all accounts, however, the height and scale of the Pinnacle will take some beating, and the same can be said for its aesthetic impact. Shaped like a tall elegant pyramid, the building seems set to become a mainstay on the itinerary of visitors to the city, who will be unable to resist its photographic opportunities. Located in the unfashionable east of the city, the building will also bring work and development to an area that has long been in need of it.

B

Though not yet finished, the Pinnacle's intrusion into our horizon ensures that most citizens are ready to offer opinions about it long before we've had the chance to work in its offices, sleep in its hotel, or visit the viewing gallery at the top. There is something about tall buildings that attracts us, as is witnessed by the queues of day trippers eagerly awaiting their chance to ride to the top of the city's current tallest building on the other side of the river. Some have questioned the Pinnacle's location in an otherwise undeveloped quarter, dwarfing as it does the eighteenth-century houses below it. But I would disagree. The graceful structure blends in remarkably well with its immediate environment, and local people have benefited from the improved public transport links that have been put in place as a result of the project.

C

Wonderfully designed it may be, but the Pinnacle is hardly a thing of beauty. More important, however, is the wider significance of the project. It's a fool who argues that a city should not grow, should be preserved as a historic monument for the benefit of the tourist industry, but to look upon the Pinnacle is to see a monumental reminder that most citizens have no stake in the way their environment is changing. There's no doubt it stands to regenerate a rather run down part of the city, but how keen are the local residents on having this monstrous structure spring up literally on their doorstep? The central business district, already the site of other high-rise structures, could surely have accommodated the intrusion more easily.

D

Despite our fascination with the rather brutal visual impact the new structure has on its surroundings, it is the wider impact of the Pinnacle that may prove to be its greatest legacy. And it's a legacy that may endure beyond the building's inevitably short-lived reign as the city's tallest structure. So many people will work in the building that the city's public transport network has had to be radically rethought in order to accommodate it, a move which will benefit commuters and locals alike for years to come, even if they never go up the tower itself. This is why the decision to build the structure in a forgotten corner of the city, originally perceived as rather unwise, has proved a stroke of genius. There can be little doubt that visitors to the city will be drawn to the east bank by the building, not only for the experience of riding in its high-speed lifts, but for the fine view of the city's other skyscrapers that can be gained from the viewing terrace on the roof.

Tip Strip

Question 37: Look for words in Extract A that refer to how the building looks, and show the writer's opinion of the design. Read the sentences before and after this word carefully. Does the writer like the appearance of the building? Which of the other writers uses similar language to talk about how the building looks?

Question 38: Look at Extract D and underline what the writer says about 'visitors to the city'. Read what the other three writers say about tourists. Which one expresses the same idea as Extract D?

Question 40: Underline the sentences in each text that talk about the part of the city where the building is. Three of the writers think it was a good place to build it – which one disagrees?

TEST 1: READING AND USE OF ENGLISH

Which writer

supports the opinion put forward in Extract A about the appearance of the building? | 37 |

expresses the same view as Extract D regarding the probable role of the building as a tourist attraction? | 38 |

disagrees with Extract D about how long the building is likely to hold a particular record? | 39 |

puts forward a different view from others about the choice of site for the building? | 40 |

Part 7

You are going to read a magazine article about a training session with a stuntman – someone who performs the dangerous and exciting actions in films. Six paragraphs have been removed from the article. Choose from the paragraphs **A–G** the one which fits each gap (**41–46**). There is one extra paragraph which you do not need to use.

In the exam, mark your answers **on the separate answer sheet**.

Learning to be an action hero

Alex Benady has a lesson in fitness from a film stuntman.

'Now see if you can touch your toes,' says Steve Truglia. As a former Army physical training instructor, he is used to dealing with less than sharp trainees. But how hard can that be? Fifteen seconds of blind confusion ensue before I finally locate my feet. The truth is I can't reach much past my knees and the effort of doing even that seems to be rupturing my kidneys.

41

These days, Steve is one of Britain's top stuntmen. You might have seen him in various well-known action movies. Although I have no real desire to enter rooms through the ceiling or drive into walls at high speed like him, I wouldn't mind looking a bit more like an action hero, so Steve is showing me exactly how he stays 'stunt fit'. 'It's a very particular, very extreme kind of fitness,' he explains, 'consisting of stamina, flexibility, strength and core stability, balance and coordination.'

42

Right now, we are working on spatial awareness, a subset of coordination which he says is key to being a stuntman. 'It's easy to get disorientated when you are upside down. But if you have a high fall and you don't know exactly where your body is, you won't be able to land safely. If you are lucky, you'll just end up with some serious injuries.' From where I'm hanging, that sounds like a pretty positive outcome. Yet it had all started so well.

43

He usually does this at the end of the session. 'On set, you can guarantee that if you have a big dangerous stunt, you won't do it until the end of the day, when you are completely exhausted. So I design my training regime to reflect that.' At first, this part of the session consists of standard strength-building exercises: dips – pushing yourself up and down on the arms of a high chair, for triceps and chest; some bench presses, again for chest; lower back exercises; and curls to build up biceps. Then Steve introduces me to the chinning bar, which involves movements for building strength in your back and arms.

44

We move on to balance and coordination, starting by walking along three-inch-wide bars. Not easy, but do-able. 'Now turn round,' says Steve. Not easy and not do-able. I fall off. Now he shows me how to jump on to the bar. Guess what? I can't do that either. Then he points to a two-inch-wide bar at about waist height.

45

Now it's outside for some elementary falls. He shows me how to slap the ground when you land, to earth your kinetic energy. He throws me over his shoulder and I arc gracefully through the air, landing painlessly. But when it's my turn, I don't so much throw him as trip him up and he smashes into the ground at my feet, well short of the crash mat. Sorry, Steve.

46

At least I'll never suffer from an anatomical anomaly – which is what happens when your thighs are so massive, the other parts of your anatomy look rather small by comparison.

Tip Strip

Question 41: Look for a word in the options that means 'weak'.
Question 43: The text before the gap says 'Yet it had all started so well.' Look for an option that talks about the beginning of something.
Question 45: The base text is talking about a bar. Find this word in the options.

A 'We'll just warm up first,' says Steve as we enter the Muscleworks Gym in East London. Five minutes on the recumbent cycle and I'm thinking this stunt lark is a piece of cake. Then we start some strength work, vital for hanging off helicopters, leaping off walls, etc.

B It's clear that I have some work to do before I am ready to amaze the world with my dripping physique and daredevil stunts. But I have taken one comforting piece of knowledge from my experience.

C Instead, we work on what he calls our 'cores'. 'All powerful movements originate from the centre of the body out, and never from the limbs alone,' he says. So we'll be building up the deep stabilising muscles in our trunks, the part of the body from the waist to the neck.

D He reckons anyone can get there with a couple of gym sessions and a couple of runs a week. 'The key is variety: do as many different types of exercise as possible. Even 20 minutes a day will do.'

E Much to my surprise, I can actually do a few. Then he says innocently: 'Just raise your legs so they are at 90 degrees to your body.' Pain, pain, pain. 'Now open and close your legs in a scissor motion.' I manage to do that once.

F You may think that this sounds a bit feeble. But I was dangling upside down at the time, suspended from a bar by a pair of gravity boots.

G With feet firmly together, he leaps on, balances himself, leaps off, on, off. For good measure he circuits the gym, leaping from one to another, using his thighs to generate the power to leap and the power to stop himself from falling when he lands. Despite his heavy build, he has the feet of a ballerina.

Tip Strip

Question 48: Look for all the years and dates in the texts. Which one is linked to 'a significant event'?

Question 51: Look for bad aspects of the jobs that have changed over the years. Which text talks about improvements?

Question 53: Look at the end of all the texts. At the end of which text do you find information about the type of people doing it?

Question 56: The question talks about Britain. Look for a reference to 'elsewhere'.

Part 8

You are going to read a magazine article about jobs in Britain that used to be common but are uncommon now. For questions **47–56**, choose from the sections of the article (**A–D**). The sections may be chosen more than once.

In the exam, mark your answers **on the separate answer sheet**.

In connection with which of the jobs are the following mentioned?

how hard it can be to find someone who does this job	47
a significant event involving people doing this job	48
the kind of people who need this kind of expertise	49
a comment on how little interest there is now in this kind of work	50
improvements that were made for people doing this job	51
a prediction that proved to be accurate	52
the kind of people still doing this job	53
a positive result of not many people doing this job anymore	54
something that people doing the job now find surprising	55
the reason why this job is no longer common in Britain but exists elsewhere	56

TEST 1: READING AND USE OF ENGLISH

THE WAY WE WORKED

Britain's disappearing jobs, and the people keeping them alive.

A Advertising signwriter

A couple of years into his career, Wayne Tanswell told his father he was in a dying trade. Having left school in 1980, to train in sign-painting, he then watched as high streets moved to plastic shop-front lettering. 'But my dad said: "Wait and stick at it; these things will come back. The more technology comes into it, the more you'll be seen as a specialist." He had a lot of foresight.'

Technology has helped Tanswell. Now that his trade has become such a rare one, he is summoned far from his home, with work ranging from period numerals by the doors of London houses to shop fronts in villages with strict planning restrictions.

Sam Roberts curates an online archive, blog and burgeoning maps of hand-painted wall ads. These signs, painted onto brickwork, once kept sign-painters in demand. Their work remains, faded but unmistakable, in many cities. 'Mention them to people and they'll look quizzical,' Roberts says, 'but next time they see you, they'll have started to spot them.'

B Typewriter repairer

Though a few thousand new electric models are still sold in Britain each year, the typewriter is not what it once was. Search online for a once-indispensable brand of correction fluid and the first page of hits will be for something completely different. Search your high street for a typewriter repairman and your chances of a result at all are ribbon-thin.

There are still a handful of typewriter repair businesses operating in Britain, mostly on the South Coast. They not only serve septuagenarian retirees and technophobes (and diehard novelists who shun PCs), but are also approached by people weaned on digital keyboards who see typewriters as relics of a distant past.

In 1986, George Blackman set up an equipment and typewriter repair shop. He trained on the old manual machines and Blackman's employees still find themselves working on those beautiful, formidably heavy old machines. 'It amazes us the price the old manual machines sell for on the internet,' one explains, and their new buyers want them spruced up when they've splashed out. They get the old machines gleaming and operational by raiding the vast collection of spare parts they've accumulated over the years (and you can't buy them any more).

C Matchgirl

There's a light that never goes out, even if it burns less brightly than it once did. Female match-makers have long been a celebrated part of British labour history. In 1888, thousands of matchgirls at the Bryant and May factory in London famously went on strike to protest over conditions. Over subsequent decades, the long hours, tiny pay packets and exposure to toxic chemicals were addressed before the industry largely relocated its production to other countries where labour was cheaper.

Today, there are still female match-makers in Britain – in Bristol, at the country's last match factory, Octavius Hunt. The company long ago diversified into other products but still makes matches. Its commercial director, Kerry Healey, says that the majority of staff are still female. 'Matches are a small part of our business, but an important one. Depending on the size of orders, we have between two and 12 people working in the department, of which two are men – so it's still mainly female.'

D Lacquerer

Since the first pieces of Oriental lacquer work arrived on the Continent in the seventeenth century, European craftsmen have attempted to replicate the incredible effects of this time-consuming process. But by the 1920s, chemical shortcuts had been developed to replace the Japanese approach of applying, sanding and polishing numerous layers of paint.

Today, there are only a handful of traditional lacquerers. Pedro da Costa Felgueiras, who runs the London Lacquer Studios, has been the capital's go-to guy for authentic lacquer work and period pigments for over a decade. In a world where even 'most paints are just plastic and dye', he's called in to provide historically accurate colours for walls and furniture from the Seventeenth to the Nineteenth century and to lacquer new things the old way, with 30 or 40 coats of paint, each being left to dry and then being polished before the next. 'I remember a friend once telling me to be careful with my recipes as someone might steal and use them,' he recalls. 'My answer was: even if I show them how to do it, no one wants to.'

TEST 1 WRITING

Guidance

About the paper

There are two parts to the paper. In each part you have to complete one task. You have 1 hour 30 minutes to complete the whole paper, and each answer carries equal marks.

Part 1

Part 1 is compulsory. You have to choose two from three points on a given topic and discuss them in an essay. You should write 220–260 words. In your essay you may have to explain which of the two points you think is most important. You will always have to give reasons for your opinions.

The focus of assessment is how well you achieve the task, which is discursive. You must cover both points required with enough detail to fulfil the task. The target reader must be able to understand your ideas and opinions, and your reasons for them.

Be careful to write a coherent and logical essay. Don't include things that are irrelevant, as this may mean that you don't cover the required points adequately. This will have a negative effect on the target reader.

Part 2

Part 2 has three questions, from which you must choose only one to answer. You should write 220–260 words.

You may be asked to write a letter, a proposal, a report or a review.

In this part you are given a clear context, an indication of what to include and a reason for writing, but you can still use your imagination and be inventive.

How to do the paper

General points

- Spend at least 10 minutes thinking about and planning your writing. Your answers should be well-organised with clear linking of ideas between sentences and paragraphs. In the exam you won't have enough time to write a rough answer and a final, neat copy, but if you plan properly this will not be necessary.
- Make sure your writing is legible. If necessary, leave a line between paragraphs so that it is clear where one paragraph ends and the next begins.
- Everything you write should have a beginning, middle and an end. Remember to use an appropriate style and layout, both for the type of text and the person you are writing to.
- Use a range of language, including both vocabulary and grammatical structures. At this level, your language should not be too simple.
- Make sure your answer is neither too long nor too short. If you write too much, you may include irrelevant information, which could be confusing and have a negative effect on the target reader. If your answer is too short, you may not cover all the required points.
- Leave enough time to read through your answer. You should check that you have included all the points necessary to answer the question and that you have given enough detail on each point. Make sure you have included all the language functions required in the task, and that you have used a range of appropriate language. You should also check for mistakes in grammar and spelling (you can use British or American spelling, but try not to mix them up).

Part 1

- Read the instructions carefully to clarify what the topic is and what you have to write about.
- Make sure you understand the situation, the context and all the points you have been given.
- Process all the information before you choose which two points you want to write about and decide what your conclusion will be. Make sure you have enough ideas to write about the points you choose and that you can think of reasons for your opinions.
- Plan your answer carefully. Make sure your conclusion follows logically from your argument. Remember you can use the opinions given in the task if you want to, but you don't have to.
- Don't copy words or phrases from the input material – just use the ideas.

Part 2

- Read through all the questions in Part 2. Before you choose which one to answer, think about what each task involves, so that you are confident that you understand everything you have to do. Always check the context, reason for writing and the target reader. Each task has a given target reader and purpose; these will determine what register and kind of language is appropriate for your answer.
- Think about what kind of writing you are best at. If you are good with more formal language and expressing your ideas concisely, you might consider writing a report or a proposal,. If you are good at writing in an interesting way, you might choose a review. However, also consider whether you have enough ideas for the topic of each task – don't just choose a task because you like that particular text type.

Part 1

Tip Strip

Question 1:
- Read all the input and choose which two points to discuss in your essay. It may help you if you think about positive and negative ideas about each one, with examples to support your views.
  Decide which one has had the most effect on people's lives. Make sure that your argument and examples support your conclusion.
- Remember to include a clear introduction to the topic, and a conclusion that follows your argument logically. Don't use words or phrases from the given opinions in your answer. If you use the ideas in the comments, rephrase them in your own words.
- Link your ideas clearly and coherently using a range of connectors.
- Use a range of vocabulary and language functions, and remember to explain and justify the points you want to make.

You **must** answer this question. Write your answer in **220–260** words in an appropriate style. In the exam, write your answer **on the separate answer sheet provided**.

1 Following a class discussion on how technology has affected the way we live today, you have made the notes below.

Which aspect of our daily lives has been affected most by technology?

- communication
- relationships
- working life

Some opinions expressed in the discussion:

'It's great to be able to communicate with people 24 hours a day.'

'It's so hard to make personal relationships – everyone's online all the time.'

'People have an easier working life because they can work from home.'

Write an essay discussing **two** of the points in your notes. You should **explain which aspect of daily life you think has been most affected** by technology, **giving reasons** in support of your answer.

You may, if you wish, make use of the opinions expressed in the discussion, but you should use your own words as far as possible.

Tip Strip

Question 2:
- Your proposal should be written in a semi-formal or formal style.
- You need to give all the information as clearly as possible, so headings may be appropriate.
- Bullet points are useful for making recommendations, but if you use them you must show a range of language in the rest of your proposal.
- Check what language functions you should use. In this task you have to describe the current situation, evaluate what new students need and suggest new activities, giving your reasons.

Question 3:
- Decide on your film, making sure that you have enough ideas about it to write a complete answer.
- Your aim in this task is to clarify why the film should be included in the set of DVDs, so think of interesting ways of expressing your ideas so that you engage the readers.
- Finish your review with a final reason why your film should be included in the set, and try to make this interesting.

Question 4:
- Decide whether Jack should apply for the job. Answer his questions based on your own experience and then explain whether you would recommend it to him or not.
- Use your imagination to provide interesting details, and use informal language as you are writing to a friend.

Part 2

Write an answer to **one** of the questions 2–4 in this part. Write your answer in **220–260** words. In the exam, write your answer **on the separate answer sheet provided**, and put the question number in the box at the top of the page.

2   You are on the social committee of your college. You have been asked to write a proposal for your college principal on the kind of social and sporting activities the college should provide for new students. You should assess the current situation, describe the needs of new students and suggest activities the college should provide.

Write your **proposal**.

3   You see the following advertisement in a film magazine:

Reviews wanted: best film ever!

We are planning to produce a set of DVDs of the ten best films of all time. Send us a review of your favourite film. What was it about? What made it so good? Why should we include it in the set of DVDs? The best reviews will be included with the set of DVDs.

Write your **review**.

4   You have received a letter from an English friend:

Hi!
I remember that you worked in a ski resort last winter, and I'm thinking of doing the same this year. Were there any drawbacks? Did you meet interesting people? What opportunities were there for skiing? Would I gain much from doing it for just four months? Should I apply for it?
Thanks for your help
Jack

Write your **letter** in reply. You do not need to include postal addresses.

TEST 1
LISTENING

Guidance

About the paper

The Listening paper lasts about forty minutes and has four parts, with a total of thirty questions. There are texts of varying lengths and types, e.g. extracts from media broadcasts and announcements, as well as everyday conversations. You hear each recording twice. You have time to read the questions before you listen.

Part 1
In Part 1, you listen to three unrelated extracts of around one minute each. Each extract has two speakers. You have to answer two three-option multiple-choice questions on each extract.

Part 2
Part 2 involves one long monologue of around two to three minutes where the speaker is talking about a particular subject. A set of eight sentences reports the main points from the listening. A word or short phrase has been removed from each sentence. You have to listen and complete the gaps.

Part 3
In Part 3, there is one long interview or discussion of around four minutes. You have to listen and answer six four-option multiple-choice questions.

Part 4
In Part 4, you hear a series of five short monologues on a theme, of around thirty seconds each. You have to complete two tasks as you listen. Each task has eight options (A–H). As you listen, you match one option from Task 1 and one option from Task 2 to each speaker. You match the gist of what the speakers say to the ideas in the prompts, e.g. their occupation, opinions, etc.

How to do the paper

Part 1
- The three extracts are not linked in any way. All three are dialogues, but there will be a variety of text types and interaction patterns.
- Before you listen to each extract, look at the context sentence. Think about who the speaker is and about the context, e.g. is it a broadcast interview, an informal chat?
- Before you listen, think about which of the speakers you are listening for in each question and underline keywords in the question stem.
- Listen first to find the correct answer to the question posed in the stem.
- Listen again to match that answer to the correct option (A–C).

Part 2
- Before you listen, read the rubric and think about the context.
- You have 45 seconds to read through the sentences before you listen. Think about the type of information that is missing in each sentence.
- Most answers are concrete pieces of information, e.g. numbers and proper nouns.
- The sentences on the page follow the same order as the information in the listening text. Use the sentences to help you keep your place as you listen.
- The words you need to write are heard on the recording. There is no need to change the form of the word or find a paraphrase.
- Write no more than three words in each gap. Most answers will be single words or compound nouns.
- Check that your answer fits grammatically and makes sense in the complete sentence.

Part 3
- Before you listen, read the rubric and think about the context.
- You have 70 seconds to read through the set of sentences before you listen.
- Underline the keywords in the question stems and options.
- The questions follow the order of the text. Listen out for discourse markers or interviewer's questions that introduce the topic of each question that you have to answer.
- Listen first to find the correct answer to the question posed in the question stem.
- Listen again to match that answer to the correct option (A–D).
- The words in the options will not be the same as those you hear in the recording.

Part 4
- There are five different speakers all talking about the same topic. You will hear all five of them and the listening extracts will be repeated.
- You have 45 seconds to read the two tasks before you listen. Read the options (A–H) in both tasks so that you are ready to choose one from each set for each speaker as you listen.
- The first time you listen, pay attention to the speaker's main idea. Mark the option closest to this idea.
- The second time you listen, check your answers. You may need to change some of them. Remember that in each task there are three options that you don't need to use.
- Don't worry if you don't understand every word. If you're not sure of an answer, then guess. You have probably understood more than you think.

TEST 1
LISTENING

Part 1

You will hear three different extracts. For questions **1–6**, choose the answer (**A**, **B** or **C**) which fits best according to what you hear. There are two questions for each extract.

In the exam, mark your answers **on the separate answer sheet**.

Tip Strip

Question 1: Listen for the phrase 'I get a buzz from that side of it'. What is he referring to when he says this?

Question 4: Listen to everything the woman says. In general, was it a positive experience or not? Which option matches this feeling?

Question 5: Listen for the phrase 'for what it's worth'. The answer comes just after it.

Extract One

You hear two people talking about their work as website designers.

1 How does the man feel about the work?

   A He finds the creativity stimulating.

   B He would like to use his academic training more.

   C He gets most satisfaction from being part of a team.

2 What do they both think about the job?

   A It's a difficult career to get started in.

   B It's important to be able to work flexible hours.

   C It's a poorly paid job for the amount of work involved.

Extract Two

You hear two cyclists talking about their sport.

3 The man thinks his success as a cyclist is due to

   A his complete dedication.

   B the age at which he started.

   C a series of great role models.

4 When talking about cycling in a velodrome, the woman reveals her

   A fear of dangerous sports.

   B inability to follow instructions.

   C willingness to accept a challenge.

Extract Three

You hear a man called Roy talking about bees on a phone-in programme.

5   Why has he phoned the programme?

   A   to raise issues not previously discussed

   B   to challenge the opinions of other contributors

   C   to lend his support to a view that's been expressed

6   When talking about gardens, he is

   A   describing what he does in his own.

   B   encouraging people to grow certain things.

   C   suggesting that people keep bees themselves.

Part 2

You will hear a student called Tim Farnham giving a class presentation about a seabird called the albatross. For questions **7–14**, complete the sentences with a word or short phrase.

In the exam, mark your answers **on the separate answer sheet**.

THE ALBATROSS

Tim thinks that the name 'albatross' comes originally from a word in
the **(7)** .... language.

There are currently thought to be a total of **(8)** .... species of albatross.

The fact that it relies on **(9)** .... explains why the albatross isn't found in some areas.

By using a locking mechanism in its **(10)** .... , the albatross can save energy when flying.

Tim explains that the albatross has a surprisingly good sense of **(11)** ....

Tim was surprised to discover that **(12)** .... attack albatross nests.

The albatross used to be hunted mostly for its **(13)** .... as well as for food.

Tim gives the example of **(14)** .... as plastic objects commonly eaten by albatrosses.

Tip Strip

Question 7: Be careful. Three languages are mentioned, but only one of them fits here.
Question 8: The words 'a total of' in the sentence tell you that you are listening for a number.
Question 9: Listen for the word 'found' when you listen. It's also in the sentence.
Question 11: What are the five senses? Which of them would you not expect a bird to use?
Question 14: Tim mentions three plastic objects, but which does he say is most common?

Part 3

Tip Strip

Question 15: Listen for when Amy says 'so creating dances was the natural way forward.' What is she referring to?

Question 18: Listen for the interviewer's question about Amy's aims. Her answer follows.

Question 19: Listen to what Amy says about students. Her answer comes here. Go back and check why the other options are wrong.

Question 20: Listen to Amy's last turn. Listen for the first and last things she says.

You will hear an interview with a woman called Amy Martles, who works as a choreographer, creating dance performances for live shows. For questions **15–20**, choose the answer (**A**, **B**, **C** or **D**) which fits best according to what you hear.

15 Amy traces her decision to become a choreographer back to

  A the advice of her first dance teacher.
  B her need to express herself through movement.
  C the emphasis placed on dance in her primary school.
  D her failure to reach a high level of sporting achievement.

16 Amy feels that, above all, a good choreographer is one who

  A remains in touch with the everyday feelings of dancers.
  B keeps dancers motivated during long tiring sessions.
  C has experience of appearing on stage as a dancer.
  D is able to join in with the dancing itself if necessary.

17 When she's creating a new dance, Amy

  A finds it easier to work directly with a composer.
  B prefers to be given clear constraints to work within.
  C keeps an open mind about how a piece might develop.
  D accepts that some of her ideas will prove to be unpopular.

18 In her work as a choreographer, Amy aims to

  A challenge the audience's ideas about what dance is.
  B feel that she is conveying a message to the audience.
  C thrill the audience with some cutting-edge dance techniques.
  D draw the audience's attention away from other elements in the show.

19 When asked about choosing dancers to work with, Amy says she

  A relies on the expertise top professionals bring to the creative process.
  B accepts the need to accommodate the feelings of sensitive people.
  C finds those with less experience an easier proposition.
  D likes to help those she has previously taught.

20 When she's working on a new production of a well-known piece, Amy

  A tries to build on the work of those who have gone before.
  B is aware of the need to update the ideas in a play.
  C is annoyed if people make unfair comparisons.
  D remains faithful to her usual guiding principles.

TEST 1: LISTENING

Part 4

You will hear five short extracts in which people are talking about how they gave up office jobs to do other types of work.

In the exam, mark your answers **on the separate answer sheet.**

TASK ONE

For questions **21–25**, choose from the list (**A–H**) what made each speaker decide to give up office work.

A	poor motivation	
B	lack of exercise	Speaker 1 □ 21
C	the regular hours	Speaker 2 □ 22
D	limited contact with people	Speaker 3 □ 23
E	overcrowded workplace	Speaker 4 □ 24
F	dull colleagues	Speaker 5 □ 25
G	few career prospects	
H	stressful deadlines	

TASK TWO

For questions **26–30**, choose from the list (**A–H**) what each speaker likes best about their present job.

A	being my own boss	
B	feeling appreciated by clients	Speaker 1 □ 26
C	being able to offer advice	Speaker 2 □ 27
D	feeling respected for my skills	Speaker 3 □ 28
E	being fully qualified	Speaker 4 □ 29
F	feeling committed to the work	Speaker 5 □ 30
G	being relatively well paid	
H	being able to help others	

Tip Strip

Speaker 1: Listen for the phrase 'The thing I couldn't stand'. What she says next explains why she decided to give up office work (Task One).
Speaker 2: Listen to what she says about clients – it helps with Task Two.
Speaker 3: What 'got him down' in his previous job? This tells you the Task One answer.
Speaker 4: When she says 'I love that feeling' about her present job, what is she referring to?
Speaker 5: Listen to the first part of what he says. What was his general feeling about his old job?

TEST 1 SPEAKING

Guidance

About the paper

The Speaking test lasts for 15 minutes and there are four parts. You take the test with a partner. There are two examiners, although only one (the interlocutor) speaks to you. The other examiner listens and gives detailed marks.

Part 1
Part 1 takes about two minutes. First the interlocutor asks each of you direct questions asking for personal information. Then the interlocutor asks you and your partner questions in turn on general topics such as your interests, daily routines and likes and dislikes.

Part 2
Part 2 lasts about four minutes, during which you each speak on your own for about a minute. You are given three photographs. You compare two of the pictures and say something more about them. You are also asked a short question about your partner's photographs after they have finished speaking.

Part 3
Part 3 is divided into two parts, and lasts around four minutes. You discuss a task with your partner for around two minutes using ideas you are given as written prompts. After two minutes, the interlocutor asks you a second question which is not written down, and you have to make a decision together connected to the topic you have been discussing. You have a minute for this part of the task.

Part 4
Part 4 takes around five minutes. The interlocutor leads a general discussion that broadens the topic of the Part 3 task by discussing more abstract questions on related issues.

How to do the paper

Part 1
- For the initial questions on personal information, you only need to give short answers; don't prepare long speeches about who you are and where you are from, but you should say a little more than *yes* or *no*.
- In the rest of Part 1 the interlocutor will ask you for your own ideas and opinions about more general topics, such as what you enjoy or what ambitions you have. Think of this as being similar to meeting someone in a social situation. You should provide enough detail to give interesting answers, without monopolising the time.

Part 2
- Listen to the interlocutor's instructions carefully. The task is also written on the paper above the photographs so you won't forget what you have to do.
- You can ask the interlocutor to repeat the task if you have to, but only do this if it is really necessary as you will lose time from your minute.
- Compare the pictures and then move on to the second part of the task. Don't describe the pictures; describing them won't allow you to show a range of language at the right level.
- Listen to what your partner says about their pictures as the interlocutor will ask you a short question about them. In your answer, you should give some detail, but don't say too much as you only have a short time for this.

Part 3
- Listen to the task carefully so that you understand exactly what to do. The task is written in the middle of the paper with prompts around it, and you have a short time to read the task before you have to start talking. You can ask the interlocutor to repeat the task if you are not sure, but this should not be necessary.
- Discuss each written prompt in turn. It doesn't matter if you don't discuss all the prompts, so make sure you say everything you can think of about each one before you move on to the next. Try to discuss the issues raised in the prompts in detail, and to use a range of language.
- Remember to ask your partner for their views as well as giving your own opinion. Really listen to what they say so that you can respond to their ideas and suggestions appropriately.
- After two minutes, you are given a minute to discuss a decision on a topic related to the one you have been discussing with the prompts.
- Continue to use a range of language in your negotiation towards your decision. Don't make your decision too quickly, or you won't talk for a minute, and remember there is no 'right' decision.

Part 4
- The interlocutor may ask questions for you both to discuss, or they may ask you each a question in turn. You can contribute to your partner's question, as long as you do this appropriately.
- The questions in this part are more abstract, and you should give longer answers than you did in Part 1. Try to develop your ideas, and give your opinions in an interesting and coherent way.
- You can disagree with what your partner says! There are no 'right' answers to the questions.

Tip Strip

Part 1:
- You should think of answers that tell the interlocutor more about you and your personal opinions. There is no 'right' answer, so relax and try to be interesting in what you say, but remember not to monopolise the time. Think of this as a social meeting!

For the first three questions, you could say:

I often have to study in the evening because that's the only time I have, but I'm more of a morning person and would prefer to study before breakfast as I feel fresh then.

I don't like organised holidays where you go round sightseeing in a group – I like travelling independently so that I can decide where I go and how long I spend in different places.

I love travelling – I love arriving at a new place and having the chance to find out about a whole new culture. But I hate it when there are delays and I get stuck in an airport departure lounge for hours because the plane is late!

Part 2:
Learning a new skill:
- Candidate A, you could say: *it's incredibly satisfying to be independent / it gives life-long pleasure / recipes can be hard to understand / it's probably hard not to be nervous / you'd really need to be well-prepared.*
- Candidate B, don't say too much, but give details, e.g. *I think ... would get most satisfaction because ...*

Entertaining others:
- Candidate B, you could say: *they're probably hoping people will give them money / busking / it looks like a school entertainment / families must feel proud / no one watches entertainment at a sports event, which must be frustrating.*
- Candidate A, you could say: *I think ... needs most practice because ...*

PART 1

The interlocutor will ask you a few questions about yourself and on everyday topics such as work and study, travel, entertainment, daily life and routines. For example:

- What's the best time of day for you to study? Why?
- What kind of holidays do you enjoy most? Why?
- Is there anything you dislike about travelling? Why?
- What kind of magazines or newspapers do you read regularly? Why/Why not?
- What do you like to do when you go out with your friends?
- Are you an organised kind of person? Why/Why not?
- Has the kind of music you enjoy changed since you were younger? Why/Why not?
- Where would you recommend tourists to visit in your country? Why?

PART 2

Learning a new skill

Turn to pictures 1–3 on page 170, which show people learning a new skill.

Candidate A, compare two of the pictures and say what you think the people might be enjoying about learning the new skill, and how easy it might be for them to master it.

Candidate B, who do you think would get the most satisfaction from learning the new skill? Why?

Entertaining others

Turn to pictures 1–3 on page 171, which show people entertaining others in different places.

Candidate B, compare two of the pictures and say why the people might be entertaining others in these different places, and how memorable it might be for the people watching.

Candidate A, who do you think would need the most practice? Why?

Tip Strip

Part 3:
- Focus your discussion on why the things are important and how important they might be in the future.
- You could say: *education is vital in the current economic climate / we need to make sure there's a planet for our grandchildren / relaxation will become increasingly important.*

Part 4:
Consider the abstract issues behind the questions. For example, you could talk about:
- *too much focus on earning money, not enough time to spend with friends/family, pressure to buy material things*
- *sports stars are highly paid, but they don't contribute to society, or help others*
- *media creates expectations, young people think they can succeed easily, the media tend to focus on lifestyles of successful people*
- *TV and magazines imply that everyone can have an expensive lifestyle, but they are the minority. This makes people think they can achieve more than is realistic, to have too high expectations*
- *life was simpler for our grandparents, they had fewer aspirations, they expected less from life, they didn't have to deal with global issues or technology but their lives were harder physically, medicine was less good, our lives are easier and more entertaining*
- *money buys a good lifestyle but not friendship, health, anything worthwhile*

PART 3

Turn to the task on page 172, which shows some things that have become important in many people's lives.

Talk to each other about why these things have become important to some people in today's world. Then decide which two things will continue to be important to people in the future.

PART 4

Answer these questions:

- Do you think that people have the right priorities in life nowadays? Why/Why not?
- Some people say that certain jobs are overvalued and overpaid. What's your opinion?
- What part does the media play in people's expectations of life nowadays?
- Do you think that people's expectations of what is achievable are too high nowadays? Why/Why not?
- Do you think that life is easier now than it was in our grandparents' day? Why/Why not?
- Some people say that it's only possible to be happy if you have a lot of money. What's your opinion?

TEST 2 READING AND USE OF ENGLISH

Guidance: Part 1–4

Testing focus

Part 1

In Part 1, there is a range of testing focuses. Most questions focus on your knowledge of vocabulary and how it is used. Questions may focus on:

- your knowledge of general vocabulary related to the topic of the text.
- the relationship between words, e.g. which preposition is used after a word, or whether it is followed by an infinitive or a gerund.
- your knowledge of fixed expressions and collocations, including phrasal verbs.
- your knowledge of linking words and phrases. This tests whether you have understood the meaning of the whole text.

Part 2

Part 2 mostly tests your knowledge of grammar and sentence structure. Questions can focus on:

- the relationship between words, e.g. which words go together to form a fixed expression or phrasal verb.
- sentence structure, e.g. asking you to insert the correct relative pronoun or a conjunction.
- other grammatical words, e.g. quantifiers, determiners, articles, etc.
- linking words and phrases to test whether you have understood the meaning of the whole text.

Part 3

Part 3 tests whether you can create the correct form of the word to fit in the sentence. Questions may focus on:

- your knowledge of prefixes and suffixes.
- your grammatical knowledge, e.g. which form of the word is needed to complete the meaning in the sentence.
- common expressions and collocations, e.g. which form of the word is used to form a common expression.
- your knowledge of compound words.

Part 4

Part 4 tests both your grammatical and lexical knowledge. Questions always have two testing points, e.g. a change to a word from the input sentence, plus a change to the word order to create a new sentence pattern.

- You are tested on your ability to express the same ideas using different grammatical forms and patterns, e.g. in a sentence that starts with a different word, or using a different part of speech.
- Questions may test your knowledge of fixed phrases and collocations by asking you to find the words that combine with those already in the target sentence.
- Your answer must be grammatically accurate.

Preparation

- Do as many practice tests as possible so that you fully understand what is expected of you and you feel confident going into the exam.
- Keep a vocabulary notebook in which you write down useful vocabulary you come across, arranged by topic.
- Try to learn words in chunks rather than in isolation. When you learn a new word, write down not only the word, but also the sentence it is used in.
- When you're doing practice tests, keep a note of items you get wrong and attempt them again two weeks later.
- Write a verb on one side of a card, and its dependent preposition on the other. Test yourself on them in your free time.
- Choose a text in English and underline all of the prepositions. Then go back through and decide which ones are part of set word patterns.
- Go through a reading text and write a list of all of the adjectives. Is there a noun in the same verb family? What about an adverb?

**TEST 2
READING AND
USE OF ENGLISH**

Guidance: Parts 5–8

Testing focus

Part 5
Part 5 tests your detailed understanding of the meaning of the text, as well as general language and reading skills. Most questions relate to specific pieces of text. The last question in a set targets the text as a whole.

There is a range of testing focuses in Part 5 questions. For example, some questions will focus on a phrase or sentence in the text, whilst others will ask you to interpret the meaning of a whole paragraph.

Look for clues in the question stems to help you find the targeted piece of text. For example, 'In the third paragraph,' is a clear indication of the piece of text you need to read; but it also tells you not to consider information and ideas from elsewhere in the text when choosing your answer.

Part 6
In Part 6, you are being tested on your ability to locate relevant parts of the text or texts and match them to the ideas in the prompt questions. Two types of reading skill are involved.

- Firstly, the ability to read through a text, understand the organisation and locate the parts relevant to a particular prompt. The prompt question will report ideas from the text, but will not use the same vocabulary and structures, so you are looking to match the meaning. This involves reading and understanding the question prompt, then locating the given writer's ideas on the topic indicated and reading this section carefully to understand the exact point of view being expressed.
- Secondly, the skill of carefully reading texts on a similar topic, where similar ideas are expressed, to understand whether or not the writers have the same ideas or different ideas on the topic.

Part 7
Part 7 tests your ability to see the links between the different parts of a text and use these to put jumbled text in the correct order. This will mean looking for the links the writer makes between paragraphs in order to tell the story, or develop the argument coherently. These links can be of different types and, often, more than one type of link will help you answer the question. Look for:

- vocabulary links between the paragraphs, especially where an idea from one paragraph is developed in the following one. Don't expect to see the same word used, however. You should look for different words with a similar meaning.
- grammatical links between the paragraphs, especially the use of pronouns and other words that summarise or refer to things already mentioned.
- logical links of topic and focus. Look for where people, places or ideas are first introduced in the base text. If these are referred to in an option, then that paragraph must fit later in the text.

You are looking for links that work, but also looking for links that don't work. For example, if a paragraph in the options seems to fit a gap logically and contains the right sort of ideas and vocabulary, you need to check whether there are any pronouns, e.g. 'his', 'these', etc., or other references in the option that don't have a point of reference in the preceding text.

Part 8
In Part 8, you are being tested on your ability to locate relevant parts of the text, or texts, and match them to the ideas in the prompt questions. Two types of reading skill are involved.

Firstly, the ability to read through a text, understand the organisation and locate the parts relevant to a particular prompt. This involves reading quickly to get a general idea of the text, without worrying about the meaning of every word or the exact point being made by the writer.

Secondly, the skill of careful reading to understand the precise meaning in both the prompt question and in the relevant part of the base text. The prompt question will report ideas from the text, but will not use the same vocabulary and ideas to do this.

Preparation

- Do as many practice tests as possible so that you fully understand what is expected of you, and you feel confident going into the exam.
- Remember that the CAE exam aims to test real life skills. The reading that you do outside the classroom will help you become a more fluent reader.
- To help with Parts 5, 6 and 8, read (online or elsewhere) texts which express people's attitudes and opinions, such as interviews with famous people. Concentrate on understanding how the people feel about the different issues discussed.
- Look at English-language news articles and note down the phrases used to link the paragraphs. This will help you with Part 7 in particular.
- Practise reading texts quickly all the way through to understand the gist. You could read online articles and summarise the main ideas or opinions in them.

TEST 2 READING AND USE OF ENGLISH

Tip Strip

Question 3: Which of the words creates an expression with 'afield' which means 'a long way away'?

Question 7: Only one of these words can be followed by the preposition 'with'.

Question 8: Only one of these words collocates with 'direct' to mean the customers' real opinions.

Part 1

For questions **1–8**, read the text below and decide which answer (**A**, **B**, **C** or **D**) best fits each gap. There is an example at the beginning (**0**).

In the exam, mark your answers **on the separate answer sheet**.

Example:

| 0 | **A** washed | **B** thrown | **C** dumped | **D** tossed |

| 0 | A ▬ | B ▭ | C ▭ | D ▭ |

Seaside Artist

Andrew Ruffhead goes out gathering rubbish on his local beach, where all sorts of interesting things are (**0**) …….. up. He later uses these as the (**1**) …….. materials for his artwork, mostly sculptures and collages in the shape of fish, like tuna, and crustaceans, (**2**) …….. crabs and lobsters. Andrews's eye-catching work, which looks equally good in kitchens, bathrooms and gardens, has been a great success with seaside fans all over the globe, with his funky fish drifting as (**3**) …….. afield as Greece and Cape Cod in New England.

(**4**) …….. as Andrew can tell you which beach the materials from each sculpture came from, he is also (**5**) …….. to know where his work will be hung. It is this interaction with the public that he particularly enjoys. Open to the public by (**6**) …….. , his small informal studio also (**7**) …….. him with an opportunity to get direct (**8**) …….. from his customers. Indeed, people often bring their own beach finds to the studio, to get Andrew's advice about how to make them into works of art.

1	**A** natural	**B** crude	**C** plain	**D** raw
2	**A** such as	**B** for instance	**C** for example	**D** much as
3	**A** distant	**B** long	**C** far	**D** remote
4	**A** Indeed	**B** Quite	**C** Rather	**D** Just
5	**A** desire	**B** fond	**C** keen	**D** wish
6	**A** schedule	**B** appointment	**C** timetable	**D** booking
7	**A** provides	**B** gains	**C** gives	**D** produces
8	**A** review	**B** feedback	**C** opinion	**D** report

Tip Strip

Question 9: Which verb is used together with the noun 'use'?
Question 10: Which word completes the comparison with 'earlier'?
Question 13: Which preposition usually follows 'similar'?
Question 15: Which word completes the fixed expression?

Part 2

For questions **9–16**, read the text below and think of the word which best fits each gap. Use only **one** word in each gap. There is an example at the beginning (**0**).

In the exam, write your answers **IN CAPITAL LETTERS on the separate answer sheet**.

Example: **0** L E D

Early Stone Tools

A recent discovery has **(0)** …….. scientists to revise their ideas about the ancestors of early humans. It seems they started to **(9)** …….. use of stone tools nearly one million years earlier **(10)** …….. had previously been thought. Archaeologists revised the date **(11)** …….. spotting distinctive marks made by stone tools on animal bones dating **(12)** …….. nearly three and a half million years. The remains, including a rib from a cow-like creature and a thigh bone from an animal similar in size **(13)** …….. a goat, were recovered from an old river bed **(14)** …….. was being excavated in Ethiopia.

The use of simple stone tools to remove meat from bones represents a crucial moment in human history. **(15)** …….. a result of turning to meat for sustenance, the early humans developed larger brains, which **(16)** …….. turn enabled them to make more sophisticated tools. The bones unearthed in Ethiopia may well represent the very beginning of that process.

Part 3

Tip Strip

Question 17: You need to add a suffix to this verb to make a noun.
Question 21: This word needs a prefix which means 'again'.
Question 22: You need to form an adverb here.
Question 24: Add a suffix to turn this verb into an adjective.

For questions **17–24**, read the text below. Use the word given in capitals at the end of some of the lines to form a word that fits in the gap **in the same line**. There is an example at the beginning (**0**).

In the exam, write your answers **IN CAPITAL LETTERS** on the separate answer sheet.

Example: | 0 | A | P | P | E | A | L | I | N | G | | | | | | |

Marathon Dreams

The idea of taking part in long-distance running races seems (0) .... After all, who hasn't watched TV **APPEAL**
(17) .... of the London or New York Marathon and been **COVER**
moved by the stories of everyday people tackling that most
epic of (18) .... races. From the comfort of your armchair, **ENDURE**
your heart swells with (19) .... for the contenders as they **ADMIRE**
cross the finish line, on the point of (20) ...., yet exhilarated. **EXHAUST**

Inspired, you vow to (21) .... your own previous fitness **GAIN**
levels and do something similar. In fact, tomorrow you'll put on
your trainers and have a go at 20 minutes around the park.

But when tomorrow comes, the motivation is not quite so strong.
(22) ...., you give up because you find the wet weather rather **POSSIBLE**
(23) ...., or you make the effort and ache terribly afterwards. **COURAGE**
This happens when you try to do too much too soon. Indeed,
top runners say that it's (24) .... to begin with a trip to the **ADVISE**
doctor to see if you are physically fit enough to embark on
the training.

Part 4

Tip Strip

Question 26: You need to create a passive sentence here.

Question 27: You need to introduce a preposition into this sentence.

Question 28: Which modal verb will you use after 'wish'?

Question 29: Which phrasal verb will match 'attend' in the input sentence?

For questions **25–30**, complete the second sentence so that it has a similar meaning to the first sentence, using the word given. **Do not change the word given.** You must use between **three** and **six** words, including the word given. Here is an example (**0**).

Example:

0   Chloe would only eat a pizza if she could have a mushroom topping.

ON

Chloe .... a mushroom topping when she ate a pizza.

The gap can be filled with the words 'insisted on having', so you write:

| **Example:** | **0** | INSISTED ON HAVING |

In the exam, write **only** the missing words **IN CAPITAL LETTERS on the separate answer sheet**.

---

25 It's difficult to say why some cars are easier to drive than others.

MAKES

It's difficult to say .... easier to drive than others.

26 Many people have blamed the hot weather for the rise in petty crime.

WIDELY

The hot weather .... for the rise in petty crime.

27 The wind was so strong that we couldn't walk along the seafront.

STRENGTH

The .... meant it was impossible to walk along the seafront.

28 Sandra regrets not being able to visit her grandmother more often.

WISHES

Sandra .... visit her grandmother more often.

29 Everyone expects a lot of people to attend the rock band's farewell concert.

TURN

A huge crowd is .... the rock band's farewell concert.

30 I want to say that I'm not at all satisfied with the service at this hotel.

MY

I want to express .... with the service at this hotel.

Part 5

You are going to read an article about a company and its employees. For questions **31–36**, choose the answer (**A**, **B**, **C** or **D**) which you think fits best according to the text.

In the exam, mark your answers **on the separate answer sheet**.

Take as much holiday time as you want

Most organisations treat vacations in the same reluctant way that parents dole out candy to their children. They dispense a certain number of days each year – but once we've reached our allotment, no more sweets for us. One US company, however, has quietly pioneered an alternative approach. Netflix Inc. is a streaming video and DVD-by-mail service that has amassed 15 million subscribers. At Netflix, the vacation policy is audaciously simple and simply audacious. Salaried employees can take as much time off as they'd like, whenever they want to take it. Nobody – not employees themselves, not managers – tracks vacation days. In other words, Netflix's holiday policy is to have no policy at all.

Back in the old days – 2004 – Netflix treated holidays the old-fashioned way: it allotted everyone 'n' days a year. You either used them up or you tried to get paid for the time you didn't consume. But eventually some employees recognised that this arrangement was at odds with how they really did their jobs. After all, they were responding to emails at weekends, they were solving problems online at home at night. And, every so often, they would take off an afternoon to ferry a child to the paediatrician or to check in on an ageing parent. Since Netflix weren't tracking how many hours people were logging each work day, these employees wondered, why should it track how many holidays people were taking each work year?

Fair point, said management. As the company explains in its *Reference Guide on our Freedom & Responsibility Culture*: 'We should focus on what people get done, not how many hours or days are worked. Just as we don't have a 9-to-5 day policy, we don't need a vacation policy'. So the company scrapped the formal plan. Today, Netflix's roughly 600 salaried employees can vacation any time they desire for as long as they want – provided that their managers know where they are and that their work is covered. This ultra-flexible, freedom-intensive approach to holiday time hasn't exactly hurt the company. Launched in 1999, Netflix is now a highly successful and growing enterprise.

Perhaps more importantly, this non-policy yields broader lessons about the modern workplace. For instance, more companies are realising that autonomy isn't the opposite of accountability – it's the pathway to it. 'Rules and policies, and regulations and stipulations are innovation killers. People do their best work when they're unencumbered,' says Steve Swasey, Netflix's Vice President for corporate communication. 'If you're spending a lot of time accounting for the time you're spending, that's time you're not innovating.'

The same goes for expenses. Employees typically don't need to get approval to spend money on entertainment, travel or gifts. Instead, the guidance is simpler: act in Netflix's best interest. It sounds delightfully adult. And it is – in every regard. People who don't produce are shown the door. 'Adequate performance,' the company says, 'gets a generous severance package.'

The idea is that freedom and responsibility, long considered incompatible, actually go together quite well. What's more, Netflix's holiday policy reveals the limits of relying on time in managing the modern workforce. In an era when people were turning screws on an assembly line or processing paper in an office, the connection between input and output was tight. The more time you spent on a task, the more you produced. But in much white-collar work today, where one good idea can mean orders of magnitude more valuable than a dozen mediocre ones, the link between the time you spend and the results you produce is murkier. Results are what matter. How you got here, or how long it took, is less relevant.

Finally, the Netflix technique demonstrates how the starting premises of workplace arrangements can shape behaviour. In his new book, *Cognitive Surplus: Creativity and Generosity in a Connected Age*, New York University scholar Clay Shirky argues that when we design systems that assume bad faith from the participants, and whose main purpose is to defend against that nasty behaviour, we often foster the very behaviour we're trying to deter. People will push and push the limits of the formal rules, search for every available loophole and look for ways to game the system when the defenders aren't watching. By contrast, a structure of rules that assumes good faith can actually encourage that behaviour.

Tip Strip

Question 32: Look in the second paragraph for the answer to this question. What does 'at odds with' mean?
Question 34: Look for Steve Swasey's name in the text. What is he quoted as saying?
Question 35: Find the word 'adult' in the text. Look at the text after this to find the answer to the question.

31 In the first paragraph, the writer emphasises

    A how popular Netflix's holiday policy is.
    B how unusual the situation at Netflix is.
    C how important holidays are to employees.
    D how hard it can be to change a holiday policy.

32 Employees at Netflix pointed out that the company's holiday policy

    A gave them less time off than they deserved.
    B was fairer for some employees than for others.
    C was not logical in the circumstances.
    D did not reflect the way their jobs had changed.

33 The management of Netflix came to the conclusion that

    A a happy workforce was the key to future success and growth.
    B employees would be willing to do some work during their holidays.
    C they should introduce both flexible working hours and flexible holidays.
    D employees' achievements were the company's top priority.

34 Steve Swasey expresses the view that company policies often

    A prevent employees from being as effective as they could be.
    B result in employees being given the wrong roles.
    C cause confusion among employees because they are so complex.
    D assume that only certain employees can make decisions for themselves.

35 The writer says that one way in which the situation at Netflix is 'adult' is that

    A competition among employees is fierce.
    B managers' expectations of employees are very high.
    C expenses allowed for employees are kept to a minimum.
    D employees are given a lot of help to improve their performance.

36 In the writer's opinion, Netflix's approach addresses the modern issue of

    A employees wanting more responsibility than in the past.
    B wasted time being more damaging than in the past.
    C good ideas taking longer to produce than mediocre ones.
    D outcomes being more important than methods.

Part 6

Tip Strip

Question 37: Reviewer A describes the book as 'engaging' and talks about 'the upbeat tone'. Which reviewer uses less positive language to talk about the style of writing?

Question 38: Look for the reference in Extract B to the main focus of the book. Which reviewer disagrees with Reviewer B's opinion about this?

Question 40: Underline the sentences in each review that talk about people in different parts of the world. Which reviewer feels that Allen's ideas may not apply in some cultures?

You are going to read four extracts from reviews of a book about the history of food. For questions **37–40**, choose from the extracts **A–D**. The extracts may be chosen more than once.

The Omnivorous Mind
Four reviews of the book by John S Allen

A

To quote John S Allen in his engaging book *The Omnivorous Mind*, 'We eat with our brains.' After this enticing assertion, Allen takes us on a fast-paced tour of world history to illustrate his point. As a neuroscientist, Allen has done extensive research into the relationship between the way we think and what we choose to eat. Indeed, the main ideas in the book will strike a chord with people around the globe, even if the detailed examples are outside their experience. Allen's principle point is that the mind has always been central in determining people's eating habits, and it's a point he returns to regularly, whether in the context of the latest fads and fashions or deeply-seated cultural traditions. Another appealing feature of the book is the upbeat tone and feeling of optimism that prevails throughout. Allen covers a lot of ground, and raises some important questions, but never gets bogged down in technicalities.

B

The human species has a very complex relationship with food. In any human society, diet is very much a key part of what makes us who we are. Why is it, Allen asks, that in every society there are certain perfectly palatable foods that people refuse to eat? Allen goes on to explore the reasons for this, and other conventions, in a way that will be accessible across cultures. The book is a thoughtful, authoritative guide to a vast and fascinating subject, touching on such issues as how food affects memory and language, and the ways foods are categorised. But it begins rather slowly, and there are moments when the casual reader will want to skip some of the long-winded explanations to get to the point. Allen often strays far from his main contention, so anyone looking for a clear focus on food may find their attention wandering.

C

Eating is so much part of our daily routine that few of us stop to think about its true social significance. John S Allen's new book takes a close look at how food forms part of our biological and cultural heritage. Allen sees this cerebral relationship with food as contributing to our uniqueness as a species, and explains why the world's cultures are so diverse in terms of their culinary traditions. Bringing together the work of food historians, anthropologists and neuroscientists, his lively narrative takes us from the diet of our earliest ancestors all the way through to modern attitudes. Even people from quite diverse cultural contexts will find familiar issues investigated along the way. *The Omnivorous Mind* examines the foods we crave and the foods we find repulsive, and our insistence on classifying all food as healthy or unhealthy. This book certainly challenges some of our preconceptions and attitudes towards eating.

D

According to Allen, the modern world presents us with complex decisions to make on a daily basis about what to eat and what not to eat. Allen eloquently describes the internal 'food model', which each of us develops to help us decide what to eat and what not to eat. Allen, however, is clearly writing for those of us living in places where food abundance is the norm rather than shortage, and this detracts from some of his broader claims about our species' relationship with what we eat. It is hard to know what people in less fortunate societies might make of them. What he does do, however, is show us that although we spend a lot of time thinking about food, there is still a great deal we don't know about our relationship with it. This book is going to help change that!

Which reviewer

doesn't share Reviewer A's opinion about Allen's style of writing? | 37 |

disagrees with Reviewer B's point about how relevant some sections of the book are to Allen's main argument? | 38 |

agrees with Reviewer D's point about the likely impact the book will have on readers? | 39 |

presents a different argument to the others regarding the extent to which Allen's ideas will be understood in different parts of the world? | 40 |

Part 7

You are going to read a newspaper article about butterflies. Six paragraphs have been removed from the article. Choose from the paragraphs **A–G** the one which fits each gap (**41–46**). There is one extra paragraph which you do not need to use.

In the exam, mark your answers **on the separate answer sheet**.

Fluttering down to Mexico

Sara Evans is enchanted by the millions of butterflies that migrate to the Sierra Madra mountains for the winter.

As golden light filters through the trees, slumbering butterflies begin to wake. Amber wings unfold and lift delicate bodies into the warm Mexican air. Gentle as wood smoke rising, butterfly after butterfly leaves the safety of oaks and fir trees, until the air fills with millions of them.

41

They are just some of the nearly 250 million or so Monarch butterflies that overwinter here in the Sierra Madra mountains, in the highlands of central Mexico. Every November, this particular patch of mountainside forest in Mexico State, 130 miles north of Mexico City, becomes a temporary retreat for Monarchs escaping the colder faraway climes of Eastern Canada and the US. Their journey here is nothing short of fabulous.

42

Our journey here has been less epic. On horseback, it has taken half an hour or so to reach the butterflies. At 12,000 ft, their roosting site lines a steep, tree-filled gully. We pause by the side of it to get a closer view. There are butterflies everywhere. From trunk bottom to the highest branch, the trees are coated in them. Boughs bend under their weight and sway softly in the breeze. The purple petals of wild lupins turn orange as butterflies smother them in search of nectar. Around pools on the ground, huge clusters of thirsty Monarchs make a fluttering carpet of wings as they drink.

43

The Aztecs once believed that Monarchs were the souls of warrior ancestors migrating through the forests on their way to the land of the dead. For centuries, local people have welcomed the arrival of the butterflies in early winter, holding special celebrations in their honour.

44

En route, generations of Monarchs mate, hatch and die. The ones that reach the US and Canada are fourth generation – the great grandchildren of those that left Mexico. These fourth-generation Monarchs then fly back to Mexico in one go, somehow finding their way here and tripling their lifespan as they do so. How and why this happens remains a mystery. What is known, though, is that this unique migration is not invincible. While the Monarch butterfly itself is not endangered (populations thrive elsewhere around the world), this migration route is.

45

This is why this pocket of forest was given UNESCO World Heritage Site status in 2008. Logging is banned here and the butterflies are officially protected. Comprised of more than 58,000 hectares, the Reserve – known as the Monarch Butterfly Biosphere Reserve – is divided into five main areas, four of which are open to the public.

46

Stretching out their evergreen branches to the millions of butterflies that flutter around them, these trees are butterfly guardians, keeping the Monarchs warm and safe until they fly north on the start of one of the Earth's most complex and beautiful migrations – a journey that continues to mystify scientists and bewitch those of us fortunate enough to witness it.

Tip Strip

Option A: What does 'this' refer to in 'much of this' at the beginning of this option? Check the base text for possible references.
Option D: Look for what 'these creatures' and 'this mass of insects' could refer to in the base text.
Option G: Look for a description of a journey in the base text.

A Much of this is down to deforestation. Quite simply, as trees tumble, so does the number of Monarchs. Without the warmth and protection of the trees, butterflies that have flown thousands of miles to avoid the ravages of northern winters find themselves folding cold wings, like icy shrouds, over their tiny bodies. They freeze to death overnight.

B It is also possible to walk or hike up to see the butterflies. Paths are well-defined, but the hour-long journey can be arduous and is at altitude, so a reasonable level of fitness is required. The best time to visit is in February, when the butterflies are at their most active.

C Fed and watered, they sky dance. Tangerine bright, they fly through the gully riding the thermals, flitting between branches and sunbeams. Moving through dappled sunlight in their millions, the Monarchs cast a nectar-fuelled spell that turns the forest into a bedazzling butterfly kingdom.

D Moving closer to the sun, these creatures – a deep orange filigreed with bold black markings – look like vast stained-glass windows and block out the blue of the sky. As the butterflies dip and soar, the sound of this mass of insects in motion rumbles like a distant waterfall.

E I'm in the newest of these, El Capulin, which is the least visited and the least affected by illegal tree-cutting. The forest here thrives. Fir trees in their thousands stand tall and solid against a bright sky.

F But it was only in the 1970s that scientists discovered that it was to this remote mountainside that the Monarchs leaving North America were headed each autumn. Later research also revealed that the Monarchs arriving back in North America, in March, are not the ones that overwinter here.

G Fluttering, dipping and soaring for over 3,000 miles at around seven and a half miles an hour, the butterflies span a continent – passing over the Great Lakes, prairies, deserts, mountain ranges, cities and motorways to get to this place. Surviving storms and burning sunshine, these fragile creatures are the stars of one of the world's most dazzling migration spectacles.

Part 8

Tip Strip

Question 52: Look for a word in the text that suggests 'investigative work'.

Question 55: Look for the names of occupations in the text.

Question 56: Look for words that mean 'upset' in the text.

You are going to read an article about an art exhibition that focuses on the subject of whether paintings are authentic or fake. For questions **47–56**, choose from the sections of the article (**A–F**). The sections may be chosen more than once.

In the exam, mark your answers **on the separate answer sheet**.

In which section of the article are the following mentioned?

information that solved a mystery about a painting known to be authentic	47
an incorrect idea about the attitude of people responsible for exhibiting pictures	48
the fundamental issue surrounding research into a picture	49
similarities in an artist's style in more than one place	50
reasons why it is understandable that a certain mistake was made	51
investigative work that showed that a picture was an unusual example of an artist's work	52
the willingness of experts to accept that their beliefs are wrong	53
the different categories of people involved in examining pictures	54
evidence from an expert outside the world of art	55
an accusation that upset the writer personally	56

Seeing through the fakes

A *Close Examination* at the National Gallery looks at 40 problematic works from the Gallery's collection – including outright forgeries, misattributions, pastiches, copies, altered or over-restored paintings, and works whose authenticity has wrongly been doubted. The curators have taken on a huge subject – the range of possibilities museum professionals take into consideration when they investigate a picture's status and the variety of technical procedures conservation scientists use to establish authorship and date. The case histories they discuss have a single common denominator. In whatever direction and to whatever conclusion the combined disciplines of connoisseurship, science and art history may lead, the study of any work of art begins with a question: is the work by the artist to whom it is attributed?

B A good example is an Italian painting on panel that the National Gallery acquired in 1923, as the work of an artist in the circle of the Italian fifteenth-century painter Melozzo da Forlì. Today, we find it incredible that anyone was ever fooled by a picture that looks like it was painted by a Surrealist follower of Salvador Dalí. But this is to forget how little was known about Melozzo 90 years ago, and how little could be done in the conservation lab to determine the date of pigments or wood panel. Even so, from the moment the picture was acquired, sceptics called its status into question. Nothing could be proved until 1960 when a costume historian pointed out the many anachronisms in the clothing. When technological advances enabled the gallery to test the pigments, they were found to be from the nineteenth century.

C Scientific evidence can be invaluable but it has to be used with caution and in tandem with historical research. For example, Corot's ravishing sketch *The Roman Campagna, with the Claudian Aqueduct* has always been dated to about 1826, soon after the artist's arrival in Rome. However, the green pigment called viridian that Corot used throughout the picture only became available to artists in the 1830s. The landscape wasn't a fake and for stylistic reasons couldn't have been painted later than the mid-1820s. All became clear when art historians did further research and discovered that the firm that sold artists' supplies to Corot in Paris started making the newly developed colour available to selected customers in the 1820s, long before it came into widespread use.

D The flipside of a fake, but capable of doing equal violence to an artist's reputation, occurs when an authentic work is mistakenly labelled a forgery. Back in 1996, I well remember how distressing it was to read an article in which the former director of the Metropolitan Museum of Art, Thomas Hoving, declared that Uccello's lovely little canvas of *St George and the Dragon* was forged. The gallery therefore X-rayed the picture and tested paint samples, before concluding that it was a rare survival of a work by Uccello dating from the early 1470s. Hoving was irresponsible not because he questioned the attribution of a much-loved work, but because he went public without first asking the gallery to carry out a thorough scientific analysis.

E Anyone can label a picture a fake or a copy, but their opinions are worthless unless they can support them with tangible proof. One picture that's been smeared in this way is Raphael's *Madonna of the Pinks*. In this exhibition, we are shown infrared photographs that reveal the presence both of major corrections which a copyist would not need to make, and also of under drawing in a hand comparable to Raphael's when he sketched on paper. The pigments and painting technique exactly match those that the artist used in other works of about the same date.

F For all its pleasures, the show also has an unspoken agenda. It is a riposte to the mistaken belief that museums have anything to gain by hiding the true status of the art they own. As the downgrading in this show of Courbet's *Self-Portrait* to the status of a posthumous copy of a picture in the Louvre shows, the opposite is the case: museums and galleries constantly question, revise, reattribute and re-date the works in their care. If they make a mistake, they acknowledge it.

TEST 2 WRITING

Guidance

Testing focus

Part 1
The focus of assessment in Part 1 is on an essay based on two points chosen from three given in the task. The target reader must be informed and able to understand your point of view. You must discuss the two points you choose, giving detailed reasons for your views, and clarifying your overall opinion. Marks are awarded for appropriate content, organisation, coherence and cohesion, range of language and the effect on the target reader. You should organise your essay clearly and use an appropriate register.

Part 2
The focus of assessment in Part 2 is on writing appropriately, coherently and answering the question. You should use an appropriate organisation and layout for the given task. Marks are awarded for suitable content, clear organisation and good coherence and cohesion (which might include using appropriate linking words). You should also use a range of language (vocabulary and structures) in the right register for the given task, and achieve the appropriate effect on the target reader.

Preparation

General points
- Practise writing tasks in the given time. There is no point in spending longer than 45 minutes when writing a practice task. In the exam, each task carries equal marks, so there is nothing to gain by spending too long on Part 1 and then not having enough time to complete Part 2.
- Practise writing only the required number of words. There is no point in writing answers that are too long as they may include irrelevant details and take too much time.
- Work with a partner so that you can help each other to spot recurring mistakes by editing each other's work. Keep a checklist of your own grammatical and spelling mistakes so that you know what to look out for.
- Get into the habit of reading the instructions carefully every time you answer a question, and always check your writing to make sure that you have included everything required.
- Make sure you understand the appropriate format and register for every type of task in the Writing paper.
- Revise connectors so that you can use these appropriately in any task.
- Don't only check for grammatical mistakes. Always read your answer through after you have written it to check that it is coherent and makes sense.

Part 1
- Read all the information before you start to write, and think about which points to choose for your essay. Do you have enough ideas for each one?
- Do as much work as you can on using a range of language. Working on the Reading and Use of English paper will also help you with this.
- Spend time thinking of issues and ideas for different topics so that you have ideas for the tasks. You could build up a file with these ideas and refer to it when you practise writing a task or revise for the exam. Topics you discuss when preparing for the Speaking paper are also useful.

Part 2
- Build up ideas about different topics in the same way as for Part 1, and practise writing in the different genres.
- Consider what your own strengths in writing are. Do you like writing lively and interesting answers, or more formal and informative answers? This will help you choose the best type of task in the exam.
- The questions in the exam may require you to use different language functions. Work on different ways of giving advice, describing, explaining, and so on.

TEST 2 WRITING

Part 1

You **must** answer this question. Write your answer in **220–260** words in an appropriate style. In the exam, write your answer **on the separate answer sheet provided**.

1 You have listened to a radio discussion programme about the importance of reading different kinds of books in modern society. You have made the notes below:

What type of book is most important to read nowadays?

- fiction
- history
- science

Some opinions expressed in the discussion:

'You learn a great deal about people by reading fiction, so it helps with relationships.'

'History is just a collection of facts – you can find out all you need to know on the internet.'

'It's important for everyone to know about science nowadays, but some ideas in books can be hard to understand.'

Write an essay discussing **two** of the points in your notes. You should **explain which type of book you think is most important** to read nowadays, **giving reasons** in support of your answer.

You may, if you wish, make use of the opinions expressed in the discussion, but you should use your own words as far as possible.

Tip Strip

Question 1:

- Read all the input and choose which two books to discuss in your essay. Think about reasons for and against each type of book you choose, with examples to support your views.
- Decide which type of book is most important for people to read, and why. Make sure your line of argument and examples support your conclusion.
- Remember to include a clear introduction to the topic of books and reading in general.
- You don't have to use the opinions given – you may have plenty of ideas of your own. If you do use them, don't use the words, just the ideas.
- Link your ideas clearly and coherently using a range of connectors and clear paragraphs.
- Use a range of language to explain and justify the points you want to make.
- Make your argument as interesting and persuasive as possible.

Part 2

Write an answer to **one** of the questions 2–4 in this part. Write your answer in **220–260** words. In the exam, write your answer **on the separate answer sheet provided**, and put the question number in the box at the top of the page.

2   You see the following announcement on a music website:

> Have you been to an interesting and unusual music festival or concert recently? Write a review for our website and tell us about it. Explain what it was, and what made it interesting and unusual. Do you think this kind of event is relevant today? We will put the most interesting reviews on our website.

Write your **review**.

3   Your friend Sarah has applied for a job in the office of an English Language College that has students from all over the world, and has asked you to write a letter of recommendation for the College Principal. Applicants should have good communication skills, be a team player and well-organised.

In your letter you should include information about your friend's relevant work experience and personal qualities, and reasons for recommending them for the job.

Write your **letter**.

4   You have just finished a short period of work in a company abroad as part of your business course. You have now been asked to write a report for your course organiser.

In your report you should explain what you did and how you benefited from the period of work, describe any problems you had and make recommendations for other students on the business course who will be working in the same company abroad later.

Write your **report**.

Tip Strip

Question 2:
- This review should be interesting and engaging for users of the website, so it should not be too formal in style. It should be clearly organised and paragraphed so that it is easy to read.
- Think of an engaging opening to catch the reader's interest, and make sure that your opinion is clearly expressed at the end.
- Use techniques such as rhetorical questions to interest and engage readers.
- In this task you must describe the festival, explain what made it interesting or unusual and justify your reasons for whether it is important or not.

Question 3:
Read the instructions carefully to identify the job, what skills are required and any other relevant information you might want to include. In this task, the job is working in a busy office, and the person required needs to be well-organised, work well with others and have good communication skills.
- Your letter should be written in a formal or semi-formal style.
- You should decide why you want to recommend your friend, give your reasons clearly and provide details of why your friend would be suitable for the job.

Question 4:
- Explain the purpose of the report in the introduction.
- Your report may have headings and some bullet points to make it easy for your tutor to pick out relevant information, but make sure that you show a range of language in the other sections.
- In this task you must say what you did and explain the benefits, describe any problems and make recommendations for other students. Your recommendations may result from the problems; make sure the reasons you give are clear so the course tutor can assess them.

TEST 2
LISTENING

Guidance

Testing focus

Part 1

There is a range of testing focuses in Part 1 questions.
- Some questions focus on a detailed understanding of parts of the text, or on the use of particular vocabulary or expressions.
- Some questions test your understanding of the text as a whole, or of the speakers' attitudes, feelings or opinions. The second question in a pair usually targets the whole text.

Part 2

Part 2 tests your ability to locate, understand and record specific information from the listening text.
- This task does not test grammar, so you don't have to change the form of the words you hear. However, you should check the grammar of the sentence to check if the word you have heard is, for example, singular or plural.
- This task doesn't test extra information. If you write too much, you risk losing the mark by not creating a good sentence.

Part 3

Part 3 tests a detailed understanding of the speakers' feelings, attitudes and opinions. Each question relates to a specific section of text and there is a range of testing focus.
- Some questions ask you to interpret the meaning of a whole long turn from the main speaker.
- Sometimes a question may ask you to listen to what two speakers say about something to understand whether or not they hold the same opinion.

Part 4

Part 4 is designed to test your understanding of what people say, as well as the ability to pick out keywords and phrases. Each of the two tasks has a separate focus and the testing focus in each task is separate. So getting the right answer for a speaker in Task One doesn't help you to get the right answer in Task Two.

Preparation

- Remember that the Advanced exam aims to test real life skills, so any listening practice you do is likely to improve your general listening skills.
- When you're doing practice tests, pay attention to synonyms and paraphrasing in questions, and try to use these techniques yourself in speaking and writing. This will help you become familiar with how these devices work and help you to spot them in the exam.
- Practise using the sample answer sheets so that you will know how to fill them in on the day of the exam.
- Search online for an English language radio programme that interests you. Listen and try to note down the key ideas as you listen.
- Watch English language DVDs with the subtitles on. Concentrate on connecting what you hear with what you read in the subtitles. Watch the film (or sections of the film) again with the subtitles turned off. This time you'll already have an idea of what's being said, and can really focus on what you hear.

TEST 2 LISTENING

Part 1

You will hear three different extracts. For questions **1–6**, choose the answer (**A**, **B** or **C**) which fits best according to what you hear. There are two questions for each extract.

In the exam, write your answers **on the separate answer sheet**.

Tip Strip

Question 1: When the woman says 'Tell me about it', she's agreeing with the man. But what is she referring to?

Question 3: Listen to the musician's first turn to find the answer. Listen to what he says about 'his music'.

Question 6: Listen to the last thing the woman says. Did she rebel or not?

Extract One

You hear two students talking about shopping for clothes.

1 What do they agree about?

   A It's better to buy inexpensive clothes.

   B Shopping for clothes is to be avoided.

   C People should respect your taste in clothes.

2 According to the man, many people see shopping as a way of

   A achieving social status.

   B making a comment on society.

   C identifying with a particular social group.

Extract Two

You hear part of an interview with a musician called Max.

3 What does he say about his music in his teenage years?

   A He wanted to keep it to himself.

   B He felt quite self-confident about it.

   C He was reluctant to ask for help with it.

4 What does he suggest about his recording contract?

   A It didn't guarantee him ongoing success.

   B It didn't mean he could give up other work.

   C It didn't have very good terms and conditions.

Extract Three

You hear part of a discussion programme in which two dancers are talking about their careers.

5   The man was inspired to train as a dancer by

   A   one reaction to a performance he gave.

   B   some encouragement from his friends.

   C   the athletic nature of the activity.

6   The woman admits that as a teenager, she

   A   behaved unreasonably at times.

   B   resented her parents' ambitions for her.

   C   managed to keep certain feelings to herself.

Part 2

You will hear a radio reporter called Sally Nelson telling a group of teenagers about how work experience schemes have helped her in her career. For questions **7–14**, complete the sentences with a word or short phrase.

In the exam, write your answers **on the separate answer sheet**.

RADIO REPORTER

At university, Sally did a degree in a subject called **(7)** ....

After graduating, Sally's first job was as a **(8)** ....

Sally uses the word **(9)** .... to describe how she felt on her first day at a radio station.

Sally was asked to join a **(10)** .... by the boss of the Brighton radio station.

Sally most enjoyed doing **(11)** .... on air during her time in Brighton.

One of Sally's colleagues in Brighton advised her to study **(12)** .... at evening classes.

At the national broadcasting company, Sally worked mostly on the **(13)** .... desk.

Sally identifies **(14)** .... as the main benefit of doing work experience.

Tip Strip
Question 7: Be careful. Three degree courses are mentioned. What was the exact name of the one Sally did?
Question 9: You are listening for an adjective that means 'rather frightened by everything around her'.
Question 10: Two schemes are mentioned. One is the name of what Sally did, the other is a comparison she makes with another scheme. Be sure to write the correct one.
Question 13: Be careful. Three desks are mentioned. Listen for the one Sally worked on most often.
Question 14: You are listening for an abstract noun that describes a quality.

Tip Strip

Question 15: Listen for the phrase 'it was pure chance'. The answer comes soon afterwards.

Question 17: Listen for the interviewer's question about 'how you work on a production' and listen to Vivienne's answer. What does she say is 'pretty vital'?

Question 19: Does Neil read reviews? How often? Why?

Question 20: Listen to the last thing Neil says. What does he prefer, films or plays? Why?

Part 3

You will hear an interview in which two people called Neil Strellson and Vivienne Barnes are talking about their work as set designers in the theatre. For questions **15–20**, choose the answer (**A**, **B**, **C** or **D**) which fits best according to what you hear.

In the exam, write your answers **on the separate answer sheet**.

15 Neil first decided he wanted to work as a set designer when

    A he went to see plays with his parents.
    B he started studying drama at university.
    C he was asked to help out on a student production.
    D he gave up on his childhood dream of becoming an actor.

16 What does Neil say about working as an assistant set designer?

    A He did it because he was short of money.
    B He saw it as a way of making useful contacts.
    C He was too young to take full advantage of it at first.
    D He appreciated the chance to put theory into practice.

17 For Vivienne, the most important aspect of starting work on a new production is

    A establishing a working relationship with the director.
    B agreeing how many scenery changes are needed.
    C feeling an involvement with the play itself.
    D doing a set of preliminary sketches.

18 Why does Vivienne prefer working on several productions at once?

    A She finds that it stimulates her creativity.
    B She feels it gives her increased financial security.
    C It means she can avoid going to all of the opening nights.
    D It stops her getting too involved in the problems of any one show.

19 Vivienne disagrees with Neil's suggestion that reviews are

    A something that set designers shouldn't take too seriously.
    B sometimes unfairly critical of the set designer's work.
    C annoying if the set isn't specifically mentioned.
    D flattering if the set is singled out for praise.

20 What does Neil say about designing film sets?

    A He finds it less challenging than the theatre.
    B He'd like the chance to work on a really good film.
    C He hasn't really worked out how to approach it yet.
    D He isn't sure whether he has the skills to do it effectively.

Part 4

You will hear five short extracts in which people are talking about a four-day hiking trip to a remote historical site in the mountains.

In the exam, mark your answers **on the separate answer sheet.**

TASK ONE

For questions **21–25**, choose from the list (**A–H**) the reason each speaker gives for going on the trip.

A to fulfil a long-held ambition

B to keep someone company   Speaker 1 [21]

C to set a personal challenge   Speaker 2 [22]

D to celebrate something   Speaker 3 [23]

E to prove someone wrong   Speaker 4 [24]

F to complete a set of experiences   Speaker 5 [25]

G to follow someone's example

H to meet like-minded people

TASK TWO

For questions **26–30**, choose from the list (**A–H**) the aspect of the trip each speaker found most memorable.

A the impressive architecture

B the view from the site   Speaker 1 [26]

C the support of companions   Speaker 2 [27]

D the historical notes   Speaker 3 [28]

E the route taken   Speaker 4 [29]

F the overnight accommodation   Speaker 5 [30]

G the food provided

H the attitude of the guide

Tip Strip

Speaker 1: Listen to what he says about his wife. It helps with Task One.
Speaker 2: When she says 'what made it for me', what is she referring to? This helps with Task Two.
Speaker 3: When he says 'I went along for her sake', what does he mean?
Speaker 4: Listen to the beginning of what she says. It helps with Task Two.
Speaker 5: When he says 'I'll never forget' …, what is he referring to?

TEST 2 SPEAKING

Guidance

Testing focus

General points
- The examiner marks in different categories – grammatical and lexical resource, discourse management, pronunciation and interactive communication. The examiner will be marking on all these aspects of the assessment criteria throughout the test.
- The interlocutor gives a global mark at the end of the test.
- It is important to remember that you are not being assessed on your actual ideas, just on the language you use to express them. Don't worry if you feel you have nothing important to say – it is the language that counts!

Part 1
- The focus is on general interactional language and social interaction. Try to be relaxed and answer the questions in an interesting way.

Part 2
- The focus is on organising a longer unit of discourse and you have to compare two pictures, express opinions and speculate about them.

Part 3
- The focus is on interacting with your partner by exchanging ideas, giving and justifying opinions, agreeing and disagreeing, suggesting, speculating and evaluating. You also have to reach a decision through negotiation with your partner. You should listen carefully to what your partner says and develop the discussion as much as possible. Try to use a range of language.

Part 4
- The focus is on giving and justifying opinions and agreeing and disagreeing with your partner's ideas. Although you may be asked individual questions, you can also join in and develop your partner's ideas as well as contributing to a discussion of the question asked.

Revision tips

Part 1
- Although you should not prepare speeches, practise talking about general topics in small groups or with your partner.
- Prepare questions for your partner on given topics, and take it in turns to ask and answer the questions.
- Practise this part for two minutes so that you feel how long your answers should be.
- Practise using different tenses in your answers, e.g. if you are asked what you like doing in the evenings, you could say that you used to play tennis, but now you prefer to watch films.

Part 2
- Practise comparing pictures from newspapers or magazines. Focus on comparing, not describing, and think about different ways of making comparisons.
- When you practise specific exam tasks, work with a partner and try to find three things to say when comparing pictures and three things about the rest of the task. This technique will help you to organise your talk in the given time.
- Practise organising your talk by linking ideas using connectors, e.g. *whereas, conversely*. Build up a list of these connectors so that you can use them confidently.
- Practise by yourself by looking at pictures and thinking of interesting things to say about them. You could practise by writing down keywords and using them to organise your talk in a logical way.

Part 3
- Practise discussing exam tasks with a partner in two minutes. You should not worry about the time in the exam, however, as the interlocutor will stop you after two minutes; you should just concentrate on everything you want to say. Don't stop discussing the prompts before the two minutes are over and the interlocutor stops you.

When you are asked to make a decision, listen carefully to the question and then discuss it in detail with your partner. Don't just point to the prompt you choose, or make your decision too quickly. Use the full minute for your negotiation; it doesn't matter if you run out of time before you have agreed on your decision as the language you use in the discussion is most important.

- Make sure you practise listening to your partner so that you can respond appropriately to what they say. It is good to refer back to what they have said when you make a point, as this shows genuine interaction.
- Think about different ways of asking your partner for their opinion, and of agreeing and disagreeing e.g. *that's interesting, but not exactly what I think.*
- It is important for you to initiate ideas as well as responding to what your partner says, so practise ways of doing that e.g. *What do you think about …*
- Practise using conversation 'fillers' to give yourself time to think if you need to, e.g. *let me think …, what I mean is …*
- Keep a list of language functions such as interrupting politely, e.g. *May I make a point here?* moving a discussion on, e.g. *Let's move on …* and reacting to what your partner says, e.g. *Absolutely.*

Part 4
- Discuss issues in the news so that you have ideas on different topics. You can also get ideas from the Advanced reading and listening texts that you study in class. Keep a note of any good ideas so that you can read them again before the exam in case that topic comes up.
- Try to contribute to general discussions in class as much as possible so that you get used to expressing your opinions clearly.
- Remember that you can disagree with your partner and that this is often very productive! Practise with a partner by making statements for your partner to agree or disagree with.
- Remember that the examiners can only mark what they hear. Try to contribute to general discussions in class as much as possible so that you get used to expressing your opinions clearly.

PART 1

The interlocutor will ask you a few questions about yourself and on everyday topics such as work and study, travel, entertainment, daily life and routines. For example:

- Do you think it would be a good idea to work in another country for a short time? Why/Why not?
- What kind of music do you enjoy listening to?
- Do you like having a routine in life? Why/Why not?
- What would your ideal job be? Why?
- If you could travel to any country in the world, where would it be? Why?
- What is your favourite way to relax?
- Have you seen any good films recently?
- Do you enjoy watching sport? Why/Why not?

PART 2

Playing games

Turn to pictures 1–3 on page 173, which show people playing games.

Candidate A, compare two of the pictures and say how people might benefit from playing games like these, and how the players might be feeling.

Candidate B, who do you think is benefiting most from playing the game? Why?

Taking a break

Turn to pictures 1–3 on page 174, which show people taking a break in different situations.

Candidate B, compare two of the pictures and say why the people might need to take a break and how relaxing these situations might actually be.

Candidate A, who seems to be finding it most difficult to relax? Why?

Tip Strip

Part 1:
- Remember to make your answers interesting, but not too long. You should not answer or add to your partner's questions in this part, nor have a discussion about their question. Questions in Part 1 are directed specifically to each of you in turn.

For these questions you could say something like:

It would be great to work in another country for a while – I'd love to work in France, because I'm learning French and it would be a good change to improve my language. It's also great to learn about business in another country.

I love listening to jazz, because my parents used to play it all the time when I was young and then I started to play the saxophone. It's great because it's always new and different, and has lots of energy.

I do like having a routine – it helps me to organise my life if I know when things are going to happen. I find it easier to remember to do things, too, which is good.

I'd love to be a journalist, because I am curious about everything and I really enjoy writing. I think it would be exciting to investigate stories in the news and then to see your articles in print.

I enjoy travelling anywhere, because it's always interesting to visit new places. But if I could choose anywhere it would be to the Antarctic; it must be amazing to see such a beautiful and different landscape, and to experience a really extreme climate.

When I need to relax, I listen to music and read one of my favourite books. Both these things are really helpful for taking away pressure after a difficult day. I also go swimming, which is relaxing too.

I don't go to the cinema very often, but I enjoy watching old films on DVD – I love Hitchcock films because they are quite thrilling and sometimes scary. I think they're better than modern films! I watched 'Psycho' recently, which was great.

Actually, I prefer playing sport to watching it – I'm more of an active person. I love playing tennis, though I don't really enjoy watching it on television. It's fun to see professional players live, though – they hit the ball so hard!

Part 2:
- Use language of speculation such as *it's possible that / perhaps it leads to …*

Playing games:
- Candidate A, you could say: *it develops powers of concentration / it could help to improve mental agility / it could lead to feelings of resentment / people usually feel triumphant when they win*

Taking a break:
- Candidate B, you could say: *sportspeople get very stressed / a break improves performance / people don't appreciate how hard it is to be a parent / it looks very difficult to relax*

Tip Strip

Part 3:

- Focus the discussion on identifying the kind of satisfaction the written prompts provide, and how satisfying they might really be.
- You could say: *Wearing fashionable clothes is important because of self-image, but it's a bit shallow/becoming rich gives you lots of options but does it really make you happy?*
- Initiate discussion and ask for your partner's opinion. You could say: *you said relationships are important, but what about money? / have you really thought that through? / what makes you think that?*

Part 4:

The general topic of these Part 4 questions is changing aspects of life. You could talk about:

- *pressure of peer groups, feeling that you belong, keeping up with new things*
- *lots of friends make you feel popular but you may not be able to trust them*
- *young people want to be successful, older people often value time, friends and family*
- *image and status is important but it's not the most important; people can do well without other people knowing about it*
- *too much money distances you from real life, too much money makes you selfish*
- *rich people should give money away to poorer people, the rich should pay higher taxes, behave well, contribute to society*

PART 3

Turn to the task on page 175, which shows some things that give people satisfaction.

Talk together about what kind of satisfaction people get from having things like these. Decide which two things would provide the most satisfaction in the long term.

PART 4

Answer these questions:

- How important is it to follow trends in fashion? Why?
- Is it better to have a few close friends or a lot of acquaintances?
- Do you think that people's interests and priorities change as they get older? Why/Why not?
- Some people say that having a high status is not the most important thing. What's your opinion?
- Is it possible to be too rich? Why/Why not?
- What kind of responsibilities do you think rich people have? Why?

TEST 3
READING AND USE OF ENGLISH

Part 1

For questions **1–8**, read the text below and decide which answer (**A, B, C or D**) best fits each gap. There is an example at the beginning (**0**).

In the exam, mark your answers **on the separate answer sheet**.

Example:

0   **A**   takes   **B**   fetches   **C**   carries   **D**   brings

0	A	B	C	D

Caving

Caving is an adventure sport that, quite literally, **(0)** …….. you to another world. But it's also quite a well **(1)** …….. secret, enjoyed by a relatively small group of devoted enthusiasts. Caving **(2)** …….. for a range of skills because it involves climbing, squeezing and squirming your way into openings in the Earth's rocks to discover the many fascinating, sometimes very large and beautiful, caverns that **(3)** …….. under the surface.

(4) …….. its rather dangerous image, largely **(5)** …….. thanks to rather sensationalist television programmes, the sport has an excellent safety **(6)** …….., so long as you go with a qualified instructor or caving club. Wearing a helmet and waterproof clothing, you're privy to a hidden world of stalagmites and stalactites, although you may have to **(7)** …….. through torrential underground rivers and negotiate thunderous waterfalls in order to **(8)** …….. the most impressive spots. The challenge of entering the unknown in the pitch dark can be terrifying, however, so it's as well to choose your location carefully.

1   **A**   cared   **B**   held   **C**   kept   **D**   minded
2   **A**   demands   **B**   calls   **C**   asks   **D**   requires
3   **A**   stay   **B**   sit   **C**   rest   **D**   lie
4   **A**   Despite   **B**   Moreover   **C**   Nonetheless   **D**   Albeit
5   **A**   accepted   **B**   acquired   **C**   assumed   **D**   admitted
6   **A**   report   **B**   history   **C**   standard   **D**   record
7   **A**   amble   **B**   wade   **C**   stroll   **D**   hike
8   **A**   manage   **B**   arrive   **C**   achieve   **D**   reach

Part 2

For questions **9–16**, read the text below and think of the word which best fits each gap. Use only **one** word in each gap. There is an example at the beginning (**0**).

In the exam, write your answers **IN CAPITAL LETTERS on the separate answer sheet**.

Example: | 0 | W | I | T | H | | | | | | | | | | |

Why are Sunglasses Cool?

Sunglasses are heavily associated (**0**) …….. images of celebrity. Sunglasses are cool, and it is a cool that seems set to endure. Have you ever wondered why this should be?

The roots of sunglasses are anything (**9**) …….. glamorous, however. Amber-tinted spectacles first appeared in the nineteenth century and were a medical remedy for people (**10**) …….. eyes were oversensitive to light. The first mass-produced versions, made by Sam Foster (**11**) …….. Foster Grant fame, were sold in the 1920s in US seaside resorts. (**12**) …….. this point, however, they remained functional objects, and were yet to acquire the cool image they now enjoy.

This (**13**) …….. about thanks to the US air force. In the 1930s, airmen started to wear anti-glare glasses called 'aviators'. In the early days of flight, these men were regarded (**14**) …….. heroes. Down on the ground, actors keen to cash (**15**) …….. on a little of that glory realised that sunglasses created an intriguing image. So it (**16**) …….. that the link between the fascination of celebrity and a pair of sunglasses was forged.

TEST 3: READING AND USE OF ENGLISH

Part 3

For questions **17–24**, read the text below. Use the word given in capitals at the end of some of the lines to form a word that fits in the gap **in the same line**. There is an example at the beginning (**0**).

In the exam, write your answers **IN CAPITAL LETTERS on the separate answer sheet.**

Example: | 0 | P | U | B | L | I | C | A | T | I | O | N | | | | |

Customer Reviews

The (**0**) .... in paperback of Matthew Quick's debut novel represented something of a milestone. The promotional material that (**17**) .... the launch featured glowing, five-star reviews such as 'charming and well-written, (**18**) .... the best book I've read this year'. Nothing so unusual in that, you might think. Except that these notices came not from the pens of (**19**) .... critics on national newspapers, but from actual readers who had bought the book on the internet, and enjoyed it enough to post a positive review on the site and whose opinions appear in an (**20**) .... form, as can be seen from the various spelling and grammatical mistakes they often contain.

It could be argued, of course, that the (**21**) .... of an informed literary critic may well be more (**22**) .... than the thoughts of one casual reader. But the site also records the cumulative star rating awarded to each title by all readers providing (**23**) .... The more people like the book, the higher the star rating. Maybe that kind of (**24**) .... speaks for itself.

PUBLISH

COMPANY

ARGUE

PROFESSION

EDIT

ANALYSE
RELY

FEED

RECOMMEND

Part 4

For questions **25–30**, complete the second sentence so that it has a similar meaning to the first sentence, using the word given. **Do not change the word given.** You must use between **three** and **six** words, including the word given. Here is an example (**0**).

Example:

0 Chloe would only eat a pizza if she could have a mushroom topping.

ON

Chloe .... a mushroom topping when she ate a pizza.

The gap can be filled with the words 'insisted on having', so you write:

Example: | 0 | INSISTED ON HAVING |

In the exam, write **only** the missing words **IN CAPITAL LETTERS on the separate answer sheet**.

---

25 A lack of work in his home area forced Frank to move to the capital.

CHOICE

Frank .... move to the capital because of the lack of work in his home area.

26 'The race is going to start in a minute,' said Rod.

ABOUT

Rod said that .... start.

27 Thanks to the success of the concert, the singer was offered a recording contract.

LED

The success of the concert .... offered a recording contract.

28 As soon as Alex finished his homework, he went out on his bike.

HAD

No .... than he went out on his bike.

29 I find it boring to watch television every evening.

SPEND

I get .... every evening watching television.

30 Sarah's father thinks she should come home earlier in the evening.

APPROVE

Sarah's father .... staying out so late in the evening.

Part 5

You are going to read an extract from a novel. For questions **31–36**, choose the answer (**A**, **B**, **C** or **D**) which you think fits best according to the text.

In the exam, mark your answers **on the separate answer sheet**.

Louisa Maguire, wedding and portrait photographer, gave her clients images of themselves as they wanted to be seen – confident and happy, with the polish of an expensive American advertising campaign. She had arrived from New York in 1993, just as Ireland was beginning to transform itself from a country of staunch Catholic conservatives into a society dominated by the neo-liberal *nouveaux riches*. In Celtic Tiger Ireland, people were no longer suspicious of success, and instead of emigrating to get rich, they were living the American Dream at home. And who better to document it than an American photographer?

Although Louisa had once harboured higher aspirations, she didn't mind doing weddings and portraits of bonny babies. After all, that was how Dutch painters had made their livings centuries before, churning out portraits that reflected their clients' prosperity. Louisa Maguire, photographer, had introduced Dubliners to high-quality black-and-white portraits in life-size formats shot with her beloved Hasselblad, which they hung on their walls like works of art. She was expensive, but that was part of her appeal.

Weddings were the other mainstay of her business. She shot them in documentary style, always telling the story of the day in a way that showed the fairytale, but she also caught the uniqueness of every occasion. Digital cameras were far easier to use than the analogue cameras she preferred, but the old-fashioned method had a timelessness and depth that digital couldn't match. And there were few things she enjoyed more than spending hours in the darkroom, fine-tuning a thousand shades of grey until she got a picture exactly right. Black and white was more evocative than colour, which stripped people of the dark sides that made them interesting …

Louisa drove into Dalkey Village and pulled up in front of her studio. Her assistant, Paul, was waiting for her. 'Hey, what's up? You're late,' he said, as he loaded Louisa's middle-aged Volvo Estate with equipment, then stretched himself out in the passenger seat. She would tell him eventually, but not yet. For now, Louisa wanted to drive without having to think. Sensing her mood, Paul put music on the CD player, sat back and closed his eyes. She found her way to the M50, then gunned the engine as she headed west, determined to make up time. Speeding along the highway that circled the city, she felt regret at the paving of Ireland; they were passing high-tech factories, warehouses and shopping malls, which made the outskirts of Dublin look like any European suburb.

'You ever visit the cairns?' Louisa asked Paul.

'The what?'

'The Bronze Age tombs in Meath. They're five thousand years old. There's one you can actually go inside, if you borrow the key from the people in the Big House. I'll never forget crawling down there. It was like going back to the very beginning. I had an eerie feeling that I'd been there before.'

'You Americans and your history. I thought you hated all that sentimental diddle-eye-doe aul' Oirlan' nonsense.'

'I do. I'm not talking about Oirlan'. I mean the real place underneath all that sentimental nonsense.'

'If I can't see it, I'm not interested. We're photographers, Lou. Surface is what we do.'

'I know it.' Too well, she realised.

They left the M50 and headed north on the N23 into countryside that was like a green quilt with grey stitching made stone by stone with muscle and sweat. The earth beneath held buried treasure – bronze goblets, gold torques, wisps of fabric and even human bodies preserved in the peat-rich soil. This was the Ireland she loved, although she usually kept her thoughts to herself. She didn't want anyone to suppose she was just another daft American looking for her roots.

31 What do we learn about Louisa Maguire in the first paragraph?

　　A　She moved to Ireland because of social changes there.
　　B　Being American helped her to get photographic work in Ireland.
　　C　The attitudes of Irish people confused her when she arrived there.
　　D　She had more success in Ireland than in America.

32 Louisa's attitude to doing weddings and portraits was that

　　A　the money she could make from that kind of work was its main advantage.
　　B　the responses of clients often made that kind of work rewarding.
　　C　she was only likely to do that kind of work temporarily.
　　D　she was not ashamed of doing that kind of work.

33 In the third paragraph, what is implied about Louisa's work for weddings?

　　A　She sometimes had to persuade clients that her methods were right for them.
　　B　She preferred photographing weddings to doing portraits.
　　C　She showed aspects of the occasion that clients had not been aware of.
　　D　She used analogue cameras for photographing weddings.

34 When Louisa met Paul at her studio and they got into the car,

　　A　he did something that annoyed her.
　　B　her mood changed.
　　C　she decided to delay answering the question he asked her.
　　D　he misunderstood how she was feeling.

35 When Lousia mentioned the cairns to Paul,

　　A　he said that her attitude to the place was typical of Americans.
　　B　he indicated that he had had a different experience at the place.
　　C　he said that he was not at all surprised by her feelings about the place.
　　D　he suggested that he did not regard it as a place worth visiting.

36 During their conversation, Louisa agreed with Paul that

　　A　his attitude to his work was more limited than hers.
　　B　she had a tendency to be too sentimental.
　　C　her attitude to aul' Oirlan' was a foolish one.
　　D　only what was visible mattered to them in their work.

Part 6

You are going to read four extracts from articles about research into the educational value of computer games. For questions **37–40**, choose from the extracts **A–D**. The extracts may be chosen more than once.

Do computer games have educational value?

Four journalists consider some recent research findings.

A   Yvonne Cheney

Nobody is claiming that computer games are going to solve the world's problems, but even the most mindless of them taps into real human abilities and emotions. Gamers may not reflect on how the characters and scenarios they engage with could help them to interact with others in the real world, but recent research at the State University suggests that the games do perform such a function. In other words, far from retreating into another world, adopting another persona and acting out fantasies unconnected with real life, gamers are taking part in meaningful interaction and developing worthwhile skills. Leaving aside for a moment the issue of whether the games are addictive or not, or how much time gets devoted to them, this meticulous study adds more weight to the growing consensus that gaming may be good for us.

B   Declan Morton

We have heard a great deal recently about the cognitive benefits of gaming. Playing computer games, even the most banal of them, would seem to keep the brain active and to replicate the kind of thought processes that are valuable in the real world. Researchers at the State University take this idea a step further, however, claiming that the games develop interpersonal skills as well as cognitive ones. Although I have no argument with the way the study was conducted, this conclusion seems to be a step too far, and I can't see too many people taking it very seriously. The evidence that gaming can become compulsive behaviour, and not just in teenagers, is quite convincing and it seems perverse to suggest that such an individualistic pastime, that takes the player off into a world of complete fantasy, could ever promote interpersonal skills in the real world.

C   Lydia Porter

New Research at the State University suggests that playing computer games may not be so bad for us after all. This is not the first study to suggest that gaming can have both social and cognitive benefits for the individual, and the claim that mental agility is promoted by gaming is well documented in the literature. Even the popular notion that gaming takes over people's lives in a negative way, stifling social development, is being questioned – and not before time. As one commentator neatly puts it: 'For today's teenager, the computer game is just as compelling and absorbing, but no more harmful, than the novels of Jane Austen were for her grandmother at the same age.' The current study would benefit from further work, however, as the researchers seem to be making quite sweeping claims on the basis of relatively thin evidence. Having said that, the idea put forward here that social skills may develop as a result of gaming is an intriguing one, that's sure to spark some lively debate.

D   Stig Strellson

For those of us who are both enthusiastic gamers and perfectly well-adjusted human beings, the accusation frequently heard that gaming is both addictive and harmful has always smacked of prejudice and ignorance in equal measure. Fortunately, recent studies into the cognitive and social benefits of gaming are now setting the record straight. The latest study, carried out at the State University, takes the argument further, claiming that gaming actively promotes real-world interpersonal skills. Although it is sure to attract quite a bit of attention, this study is clearly just scratching the surface of a big issue. The fact that only a small geographical area was studied detracts a little from the findings. It is nonetheless, a further step in the right direction in terms of dispassionate debate on this emotive subject.

Which writer

has a different view from Cheney regarding the social benefits of gaming? | 37 |

doesn't share Morton's opinion about the addictive nature of gaming? | 38 |

agrees with Porter's point regarding the researcher's methodology? | 39 |

presents a different argument to the others regarding the likely impact of the research? | 40 |

Part 7

You are going to read an article about a competition in Britain in which the winners are the towns and cities considered the most attractive, particularly with regard to flowers and plants. Six paragraphs have been removed from the article. Choose from the paragraphs **A–G** the one which fits each gap (**41–46**). There is one extra paragraph which you do not need to use.

In the exam, mark your answers **on the separate answer sheet**.

The 'Britain in Bloom' competition

Every year, more than 1,000 towns and villages across Britain are in fierce competition to reap the benefit of the Britain in Bloom awards. William Langley reports.

Another town, another riot of begonias, hollyhocks and lupins. Cruising down streets thick with hanging baskets, planted tubs and flower-filled horse troughs, Jim Buttress, the Head Judge of the annual Britain in Bloom competition, needs no reminding that his verdict can make or break the place where you live. A nod from Jim can raise house prices, attract businesses, bring in tourists and secure council grants. Towns will do a lot to please him.

41

From barely noticed beginnings nearly half a century ago, Britain in Bloom has become a cultural phenomenon, stoking passions and rivalries that are changing the way the country looks and, as a consequence, refashioning our sense of what makes a place appear attractive. More than 1,000 towns, villages and cities now enter and the event has grown into the most fiercely contested of its kind in the world. Last week, the judging entered its tense final stages and Jim was weighing up the contenders for the biggest prize of all, the Champion of Champions trophy. In the early days, according to Jim, winning depended more or less on how many flowers you could plant and how much colour you could create.

42

The competition's influence extends far beyond the committees that enter it. Extravagant manifestations of floweriness have become a part of the country's visual texture. Traffic roundabouts have been turned into giant bouquets; ornamental gardens are springing up in industrial wastelands. Hanging baskets were relatively rare in Britain until the competition began. Now it's hard to find a high street in the country that isn't awash with them.

43

The competition's defenders consider such criticisms over the top or, at least, out of date. Since 2001, it has been run by the Royal Horticultural Society, with the aim of supporting 'environmentally sustainable, socially responsible, community-based' programmes. The old tricks of concealing urban grime beneath forests of fuchsias or creating rustic pastiches in built-up suburbs no longer work.

44

However badly these developments go down with the traditionalist element, the competition has become too important for many communities to ignore. A spokesman in Stockton-on-Tees, which won the Champion City award three years ago, says: 'Say you're a business trying to recruit staff and your town's won Britain in Bloom. It's very helpful in image terms. It makes people feel happier about living here.'

45

With so much at stake, the competitive tempo of Britain in Bloom has risen to a point that has started to cause alarm. Tales of dirty tricks abound. Recently, the village of Cayton, winner of several prizes, awoke to find that a mystery attacker had destroyed its prized flower beds. Jealous local rivals were rumoured to be responsible, though nothing has been proved. Some years earlier, in one village a water bowser used for irrigation was spiked with toxic chemicals.

46

Last week found Jim on his final tour before the results are announced in a month's time. 'It's been great,' he says. 'You see a lot of things when you do this job, and what I've seen most of is pride.'

A This is because, over the past decade, the judging criteria have been subtly changed. They now take into account 'conservation and biodiversity', 'recycling and limiting demand on natural resources' and 'community awareness and understanding'.

B It's not always like that, however, says Jim. 'I arrived somewhere on the train once, and there were flowers planted all around the station. It looked fantastic. When I got in the taxi, the driver said: "I don't know where all these flowers came from, they weren't here yesterday."'

C 'Some of this is exaggerated,' says Jim. 'There are rivalries, but there's a good spirit too. The competition brings out the best in communities. Go to places where there's poverty, vandalism, drugs, and you will see people working together, trying to make their surroundings look better.'

D Sometimes too much. One hired a stretch limousine to ferry him around in luxury. 'The thing had blacked-out windows,' he huffs. 'I couldn't see a thing.'

E Not everyone is thrilled, though. In a celebrated attack some years ago, the eminent historian and gardener Roy String accused Britain in Bloom of burying the country beneath an avalanche of flowers, which, he claimed, was destroying the character of otherwise perfectly attractive communities.

F Aberdeen, long wreathed in a reputation for charmlessness, has invested a great deal of money in reviving its image through the competition. Four years ago, it was awarded a gold award and a citation that described it as 'providing an outstanding combination of floral displays, wonderful trees, and numerous lovely parks'. Once known as the Granite City, the tourist-hungry city now styles itself the 'City of Roses'.

G 'But it's much more sophisticated, much more competitive now,' he says. 'People are in this thing to win it. There's a lot at stake. That sign on the way into town that says "Britain in Bloom Winner" is a real asset.'

Part 8

You are going to read a magazine article about the use of gadgets by people doing outdoor activities. For questions **47–56**, choose from the sections of the article (**A–D**). The sections may be chosen more than once.

In the exam, mark your answers **on the separate answer sheet**.

In which section of the article are the following mentioned?

why people were willing to suffer outdoors in the past	47
the need to understand certain terminology	48
a belief about what the reason for doing outdoor activities should be	49
a feeling of reassurance provided by a certain gadget	50
how many people have taken up outdoor activities because of gadgets	51
a criticism of the motivation of people who get a lot of gadgets for outdoor activities	52
a belief that gadgets may prove not to be useful	53
a belief that someone with gadgets would not be a good companion in certain circumstances	54
the high level of demand for gadgets connected with outdoor activities	55
an advantage of outdoor gadgets in addition to the benefits for users	56

On the trail of Kit Man

Gadgets that bring home comforts to the great outdoors have given rise to a new breed of outdoor adventurer. But purists are unconvinced.

A

Up there, in the clear fresh air, it isn't just the stars that are glowing. You can climb a mountain and find at the top of it a bleeping nightmare of hi-tech gadgetry and hardship-avoidance devices. Worried about getting lost? Relax with a handheld GPS unit, featuring 3D and aerial display, plus built-in compass and barometric altimeter. Even the sacred covenant between outdoor types and wet socks has come unravelled with the development of 'hydrophobic' fabrics which repel all moisture. At next month's Outdoors Show in Birmingham, all this kit and more will be on display for an audience which seemingly can't get enough of it. 'When we ask people what they come to the show for, they list two things,' says the event's sales manager, Mike Simmonds. 'One is the inspiration to get outdoors in the first place, and the other is to see the new gear, the gadgets, the breakthroughs. That's what they love.' The event, the showcase of Britain's booming adventure business shows everything the tech-savvy adventurer could wish for, from solar-heated sleeping bags to remote-controlled lanterns.

B

The rise of Kit Man, as the gizmo-fixated menace of the 21st-century mountains has been christened, reflects both changing social trends and the dizzying speed of scientific advance. Modern hikers have moved on from the Spartan routines of 50 years ago, when discomfort, bad food and danger were seen as part of the authentic outdoor experience. They also have more money and a conditioned attachment to life's luxuries. However, basic pioneering disciplines – map-reading, camp-laying, First Aid – have declined, to be shakily replaced by the virtual skills offered by technology. With so much gear now available, Kit Man and his kind stand accused by the old-schoolers of being interested only in reaching the summits of gadgetry.

C

'I think these people are completely missing the point,' huffs author and TV presenter Guy Grieve, who spent a year living alone in the Alaskan wilderness. 'The whole idea of going into the wild is to get away from the things that tie you in knots at home. I'd prefer to take as little as possible – a tent, a rifle, and a few pots and pans. All this technology, I mean, it might look fantastic on paper, but when there's a real problem, it's almost certainly going to let you down. What will see you through is the old stuff, the maps and the bits of rope. There are times when you need that kind of dependability. Who'd want to be stranded out in the wild with a gadget freak?' Travel and adventure writer Clive Tully agrees. 'Be suspicious of anything that claims to make your life easier,' he warns. 'My experience is that people who depend on technology are woefully ill-prepared in other ways. You still need to be able to read a map and do the basic stuff.'

D

None of which is enough to keep Kit Man from his toys. The mountains and hills are alive with the sound of ringing mobiles, beeping biometric pressure metres, clicking ultra-violet radiation sensors and the whirring of the current ultimate in gadget chic – a micro-helicopter which can be controlled from an iPod to send back live pictures of the route ahead. Thus tooled up, Kit Man must consider what he is to wear. And as any visit to a contemporary outdoor store shows, this involves not only acquiring new clobber, but new jargon. When he asks about a pair of pants, he will learn about Moisture Vapour Transfer Rate, Hydrostatic Heat Resistance and Wickability. It is tempting to scoff at Kit Man, but not everyone sides with the romantics. Many in the adventure business say gadgets have encouraged thousands who would otherwise not have ventured into the great outdoors. Evidence from the American market also suggests that technology has had a positive environmental impact, and increased safety standards.

Part 1

TEST 3 WRITING

You **must** answer this question. Write your answer in **220–260** words in an appropriate style. In the exam, write your answer **on the separate answer sheet provided**.

1 You have listened to a radio discussion programme about further education courses that should receive extra financial support from the government. You have made the notes below.

Which type of further education course deserves extra financial support from the government?

- art
- sport
- music

Some opinions expressed in the discussion:

'Art is a way to maintain a country's cultural heritage, so new artists are needed.'

'It's important that sportsmen and women represent the country internationally.'

'Music develops personal skills like co-operation and empathy necessary in the business world.'

Write an essay discussing **two** of the courses in your notes. You should **explain which type of course deserves extra financial support** from the government, **giving reasons** in support of your answer.

You may, if you wish, make use of the opinions expressed in the discussion, but you should use your own words as far as possible.

Part 2

Write an answer to **one** of the questions **2–4** in this part. Write your answer in **220–260** words. In the exam, write your answer **on the separate answer sheet provided**, and put the question number in the box at the top of the page.

2   You have received a letter from an English friend.

> I'm thinking about coming to live in your town for a while and learn your language! What kind of accommodation would I be able to get? And you know how keen I am on sport – any chance of learning a new one while I'm there? The problem is, I'll need to get a part-time job to pay for it all – is that going to be easy?
>
> Let me know – it would be great if I could do it all!
>
> Joe

Write your **letter** in reply. You do not need to include postal addresses.

3   You see this announcement on a media website.

> ## Best TV series ever!
>
> We want to find out what people think is the best TV series they've ever seen. Help us compile a list of the top ten! Submit a review of your own favourite TV series, explaining why it appeals to you and giving reasons why it should be included in our top ten list.

Write your **review**.

4   You see this announcement on your college noticeboard.

> ## Language students – let us improve what we do for you!
>
> Unfortunately, we can't spend much money, but we'd like to improve what we provide for our language students. Submit proposals to us explaining what is useful about the current facilities we provide, describe any problems you have with them and make recommendations for how we can improve them, giving reasons to support your ideas.

Write your **proposal**.

TEST 3 LISTENING

Part 1

You will hear three different extracts. For questions **1–6**, choose the answer (**A**, **B** or **C**) which fits best according to what you hear. There are two questions for each extract.

In the exam, write your answers **on the separate answer sheet**.

Extract One

You hear part of a discussion programme in which two artists are talking about their work.

1 What do they agree about inspiration?

   A An artist must know where it comes from.

   B Non-artists are unlikely to understand it.

   C Not all artists are willing to talk about it.

2 In his latest work, the man is exploring whether

   A holiday brochures are actually works of art.

   B the visual material in holiday brochures is effective.

   C we are misled by the image projected in holiday brochures.

Extract Two

You hear two club DJs talking about their work.

3 What did the man dislike about his previous job as a radio DJ?

   A He lacked the necessary background knowledge.

   B He didn't have one of the key skills required.

   C He often disagreed with the management.

4 What do they agree about being a club DJ?

   A It's difficult to make enough money to live well.

   B It's best not to play music you don't like personally.

   C You have to be responsive to the needs of the audience.

Extract Three

You hear part of an interview with the owner of a new cake shop.

5 What does she say about cake making?

   A It's always been her dream to do it professionally.

   B It appealed to her because it calls for a range of skills.

   C It was something she learnt to do as part of her first job.

6 How does she feel about her new business?

   A confident in her own judgement

   B relieved that she followed expert advice

   C concerned that its early success will not last

Part 2

You will hear a man called Paul Osborne giving a careers talk about his work as a computer game designer. For questions **7–14**, complete the sentences with a word or short phrase.

In the exam, write your answers **on the separate answer sheet**.

COMPUTER GAME DESIGNER

Paul says that people often think that he's a game **(7)** .... rather than a designer.

As part of his degree, Paul did a course in **(8)** ....
which has proved the most useful in his career.

In his first job, Paul was designing **(9)** .... most of the time.

Paul worked on what are known as **(10)** .... in his first job.

Paul mentions a game with the name **(11)** ....
as the one he's enjoyed working on most.

Paul uses the word **(12)** .... to describe what multi-players
in a game can create for themselves.

Paul says that achieving the correct **(13)** .... is the biggest challenge
when designing a game.

Paul feels that **(14)** .... is the most important personal
quality that a game designer needs.

Part 3

You will hear an interview with an archaeologist called Julian Radwinter. For questions **15–20**, choose the answer (**A**, **B**, **C** or **D**) which fits best according to what you hear.

15 Julian attributes his interest in archaeology as a teenager to

    A a wish to please his father.
    B his natural sense of curiosity.
    C a need to earn some spare cash.
    D his dissatisfaction with life on a farm.

16 What aspect of archaeology still excites Julian today?

    A the methodical nature of much of the work
    B the satisfaction of solving long-standing mysteries
    C the opportunity to use sophisticated equipment to date objects
    D the process of building up a theory around a few known facts

17 Julian feels that the public perception of archaeology

    A fails to acknowledge its scientific value.
    B has been negatively influenced by fictional accounts.
    C underestimates the gradual nature of the research process.
    D has tended to concentrate on the physical hardships involved.

18 How does Julian feel about his current research post?

    A He regrets having relatively few opportunities to travel.
    B He wishes his colleagues would take it more seriously.
    C He admits that the problems can get him down.
    D He suggests that it is relatively cost effective.

19 What does Julian hope to show as a result of his current research?

    A population levels in England in different periods
    B the length of time certain villages have existed
    C how wider trends affected local communities
    D the range of ancient agricultural methods

20 Julian's project on humour in archaeology aims to

    A celebrate an otherwise unrecorded aspect of archaeologists' lives.
    B compare archaeological findings with anecdotal evidence.
    C create a database of jokes connected with archaeology.
    D make archaeological reports more widely accessible.

Part 4

You will hear five short extracts in which college students are talking about being a member of a club.

In the exam, write your answers **on the separate answer sheet.**

TASK ONE

For questions **21–25**, choose from the list (**A–H**) what made each speaker decide to join the club.

A the advice of a friend

B seeing an advertisement   Speaker 1 [ ] 21

C wanting to meet people   Speaker 2 [ ] 22

D a desire to try something new   Speaker 3 [ ] 23

E hoping to learn a skill   Speaker 4 [ ] 24

F a need for exercise   Speaker 5 [ ] 25

G wishing to please someone else

H going along with a group decision

TASK TWO

For questions **26–30**, choose from the list (**A–H**) the main disadvantage of being a club member which each speaker mentions.

A the cost   Speaker 1 [ ] 26

B the regular commitment   Speaker 2 [ ] 27

C the attitude of other members   Speaker 3 [ ] 28

D the location   Speaker 4 [ ] 29

E the way it's organised   Speaker 5 [ ] 30

F the level of challenge

G the timing of sessions

H the lack of feedback on progress

TEST 3 SPEAKING

PART 1

The interlocutor will ask you a few questions about yourself and on everyday topics such as work and study, travel, entertainment, daily life and routines. For example:

- Where is a good place to visit in winter in your country? Why?
- Do you think you spend more or less time watching television now than you did in the past? Why?
- Do you think it's a good idea to have a daily routine? Why/Why not?

PART 2

Experiencing emotions

Turn to pictures 1–3 on page 176, which show people feeling emotional in different situations.

Candidate A, compare two of the pictures and say why the people might be feeling emotional, and how long the feeling might last.

Candidate B, which situation do you think is the most emotional? Why?

Dealing with difficult situations

Turn to pictures 1–3 on page 177, which show people dealing with difficult situations.

Candidate B, compare two of the pictures and say what might be difficult for people to deal with in these situations, and how important it might be for them to deal with the situations well.

Candidate A, which situation do you think is most difficult for the people to deal with? Why?

PART 3

Turn to the task on page 178, which shows how technology has changed people's lives.

Talk to each other about whether technology has had a positive or negative impact on people's lives today.

Decide which kind of technology has brought about the greatest change in people's lives today.

PART 4

Answer these questions:

- What do you think is the most positive aspect of technology? Why?
- Some people dislike using technology. Why do you think this is?
- Do you think that life is generally easier now than it was in the past? Why/Why not?
- Some people say that computers are the biggest time-saving device in modern life. What do you think?
- The popularity of mobile phones means that people are always contactable. Is this a good thing?
- What effect do you think social networking sites have had on relationships?

TEST 4
READING AND USE OF ENGLISH

Part 1

For questions **1–8**, read the text below and decide which answer (**A, B, C or D**) best fits each gap. There is an example at the beginning (**0**).

In the exam, mark your answers **on the separate answer sheet**.

Example:

| 0 | A | hardly | B | seldom | C | improbably | D | unlikely |

0 A ■ B ☐ C ☐ D ☐

Ceramics Fair

The sleepy village of Bussiere-Badil is **(0)** …….. the place where you'd expect to find an internationally famous ceramics exhibition attracting fifteen thousand visitors each year. Yet when a pottery fair was first held there over thirty years ago, it was the only one in all of France, and it is still one of the most important.

But why here? There is a seam of clay which runs through the area, but it is red clay of the type used to make tiles and bricks as **(1)** …….. pots, so there is no **(2)** …….. tradition of art pottery. The idea of the fair started when a Portuguese potter by the name of Miguel Calado **(3)** …….. a studio in the village at the **(4)** …….. of the mayor, himself a local tile-maker, who was **(5)** …….. to put the region on the map.

And he has certainly succeeded. Every year, up to 40 potters from all over France and beyond **(6)** …….. on the village to display their wares in a huge purpose-built shed. **(7)** …….. on show range from the utilitarian to the decorative, with every nuance in between. And the crowds come to look, to **(8)** …….. at the potters' art, and to buy.

1	A	opposed to	B	rather than	C	instead of	D	apart from
2	A	certain	B	particular	C	exact	D	individual
3	A	turned up	B	took up	C	made up	D	set up
4	A	instigation	B	advice	C	encouragement	D	persuasion
5	A	convinced	B	determined	C	dedicated	D	committed
6	A	gather	B	assemble	C	converge	D	collect
7	A	Issues	B	Items	C	Matters	D	Topics
8	A	astonish	B	fascinate	C	amaze	D	marvel

Part 2

For questions **9–16**, read the text below and think of the word which best fits each gap. Use only **one** word in each gap. There is an example at the beginning (**0**).

In the exam, write your answers **IN CAPITAL LETTERS on the separate answer sheet**.

Example: **0** O T H E R

Cheating at Computer Games

Computer games try to strike a balance between providing a challenge on the one hand, and allowing you to win through on the **(0)** ……… . Inevitably, however, you get stuck sometimes. But all is not lost. Many other gamers have figured **(9)** ……… what to do and posted the solution online. The answer is just a **(10)** ……… clicks away.

Purists say this is cheating. They argue that solving a puzzle yourself, **(11)** ……… gamers had to do in the old days, might have **(12)** ……… longer, but it was more satisfying. **(13)** ……… you know that detailed 'walkthroughs' are available online, free of charge, for almost any game, the temptation is to ask for virtual help at the first sign of trouble, **(14)** ……… robs players of a true sense of achievement.

I say this is rubbish. Doing a search and downloading a solution **(15)** ……… me more likely to finish games, so I get better value for money. But it's also a reminder that I'm a member of a broader community, many of **(16)** ……… have been this way before.

Part 3

For questions **17–24**, read the text below. Use the word given in capitals at the end of some of the lines to form a word that fits in the gap **in the same line**. There is an example at the beginning (**0**).

In the exam, write your answers **IN CAPITAL LETTERS** on the separate answer sheet.

Example: | 0 | E | S | S | E | N | T | I | A | L | | | | | | |

Trolley Bags

Wheeled trolley bags have become an (**0**) .... item of luggage amongst frequent travellers. The compact version proves particularly (**17**) .... as a piece of hand luggage. Carried onboard aeroplanes, it allows you to avoid the queues at the baggage check-in counters on your (**18**) .... journey and waiting at the baggage carousel on your way home. These days, there are (**19**) .... guidelines regarding the maximum size for hand luggage on flights, and these stipulated (**20**) .... are continuously subject to change. Policies also vary between airlines and airports as well as being influenced by your (**21**) .... destination. The outcome of all this is that travellers are recommended to check out the latest luggage (**22**) .... before setting out for the airport.

What's more, before investing in a trolley bag, bear in mind that you're likely to be negotiating (**23**) .... surfaces as well as the smooth flooring of airport lounges, and that larger wheels are better able to absorb bumps than their smaller (**24**) ....

ESSENCE

USE

OUT

OFFICE

MEASURE

EVENT

RESTRICT

EVEN

COUNTER

Part 4

For questions **25–30**, complete the second sentence so that it has a similar meaning to the first sentence, using the word given. **Do not change the word given.** You must use between **three** and **six** words, including the word given. Here is an example (**0**).

Example:

0 Chloe would only eat a pizza if she could have a mushroom topping.
ON

Chloe .... a mushroom topping when she ate a pizza.

The gap can be filled with the words 'insisted on having', so you write:

Example: | **0** | INSISTED ON HAVING

In the exam, write **only** the missing words **IN CAPITAL LETTERS on the separate answer sheet**.

---

25 Even if she runs really fast, Tina won't get to school on time.
HOW

No .... , Tina won't get to school on time.

26 Penny was unwilling to admit that the accident had been her fault.
BLAME

Penny was .... for the accident.

27 Clarice's mother told her not to spend the money under any circumstances.
MUST

'Whatever .... that money, Clarice,' said her mother.

28 Joe was very surprised to see Melanie walk into the room.
TAKEN

Joe .... Melanie walked into the room.

29 In the office, Tom is responsible for all aspects of the updating of the company's website.
OVERALL

In the office, Tom has .... the company's website up to date.

30 It's quite common for students at the school to go on to win Olympic medals.
MEANS

It's .... for students at the school to go on to win Olympic medals.

Part 5

You are going to read an article about happiness. For questions **31–36**, choose the answer (**A**, **B**, **C** or **D**) which you think fits best according to the text.

In the exam, mark your answers **on the separate answer sheet**.

The impossible moment of delight

A recent survey has examined the well-trodden ground of the relationship between pleasure and money. Many studies have examined this, from any number of starting points, often concluding, in the oldest of old clichés, that money can't buy you happiness or, in more sophisticated terms, that happiness and pleasure often reside, not in riches in absolute terms, but in being richer than the people who happen to live to your left or your right. Other studies have claimed that comparison with the wealth of others leads to a 'set-up for disappointment' and that a good attitude is all that matters.

This most recent study inquired into the well-being of 136,000 people worldwide and compared it to levels of income. It found, overall, that feelings of security and general satisfaction did increase with financial status. Money, however, could not lift its possessors to the next level, and was unable to provide enjoyment or pleasure on its own. The survey, published in the *Journal of Personality and Social Psychology*, examined large numbers of people from almost every culture on Earth, and found much the same thing. The stereotype of the rich man who finds life savourless and without pleasure was not invented simply to keep the poor happy with their lot.

Paul Bloom addresses the same issue in his book *How Pleasure Works*. According to Bloom, at the point when people get the thing they really want, they enter a state of perfect pleasure. Both Bloom's book and the enormous survey concentrate on status and on the moment of getting possession of something we want. Are we satisfied and filled with pleasure when we get what we want? Bloom, looking at eager consumers, would say 'yes'; the survey tends to say 'not necessarily'. In my view, it's rare that we can actually pin down the specific moment when the feeling of pleasure is at its clearest.

Take the teenager determined to buy the latest must-have gadget, a woman setting out to get a new handbag, or a prosperous businessman who wants to add to his collection of Japanese *netsuke*. The setting out with the happy intention of spending; the entering of the shop; the examination of the wares; the long decision; the handing over of the money; the moment when the ownership of the goods is transferred; the gloating at home; the moment when the object is displayed to others. All these steps form a process in enjoyment, but almost all of them are redolent with anticipation or with retrospective glee. The moment where bliss is at its peak is over in a flash, and hardly exists at all. Everything else is expectation or memory.

Composers have always known this simple, basic truth: pleasure is half anticipation and half blissful recollection, and hardly at all about the fulfilment of the promise. The great musical statements of ecstasy, such as Wagner's *Tristan and Isolde* or Schubert's first *Suleika* song, are literally all half crescendo and half languid recall. We look forward to pleasure; we look back on it. The moment of pleasure itself is over in a flash, and often rather questionable.

The hairband and geegaw emporium Claire's Accessories has a thoughtful, rather philosophical slogan to tempt its young customers. It sells itself under the strapline 'where getting ready is half the fun'. That is honest and truthful. A group of 14-year-old girls in their party best is nowhere near as successful an enterprise of pleasure as exactly the same girls putting on and trying out and discussing their hopes for the party in advance; not as successful either as talking it over the next day. The party itself, from the beginning of time, has consisted of a lot of standing around and gawping and giggling, and someone crying in the lavatory.

So any notion of fulfilled pleasure which insists on the moment of bliss is doomed to failure. Mr Bloom and the researchers of the *Journal of Personality and Social Psychology* were clearly happiest when undertaking their research, during which time they were looking forward to coming to a conclusion. And now they can sit back and start to say 'Yes, when I concluded my theory of pleasure and satisfaction ...' Even for philosophers of pleasure, another ancient and well-handled cliché about travel and life is true: getting there really is half the pleasure.

31 The writer says that previous studies of happiness have differed on

　A whether having more money than others makes people happy.
　B why people compare their financial situation to that of others.
　C what makes people believe that money brings happiness.
　D how important it is for people to think that they are happy.

32 According to the writer, the most recent survey

　A confirmed a common belief about wealth and happiness.
　B produced results that may surprise some people.
　C provided more accurate information than many other surveys.
　D found that there was no connection between money and happiness.

33 In the third paragraph, the writer says that his own opinion on the subject

　A has been influenced by the results of the survey.
　B is based on his personal feelings rather than on research.
　C differs from what Bloom concludes in his book.
　D might not be widely shared by other people.

34 The writer says that the musical works he mentions

　A are not intended to produce feelings of intense happiness.
　B sometimes disappoint people who listen to them.
　C perfectly illustrate his point about pleasure.
　D show how hard it is to generalise about pleasure.

35 The writer says that the company Claire's Accessories understands that

　A parties are less enjoyable for girls than getting ready for them.
　B girls enjoy getting ready for parties more than any other aspect of them.
　C looking good at parties makes girls happier than anything else.
　D what girls wear for parties affects their memories of them.

36 The writer concludes that both Bloom and the researchers

　A would agree with his own theory of pleasure.
　B would agree with a certain cliché.
　C have made an important contribution to the study of pleasure.
　D have gone through a process he has previously described.

Part 6

You are going to read four extracts from articles about research into workspaces. For questions **37–40**, choose from the extracts **A–D**. The extracts may be chosen more than once.

The Perfect Workspace
Four commentators review recent research into workspaces.

A   Delphine Bartlett
Whether we work in an architect-designed office complex or the spare room at home, many of us spend the greater part of our working lives sitting at the same desk in the same room. Recent studies by psychologists confirm that the nature of that space, and how a worker relates to it, can have serious consequences for that person's sense of well-being. Less convincing is the claim made in one study that productivity improves if each individual is given a measure of control over their own workspace. Some firms encourage family photos and desk toys whilst others forbid them, but does this really affect the way people work? What's more, clearly some people thrive on clutter, whilst others perform better if surrounded by order, and this is true across a range of occupations. And although research suggests that when management tries to impose a 'tidy-desk' policy, this can be counter-productive in terms of levels of creativity, I've seen little evidence of this in practice.

B   Brian O'Malley
A recent study by workplace psychologists suggests that giving employees a say in how their working environment is designed and organised can lead to real improvements in self-esteem. Features such as low ceilings and small windows can have the opposite effect, and add to the impression of merely being a small cog in a big wheel. I'd go further and suggest that there are also implications for efficiency and output, having observed many such instances myself. By encouraging workers to do things like choose the colour scheme or giving them the freedom to surround themselves with disorderly piles of papers if they so choose, firms can encourage them to do their best. And although it's a cliché to suggest that new ideas are more likely to emerge from chaos than from proscriptive order, innovation can be stifled by other aspects of the physical working environment.

C   Agnetha Gomez
You would expect an artists' studio to be a bit messy and an accountant to finish the day with a clear desk in a state-of-the-art smart building – but I suspect that there are individuals engaged in both professions who would feel uncomfortable in such stereotypical surroundings. And why shouldn't they? Nonetheless, there is something about rows of figures and the whole idea of reconciliation that seems to suggest that the disorderly accountant may be in the wrong job, and recent research does point to some correlation between tidiness and accuracy. Photographic evidence meanwhile reveals that Einstein had an incredibly messy desk, suggesting that disorder in the workplace doesn't obstruct the ability to come up with new ideas. What a workspace does clearly reflect, however, is someone's personality. Most of us want to settle down to work in congenial surroundings, and most companies respect this and allow some personal touches to be introduced.

D   Rory Lin
There can be little doubt that the design of office buildings can have a great effect on the well-being of those working inside. Cramped offices with a lack of natural light aren't conducive to happy working relationships, whereas a building designed to facilitate interaction and positive attitudes is a good investment for forward-thinking companies with cash to spare. But recent research suggests that even in the best designed building, employees welcome the chance to endow their own particular workspace with personal touches. Furthermore, a slick, minimalist environment, however fashionable, does not necessarily meet the needs of all groups of employees. Some creative people need to experiment in real space and time, and there are still limits to what can be confined to a computer screen. In the end, a good office building has got to accommodate everybody comfortably.

Which writer

expresses a different view from Bartlett's concerning the probable outcome
of attempts by companies to influence how individuals organise their workspace? **37**

makes a similar point to Gomez regarding the extent to which the physical
appearance of a workspace needs to reflect the type of work being done there? **38**

shares Lin's view on the possible effects of architectural features on staff morale? **39**

presents a different argument to the others on the subject of possible links
between tidiness and creativity? **40**

Part 7

You are going to read an article about a series of books. Six paragraphs have been removed from the article. Choose from the paragraphs **A–G** the one which fits each gap (**41–46**). There is one extra paragraph which you do not need to use.

In the exam, mark your answers **on the separate answer sheet**.

Publishing's natural phenomenon

The 'Collins New Naturalist' series is as famous for its covers as its content. Peter Marren looks at how the unique jackets have taken on a life of their own.

They fill a large bookcase like a paper rainbow. The *Collins New Naturalist* series (or 'library', as its editors prefer) has been a publishing phenomenon for many decades. It has rolled on, in fits and starts, from the late 1940s and is currently enjoying a sprint, with four new titles in the past 12 months. Numbering 111 books in all, and with plenty more in the pipeline, the *New Naturalist* is probably the longest running specialist series in the world. What is its secret?

41

There is nothing quite like them. From the start, they were based not on strictly natural photography but on lithographic prints. The artists preferred bold, simplified forms that were symbolic rather than strictly illustrative.

42

These quirky designs were the work of Clifford and Rosemary Ellis, a husband-and-wife artistic partnership who normally signed their work with a cipher: 'C&RE'. They generally used a limited palette of colours broadened by printing one on top of another. Both were well-versed in animal drawing, in Rosemary's case from sketching livestock on the farm where she lived as a girl, in Clifford's from studying animals at the London Zoo.

43

But the technology for producing those in colour was in its infancy in the 1940s and the available stock was unimpressive. Instead, with the tacit support of William Collins, the Ellises were commissioned to produce a jacket for the first title, *Butterflies*. Collins liked it. The books' scientific editors, led by James Fisher and Julian Huxley, did not. But, since the jacket was part of the sales process, not the science, Collins had his way. The Ellises then produced a common design for every book in the series.

44

They were seen to best advantage when the books were displayed together in the shop, becoming ever more eye-catching as the series took off during the late 1940s and 1950s. The jackets were printed by lithography in three or four colours on expensive art paper. Initially, the artist's life-size sketch was transferred to the printing plate with great skill by artisan printers in London.

45

The jackets effectively became an extended work of art, until the Ellises had completed 70 designs (plus 22 more for the series of single-species monographs). Their last one was published the year Clifford Ellis died, in 1985. Fortunately, his shoes were filled by Robert Gillmor, the highly acclaimed bird artist, who since then has produced dazzling jackets to the same overall design. Originally printed by lithography, Gillmor's designs are now based on linocuts, and they evoke the contents of the book as well as ever. To celebrate these unique jackets, Collins commissioned Gillmor and me to write a book discussing each design, one by one.

46

Our book, *Art of the New Naturalists*, has now been published. We hope people agree that it commemorates something special: commercial art inspired by natural forms, a riotous dance of biodiversity and imagination.

A Later, an even more demanding production method was devised, which separated out each colour for combining on the press. Great trouble was taken to get each one exactly right, and every design was the product of many weeks of sketching and colour trials.

B For example, the jacket of *The Sea Shore* shows a broken crab's claw resting on the beach; nothing more. The fox on the jacket of *British Mammals* is a green-eyed blur, and the eye of the rabbit it is stalking is repeated three times on the spine.

C In the process, some buried treasures came to light. These included the original artwork, long lost to sight in a warehouse, preparatory sketches and discarded alternate designs. There was even artwork for books that never were; striking jackets for the unpublished *Bogs and Fens, The Fox* and the intriguingly titled *Ponds, Pools and Puddles*.

D This had the title printed on a broad band of colour (at first in handcrafted letters) and the book's number in the series at the top of the spine. A specially designed colophon with two conjoined 'N's smuggled itself inside an oval at the bottom.

E Partly it was, and is, its scientific quality. The series is at the high end of popular natural history, unafraid to tackle difficult cutting-edge science. These books are also collector's items. And the reason they are collected is their jackets.

F The proof of this is that the cover illustrations have become iconic. They have given the books a highly distinctive style that has inspired nature enthusiasts for many decades and they have helped to make the books become highly collectible.

G They came to the series largely by chance. The original plan had been to wrap the books in photographic jackets, in keeping with the publisher's intention to 'foster the natural pride of the British public in their native fauna and flora'.

Part 8

You are going to read a magazine article about interns – young people doing work placements for a limited period, usually without pay. For questions **47–56**, choose from the sections of the article (**A–D**). The sections may be chosen more than once.

In the exam, mark your answers **on the separate answer sheet**.

Which intern mentions

her feeling when discovering something at work?	47
the fact that some of her work can be seen?	48
having no idea how to carry out a certain task?	49
her feeling about the people she works with?	50
having no regrets about a choice she made previously?	51
what is considered normal in her area of work?	52
the outcome of some of the work she does?	53
a desire not to be in the same situation in the future?	54
something she regarded as unpredictable?	55
a preference concerning the work she does as an intern?	56

The intern's tale

Many workplaces have interns. Is it useful work experience or an unpaid waste of time?
Sarah Barnes meets four young interns.

A   Jessica Turner: Future Films

Working on scripts that you know are going to become films one day is really exciting. We get a broad variety of genres sent to us here. Personally, I love anything that's been adapted from a book, especially if I've read it. I read scripts, sometimes I attend meetings with writers, and I've also researched potential writers and directors online. My placement was due to come to an end this month but I've just been offered the paid role of production and development assistant. I'm pleased to be able to stay – I didn't want to leave everyone. It's been tough getting to this point, but you can't expect too much because it's a competitive industry. Because my degree was in film theory, I didn't come away with the practical experience of being able to go on set and know what's what. Maybe I would have progressed more quickly if I had.

B   Rasa Abramaviciute: Vivienne Westwood fashion company

I work in the same department as Vivienne Westwood, so I see her almost every day. She treats everyone equally, whether they are paid staff or interns. My main task is tracing patterns. I was shocked by how big they are; so much fabric goes into making a Westwood dress. When I started, I was working on the archive, so I had the opportunity to see past collections up close. I work five days a week, 10a.m. to 6p.m., but the days get longer and more stressful as we approach Fashion Week. I'll stay for another three months, and then I'll go straight back to university to complete my final year. In fashion, if you want to establish yourself over the competition, you have to work hard and for free, because that's what everyone else is willing to do.

C   Hannah Sanderson: Merlin

Over the past few years I've been doing volunteer work in Calcutta, Bogotá and Teheran, so it's quite hard to adjust to being back in the UK. Most of my friends are buying houses, have cars and go on holidays. But I never feel I've missed out because I'm doing what I've always wanted to do. I work three days a week, receiving a small sum to cover expenses. Money from my father has gone towards funding my placement and I'm really fortunate that I can live with my mum, although it does mean my commute can take up to two hours. Without my family, I don't think I could be doing this. Next month I'm starting a six-month placement in Myanmar, monitoring the health facilities the charity supplies there. After that, I might actually be in a position to earn a salary. If I was 35 and still working unpaid, I'd think 'What am I doing?'

D   Paula Morison: Whitechapel Gallery

I came to London with no plans. I didn't know how long it would take to get a job. I'd saved up some money and resigned myself to staying on a friend's sofa for a while, but luck was on my side and I found a job as a seamstress within a couple of weeks. My placement at the gallery came along a week later. I've helped install exhibitions and create gallery publications. One of the most exciting tasks was helping the artist Claire Barclay create the installation that's now on display in the gallery. Because some of the piece is sewn, my seamstress skills came in handy. The hardest thing is at the start, when you don't know anything. Someone asks: 'Can you courier this?' and you have to ask so many questions, like 'Which courier company?' and 'Where are the envelopes?' I'm about to finish my placement and I'm planning my own curatorial project with a friend. It will be a lot of work but I think I have to go for these things now, otherwise I'll regret it later.

Part 1

You **must** answer this question. Write your answer in **220–260** words in an appropriate style. In the exam, write your answer **on the separate answer sheet provided**.

1 Your class has had a discussion on the value of competitive sport for young people. You have made the notes below.

> **What is the greatest value of competitive sport for young people?**
>
> - positive attitude
> - healthy lifestyle
> - use of time

> Some opinions expressed in the discussion:
>
> 'It can make young people overly competitive, then they don't help each other or learn to co-operate.'
>
> 'It's good to exercise because a healthy body means a healthy mind – winning's irrelevant.'
>
> 'It takes up too much time and takes young people away from more important things like studying.'

Write an essay discussing **two** of the points in your notes. You should **explain which is the greatest value** of competitive sport for young people, **giving reasons** in support of your answer.

You may, if you wish, make use of the opinions expressed in the discussion, but you should use your own words as far as possible.

Part 2

Write an answer to **one** of the questions **2–4** in this part. Write your answer in **220–260** words. In the exam, write your answer **on the separate answer sheet provided**, and put the question number in the box at the top of the page.

2   You see this announcement in an international magazine.

> ### The best of friends!
> As part of our series of letters on relationships in the twenty-first century, we want readers to tell us what they think makes someone a good friend, and how such a relationship can be maintained today. Write us a letter about a friend you feel is special. Tell us how you maintain this relationship, and whether you feel it has changed over the years. We'll publish the best ones on our Letters Page.

Write your **letter**. You do not need to include any postal addresses.

3   Your school wants to do more to help its language students improve their communication skills and has asked current students to write proposals making suggestions for what the school could do.

In your proposal you should explain what language students currently do to improve their communication skills, describe any problems they have and recommend any activities or facilities that the school should provide.

Write your **proposal**.

4   You have been helping to run a new music club at your college. Now the college principal wants to get more people involved with the club and attract new members. The club organiser has asked you to write a report for the principal outlining what the club currently does, explaining the club's future plans and suggesting ways of getting more people involved with the music club.

Write your **report**.

TEST 4
LISTENING

Part 1

You will hear three different extracts. For questions **1–6**, choose the answer (**A**, **B** or **C**) which fits best according to what you hear. There are two questions for each extract.

In the exam, write your answers **on the separate answer sheet**.

Extract One

You hear a man talking to a friend who's just arrived at an airport.

1   They disagree about whether the woman's flight

   A   represented good value for money.

   B   managed to keep to the schedule.

   C   offered a good level of comfort.

2   What is the man suggesting for the future?

   A   changing the airline

   B   changing the arrival airport

   C   changing the means of transport

Extract Two

You hear a science teacher telling a friend about her work.

3   What does she say about kids using the internet as a source of information?

   A   It has changed the nature of the teacher's role.

   B   It should only happen with the teacher's guidance.

   C   It can't take the place of the teacher's input on a subject.

4   How does she feel about the type of teaching she does?

   A   keen to keep changing it to meet students' needs

   B   sorry that other teachers don't want to adopt it

   C   convinced that it is proving to be effective

Extract Three

You hear a new album being reviewed on a music radio station.

5   What aspect of the recording made the greatest impression on the woman?

   A   where it was made

   B   the style of the finished product

   C   the range of instruments used on it

6   What does the man feel is different about this band?

   A   the originality of their sound

   B   the consistent quality of the tracks

   C   the way they've blended various musical influences

Part 2

You will hear a student called Jon giving a class presentation about the llama, an animal that comes originally from South America. For questions **7–14**, complete the sentences with a word or short phrase.

In the exam, write your answers **on the separate answer sheet**.

THE LLAMA

Jon says that llamas and alpacas are generally distinguished by the shape of the
(7) ....

Jon discovered that the wild ancestor of the llama was mostly (8) .... in colour.

In ancient times, domesticated llamas most often worked in (9) .... areas.

Jon says that the word (10) .... is most often used by humans when talking about llamas.

Jon found out that well-trained llamas only spit and kick if they feel (11) ....

Jon describes the noise made by llamas for usual communications as a (12) ....

Jon says that llama fleece is popular with weavers because it contains no (13) ....

The commonest products made from llama hair are (14) ....

94   TEST 4: LISTENING

Part 3

You will hear an interview with a young film director, Lauren Casio, who is talking about her life and work. For questions **15–20**, choose the answer (**A**, **B**, **C** or **D**) which fits best according to what you hear.

In the exam, write your answers **on the separate answer sheet**.

15 Lauren was encouraged to follow a career as a film-maker because her teachers

    A could see that she had potential.
    B found her early attempts highly original.
    C were impressed by her level of motivation.
    D appreciated her ability to work within a budget.

16 How does Lauren respond when asked about critics of film school?

    A She thinks they would benefit from going to one.
    B She defends the record of the one that she attended.
    C She agrees that it's less useful for certain types of work.
    D She regrets that it is the only option for poorer students.

17 Lauren didn't start making full-length feature films sooner because

    A she wanted to be sure of her ability first.
    B she had a bad experience with an early attempt.
    C she wasn't lucky enough to have the opportunity.
    D she didn't manage to find the financial backing she needed.

18 What does Lauren say about the characters in her films?

    A She tries to surprise her audience with them.
    B She likes them to fit into well-defined types.
    C She accepts that the men may be more interesting.
    D She sets out to make them as complicated as possible.

19 How does Lauren feel now about the film *Hidden Valley Dreams*?

    A She regrets the setting she chose for it.
    B She regards it as being far from perfect.
    C She's surprised that it's proved so popular.
    D She wishes she'd spent more time on the plot.

20 How does Lauren feel when she goes to give talks in schools?

    A unsure whether to reveal her humble background
    B worried that she might give the kids unrealistic ambitions
    C slightly uncomfortable with the idea of being a role model
    D concerned that she may not command the respect of the students

TEST 4: LISTENING

Part 4

You will hear five short extracts in which people are talking about falling asleep in a public place.

In the exam, write your answers **on the separate answer sheet**.

TASK ONE

For questions **21–25**, choose from the list (**A–H**) the reason each speaker gives for falling asleep in the place they did.

A   to keep someone company

B   as a result of physical exertion   Speaker 1   [21]

C   to save money   Speaker 2   [22]

D   as preparation for physical activity   Speaker 3   [23]

E   to avoid inconveniencing others   Speaker 4   [24]

F   as a result of some treatment   Speaker 5   [25]

G   to avoid a long walk home

H   to prove something to themselves

TASK TWO

For questions **26–30**, choose from the list (**A–H**) how each speaker felt afterwards.

A   embarrassed by the situation

B   aware of physical discomfort   Speaker 1   [26]

C   offended by the reactions of others   Speaker 2   [27]

D   pleased to have had some rest   Speaker 3   [28]

E   worried about the risk taken   Speaker 4   [29]

F   grateful for a way of passing the time   Speaker 5   [30]

G   happy to have followed local customs

H   disgusted by the conditions

TEST 4: LISTENING

TEST 4 SPEAKING

PART 1

The interlocutor will ask you a few questions about yourself and on everyday topics such as work and study, travel, entertainment, daily life and routines. For example:

- What would you like to be doing in five years' time? Why?
- Do you enjoy listening to the same kind of music as your friends?
- When is the best time of day for you to relax? Why?

PART 2

Challenging activities

Turn to pictures 1–3 on page 179, which show people doing activities that can be challenging.

Candidate A, compare two of the pictures and say why the people might be finding these activities challenging, and which activity might give them the most satisfaction.

Candidate B, which activity do you think is the most challenging? Why?

Learning about the past

Turn to pictures 1–3 on page 180, which show people learning about the past.

Candidate B, compare two of the pictures and say what the advantages are of learning about the past in these ways, and who might actually learn most about the past.

Candidate A, which do you think is the least effective way to learn about the past? Why?

PART 3

Turn to the task on page 181, which shows some special qualities or skills people might need to be successful at work nowadays.

Talk to each other about why people might need special qualities or skills to be successful at work nowadays.

Decide which quality is the most important for employers when they take on new employees.

PART 4

Answer these questions:

- Which is more important in any job: qualifications, personality or practical experience?
- What type of jobs should be most highly-valued and paid? Why?
- Do you think it's better to do one job all your life or change jobs frequently? Why?
- Should there be a compulsory retirement age or should people be allowed to work as long as they like? Why/Why not?
- Do you think that people can be taught to be good leaders in the workplace? Why/Why not?
- Some people say that it doesn't matter what job you do – the most important thing is to enjoy doing it. What do you think?

TEST 5 READING AND USE OF ENGLISH

Part 1

For questions **1–8**, read the text below and decide which answer (**A, B, C** or **D**) best fits each gap. There is an example at the beginning (**0**).

In the exam, mark your answers **on the separate answer sheet**.

Example:

0   A   fulfil   B   accomplish   C   manage   D   perform

0	A	B	C	D
	▬	▭	▭	▭

Book Review
Galapagos: The islands that changed the world

I was lucky enough to **(0)** …….. an ambition and visit the Galapagos Islands two years ago. **(1)** …….. no substitute for a visit, this superbly attractive book provides a fascinating commentary and scientific background to the Galapagos experience. BBC books have **(2)** …….. their usual high-quality job in producing the volume that will accompany their TV series of the same name.

Nothing can compare to exploring the strange landscapes, **(3)** …….. up close and personal with the unique wildlife and witnessing the rich biological and environmental history that is so very apparent on the islands. However, this book does **(4)** …….. close. The superb descriptive prose of award-winning cameraman Paul Stewart is another plus **(5)** …….., as is the fact that this is punctuated by his iconic photography. This book **(6)** …….. in celebrating the weird and wonderful sights but don't **(7)** …….. read this book as an alternative to actually going, use it as the **(8)** …….. of inspiration for your own trip, a useful guide once you're there and a stunning reminder on your return.

1	A	Despite	B	However	C	Whilst	D	Whereas
2	A	set	B	done	C	made	D	given
3	A	getting	B	reaching	C	arriving	D	gaining
4	A	run	B	come	C	go	D	pass
5	A	spot	B	point	C	mark	D	tip
6	A	attains	B	succeeds	C	achieves	D	obtains
7	A	barely	B	hardly	C	merely	D	scarcely
8	A	base	B	cause	C	origin	D	source

Part 2

For questions **9–16**, read the text below and think of the word which best fits each gap. Use only **one** word in each gap. There is an example at the beginning (**0**).

In the exam, write your answers **IN CAPITAL LETTERS on the separate answer sheet**.

Example: | 0 | A | S | | | | | | | | | | | | | | |

A history of table tennis

Like many other sports, table tennis started out **(0)** …….. a mild social diversion. It was popular in England in the second half of the nineteenth century under its present name and various trade names like Whiff-Whaff and Ping-Pong, **(9)** …….. sought to imitate the sound **(10)** …….. by the ball striking the table. The game soon **(11)** …….. something of a craze and there are many contemporary references to it and illustrations of it **(12)** …….. played, usually in domestic surroundings.

(13) …….. the early twentieth century, the sport had already acquired some of its present-day complexities, **(14)** …….. it was still seen by many as an after-dinner amusement **(15)** …….. than a sport. An account published in 1903 found it necessary to warn players **(16)** …….. the wearing of evening dress, but went on to give detailed technical advice about the pen-holder grip and tactics.

Over the next 60 years, table tennis developed into a worldwide sport, played by up to 30 million competitive players.

Part 3

For questions **17–24**, read the text below. Use the word given in capitals at the end of some of the lines to form a word that fits in the gap **in the same line**. There is an example at the beginning (**0**).

In the exam, write your answers **IN CAPITAL LETTERS on the separate answer sheet**.

Example: **0** H I S T O R I A N S

Dancing is good for you

Since the dawn of civilisation, dance has been an important part of life, and dance (**0**) .... struggle to identify the first evidence of dance as it has always been an intrinsic part of human (**17**) .... The earliest recorded dances, discovered in the 9,000-year-old Bhimbetka rock paintings in India, were used to tell stories and celebrate (**18**) .... events, whilst also serving as a way of passing on information to future generations.

But why has dance, something which can make someone look utterly (**19**) .... if done wrong, always seemed to be natural to our DNA? Experts argue that its psychological and physiological benefits are the cause. (**20**) .... studies have discovered that dancing is not only an (**21**) .... form of non-verbal communication, but is also a mood-boosting cure that can alleviate (**22**) ...., improve interpersonal (**23**) .... and cure illnesses. Physically, dancing makes us happy because, as with any repetitive exercise, it releases endorphins. Also it's a socialising event, (**24**) .... us to be physically close to people and more emotionally connected to them.

HISTORY

BEHAVE

SIGNIFY

RIDICULE

NUMBER
EFFECT

DEPRESS
RELATION

ABLE

Part 4

For questions **25–30**, complete the second sentence so that it has a similar meaning to the first sentence, using the word given. **Do not change the word given.** You must use between **three** and **six** words, including the word given. Here is an example (**0**).

Example:

0 Chloe would only eat a pizza if she could have a mushroom topping.
  ON
  Chloe .... a mushroom topping when she ate a pizza.

The gap can be filled with the words 'insisted on having', so you write:

| Example: | 0 | INSISTED ON HAVING |

In the exam, write **only** the missing words **IN CAPITAL LETTERS on the separate answer sheet**.

---

25 The village shop is now being managed by a national supermarket chain.
  TAKEN
  A national supermarket chain .... of the village shop.

26 This door is an emergency exit and must never be locked for any reason.
  ACCOUNT
  On .... be locked because it is an emergency exit.

27 Melvin's friend recommended that website where he bought the camping equipment.
  ON
  Melvin bought equipment from that website .... a friend.

28 We never imagined that Julian might be planning to resign from his job.
  OCCURRED
  It never .... Julian might be planning to resign from his job.

29 As long as he could see, Kevin really didn't mind where he sat in the stadium.
  DIFFERENCE
  As long as he could see, ... where he sat in the stadium.

30 Unfortunately, I don't have enough time to visit the gym regularly.
  ABLE
  If I had more time, ... more regular visits to the gym.

Part 5

You are going to read an article about a management theory book. For questions **31–36**, choose the answer (**A**, **B**, **C** or **D**) which you think fits best according to the text.

In the exam, mark your answers **on the separate answer sheet**.

The new management gurus
What can animals tell us about business?

Bees. Ants. Reindeer. Not the usual topic of conversation at an average board meeting. But if Peter Miller's debut book, *Smart Swarm*, is anything to go by, the creatures could revolutionise the way we do business. In the latest in a series of books that challenge leaders to think differently, *Smart Swarm* explores the habits, actions and instincts of animals and how they can be applied to business. The book is set to become the most talked about in management circles after Miller, a senior editor at *National Geographic Magazine*, wrote an article on the subject a few years ago, which was read by 30 million people globally.

It follows a string of 'business thinking' books that have hit the shelves in recent years, all searching for new answers on how to run organisations effectively. *Obliquity*, published in March, told us that the most profitable companies are not the most aggressive in chasing profits, *Wikinomics*, a bestseller, demonstrated new models of production based on community and collaboration. Miller believes his book is the first time anyone has laid out the science behind a management theory. 'The biology of how ant colonies or beehives work are appealing models for organisations and systems that can be applied in a business context,' he says.

So how exactly can bees help run board meetings? 'By the way they work independently before they work together,' Miller says. 'Picture a huge beehive hanging on the branch of a tree, with about 5,000 bees vying for space and protection. They know their colony is getting too big and leaving them vulnerable. They must find a new home – and fast – but in a way that everyone agrees with. In today's business environment, managers need to be able to make the right decisions under huge amounts of pressure. Yet, it is clear that some of the best-paid leaders in some of the biggest organisations can get it dramatically wrong. How is it that they can fail to make efficient business decisions when a swarm of bees can make a critical decision about their hive in just a few seconds?'

According to Miller, 'swarm theory' can help managers in three simple steps: discover, test and evaluate. The bees first realise they have a problem. They then fly into the neighbourhood to find potential new sites. They come back and perform a 'dance' to get other bees to follow them. Eventually, the bees with the best dance attract the most votes – and a decision is made. Back to the board meeting. Managers that encourage debate, and then have a ballot over which idea is best, stand a better chance of getting it right, Miller says. 'The bee example tells you that you need to seek out diversity in your team. You need to have a way of gathering up very different approaches and ideas so you can make sure you pick the right one.'

Ants, in addition, can help businesses organise workflow and people. In an ant colony, there is no leader. Ants are self-organised, and respond to their environment and each other. One ant on its own could not raid a kitchen cupboard, but one ant telling the next one that it's worth following him to find food ends up creating a food chain. 'In an ant colony, you get the right number going in and out searching for food, you get the right number taking care of the babies,' Miller says. 'As a manager, this can tell you your hierarchy, your bureaucracy, is getting in the way of getting the work done.'

The airline industry has already flirted with the idea that ants can help make flying stress-free. Southwest Airlines, an American low-cost airline, was concerned its 30-year-old policy of letting customers choose where they sit once they boarded a plane was slowing down the process. By creating a computer simulation of people loading on to a plane, based on what ants would do, the company was able to show that assigned seating would only be faster by a few minutes. It was not worth scrapping their first-come, first-served policy, which was a key part of the company's brand.

Miller says: 'If you are concerned about surviving the next business cycle, in other words giving your company the resilience and ability to bounce back from challenges that you can't anticipate, then Nature is a great model.'

31 What does the writer say about *Smart Swarm* in the first paragraph?

  A It has already attracted a great deal of attention.
  B It is one of several books on animal behaviour and business.
  C It concerns a topic that a great many people are interested in.
  D It reflects what is already happening in some businesses.

32 Miller believes that his book differs from other 'business thinking' books because of

  A the evidence given in support of the theory.
  B the ease with which the theory can be implemented.
  C its focus on behaviour rather than profit or production.
  D its emphasis on practical action rather than theory.

33 In the third paragraph, the writer says that the behaviour of bees can show managers

  A the consequences of making the wrong decisions.
  B how to pinpoint exactly what a problem is.
  C how to arrive at the correct conclusions very quickly.
  D the need to act decisively when under great pressure.

34 According to the 'swarm theory', managers need to

  A consider the effect of a decision on a variety of other people.
  B be able to persuade others that their proposed decisions are right.
  C regard decision-making as a collaborative process.
  D accept criticism of decisions they have made.

35 The example of ants raiding a food cupboard illustrates

  A the need to create the right kind of hierarchy and bureaucracy.
  B the differences between how managers and employees think.
  C the belief that aims can be achieved in various different ways.
  D the effectiveness of employees making decisions for themselves.

36 Looking at the behaviour of ants caused Southwest Airlines to

  A improve one of its practices.
  B speed up one of its processes.
  C retain one of its policies.
  D increase customer choice.

Part 6

You are going to read four extracts from articles in which art historians are talking about the value of works of art over time. For questions 37–40, choose from the extracts A–D. The extracts may be chosen more than once.

Worth its weight in gold?

Four art historians consider the value of works of art over time.

A   Audrey Anson

It can be particularly challenging to identify the kind of art that will maintain its reputation and value over decades and centuries. Historically many collectors of fine art were entirely self-centred in their approach, purchasing particular works simply to impress others with evidence of their wealth and taste, but with hardly a thought as to what might endure to impress subsequent generations. Such collectors tended to be conservative by nature, often assuming that trends and fashions in art were passing phases and that traditional quality would stand the test of time. Judging the long-term value of contemporary art cannot be an exact science, however, and it is easy to see in retrospect who had a good eye for the art of the future and who had not. Much harder is the business of predicting which of today's artists will be appreciated in years to come, as many disillusioned art collectors have learnt to their cost. What is not in doubt, however, is that some will end up being counted amongst the all-time greats.

B   Justin Bellamy

It's the need to distinguish the truly worthwhile from the merely fashionable that drives those aiming to establish meaningful art collections today. Their aim is to seek out those contemporary works of art which might be expected not only to retain their value, but also in the fullness of time quite rightly come to be regarded as definitive examples of a trend or period. Some historians argue that every age is defined by the art it inspires, be it sculpture, painting or whatever. But this is a gross simplification. Until relatively recent times, very few of those commissioning or purchasing such works as new did so with a view to the future. They were more interested in the prestige that owning such works brought them. What's more, a famous picture may come to be more memorable than the event it depicts, distorting our true understanding of the event itself.

C   Anita Crouch

Critics and commentators find it hard enough to agree on what represents the finest in the artistic output of their own times, let alone predict the tastes of the future. In their relentless search to identify the cutting edge, they risk heaping praise on work that is merely of transitory interest, and sadly this risk was never greater than in our present age, when mediocrity seems to be the norm. But it wasn't always so. In the past, there was much wider consensus regarding what represented notable artistic achievement in whatever style prevailed in a given period. The purchase and exhibition of such works represented a status symbol for those in positions of power and influence, and although over time collections accumulated, it was largely short-term goals that triggered the process. In the end, history judges whether such collections have long-term artistic value or not.

D   Dario D'Amico

When people consider what we can pass on to future generations, they come up with various answers ranging from ideas to technology to works of art. And it is the latter that some people feel truly reflect the mood and atmosphere of their time. This will be just as true of our own age, however eccentric the contemporary art scene might appear on the surface. Down through the centuries, people have bought and passed on to future generations, those works of art that seemed to embody the spirit of their age and would have lasting value. More often than not, this turned out to be a self-fulfilling prophecy because for periods predating the advent of mass communications and photography, the art helps form a view of both what life was like and how people thought at the time. Some people go further, claiming that art continues to resonate long after detailed memories of momentous events have been lost.

Which art historian

doesn't have the same opinion as Anson about why people in the past collected works of art? 37

shares Crouch's view regarding how successfully the best contemporary works of art can be identified? 38

holds a different view to Bellamy regarding the value of art in the study of history? 39

has a different opinion from the others regarding the lasting value of current trends in art? 40

Part 7

You are going to read a newspaper article about a very young artist. Six paragraphs have been removed from the article. Choose from the paragraphs **A–G** the one which fits each gap (**41–46**). There is one extra paragraph which you do not need to use.

In the exam, mark your answers **on the separate answer sheet**.

Is Kieron Britain's most exciting artist?

Peter Stanford watches an amazing seven-year-old artist at work.

All the time we are talking, Kieron Williamson is busy sketching on the pad in front of him with quick, fluid movements of his pencil. He is copying from a book of pen and ink illustrations by Edward Seago, the twentieth-century British artist, before he adds touches of his own to the sketches.

41

Kieron is clearly caught up in what he is doing, his blonde head a study in concentration as he kneels in the front room of his family home. But he's not so distracted that he doesn't sometimes look me in the eye and put me right. 'You've added a bit more detail here,' I say, as he is reproducing Seago's sketch of an old man in an overcoat. 'Seago's', I explain, 'is lighter.' 'Not lighter,' Kieron corrects me. 'You call it looser. Loose and tight. They're the words.' Seven-year-olds don't often give adults lessons in the terminology of fine art.

42

Kieron actually can and does, and has been hailed as a 'mini-Monet', on account of his neo-Impressionist style, or the next Picasso. Recently, buyers from as far afield as South Africa and America queued up outside his modest local art gallery – some of them camping out all night – to snap up 33 paintings in just 27 minutes, leaving Kieron £150,000 better off. How did it feel? 'Very nice,' he replies politely. 'Did you talk to any of the buyers?' 'Yes, they kept asking me what else I do.' And what did you tell them? 'That I go to school, that I play football for my school and that I am the best defender in the team.'

43

His exhibition – the second to sell out so quickly – has brought him a lot of attention. Several American TV networks have filmed him in the family flat already and today a camera crew is squeezed into the front room with me, Kieron's mum, Michelle, his younger sister, Billie-Jo, and two sleeping cats.

44

'These are ones I did last night when I was watching the television with Billie-Jo,' he says, handing me a sketchbook. It falls open on a vibrant fairground scene. Kieron finds the page in the Seago book that inspired him. There is the same carousel, but he has added figures, buildings and trees in his drawing in the sketchbook.

45

As accomplished as Kieron's paintings are, part of their appeal is undoubtedly the story of precocious talent that goes with them. If he's doing similar work when he's 28, it may prompt a different reaction.

46

But Kieron is having none of it. He looks up sharply from his sketching. 'If I want to paint,' he says, 'I'll paint.'

A An example is his pastel *Figures at Holkham*, an accomplished composition with big blues skies, a line of sand dunes framing to either side and two figures, one with a splash of red in the centre to draw the eye in. There is such an adult quality to his work that you can't help wondering if someone older has been helping him.

B Standard seven-year-old boy stuff there. Kieron, however, is being hailed as a child prodigy. 'They only come along once in a generation,' artist Carol Pennington tells me later, as she explains how she helped nurture this early-blooming talent, 'and Kieron is that one.'

C Michelle Williamson is aware of this. 'I fully expect Kieron in a few years' time to focus on something else as closely as he is focusing on art right now,' she says. 'Football or motor racing. There may well be a lot more ahead for him than art.'

D Yet, in the centre of the melee, Kieron seems utterly oblivious and just gets on with what he does every day, often rising at 6 a.m. to get on to paper a picture that is bursting to get out of his head. He will be painting every day of the school holidays, relishing the freedom denied him during term time.

E Each one takes him only a few minutes – horses, figures huddling in a tent, men and women in unusual costumes. 'I'm going to do this one, then this one, then this one,' he tells me, 'but not this one – the eyes aren't looking at anyone – or this one – it's too messy.'

F This, it is clear, is no mechanical exercise in reproduction. To underline the point, Kieron takes it back off me and adds a smudge of dark under one of the groups of people.

G But then Kieron Williamson is not your average boy. Aside from his precocious articulacy, he is single-handedly illustrating that familiar remark, made by many a parent when confronted with a prize-winning work of modern art, that 'my seven-year-old could do better than that'.

Part 8

You are going to read an article about the Royal Society, a British scientific institution. For questions **47–56**, choose from the sections of the article (**A–E**). The sections may be chosen more than once.

In the exam, mark your answers **on the separate answer sheet**.

In which section of the article are the following mentioned?

a belief that a certain development has been of particular use to scientists	47
the variety of ways in which the Royal Society encourages people who are not scientists to consider scientific issues	48
a rapid reaction to research being made public	49
a particular development that requires urgent action to improve it	50
a resource for information on past scientific discoveries	51
a lack of understanding of scientific matters among people in general	52
a system that the Royal Society introduced	53
the fact that scientists do not always reach firm conclusions	54
a problem that is not limited to the world of science	55
the belief that certain things that are possible are not desirable	56

The unstoppable spirit of inquiry

The president of the Royal Society, Martin Rees, celebrates the long history of one of Britain's greatest institutions.

A

The Royal Society began in 1660. From the beginning, the wide dissemination of scientific ideas was deemed important. The Society started to publish *Philosophical Transaction*, the first scientific journal, which continues to this day. The Society's journals pioneered what is still the accepted procedure whereby scientific ideas are subject to peer review – criticised, refined and codified into 'public knowledge'. Over the centuries, they published Isaac Newton's researches on light, Benjamin Franklin's experiments on lightning, Volta's first battery and many of the triumphs of twentieth-century science. Those who want to celebrate this glorious history should visit the Royal Society's archives via our *Trailblazing* website.

B

The founders of the Society enjoyed speculation, but they were also intensely engaged with the problems of their era, such as improvements to timekeeping and navigation. After 350 years, our horizons have expanded, but the same engagement is imperative in the 21st century. Knowledge has advanced hugely, but it must be deployed for the benefit of the ever-growing population of our planet, all empowered by ever more powerful technology. The silicon chip was perhaps the most transformative single invention of the past century; it has allowed miniaturisation and spawned the worldwide reach of mobile phones and the internet. It was physicists who developed the World Wide Web and, though it impacts us all, scientists have benefited especially.

C

Traditional journals survive as guarantors of quality, but they are supplemented by a blogosphere of widely varying quality. The latter cries out for an informal system of quality control. The internet levels the playing fields between researchers in major centres and those in relative isolation. It has transformed the way science is communicated and debated. In 2002, three young Indian mathematicians invented a faster scheme for factoring large numbers – something that would be crucial for code-breaking. They posted their results on the web. Within a day, 20,000 people had downloaded the work, which was the topic of hastily convened discussions in many centres of mathematical research around the world. The internet also allows new styles of research. For example, in the old days, astronomical research was stored on delicate photographic plates; these were not easily accessible and tiresome to analyse. Now such data (and large datasets in genetics and particle physics) can be accessed and downloaded anywhere. Experiments and natural events can be followed in real time.

D

We recently asked our members what they saw as the most important questions facing us in the years ahead and we are holding discussion meetings on the 'Top Ten'. Whatever breakthroughs are in store, we can be sure of one thing: the widening gulf between what science enables us to do and what it's prudent or ethical actually to do. In respect of certain developments, regulation will be called for, on ethical as well as prudential grounds. The way science is applied is a matter not just for scientists. All citizens need to address these questions. Public decisions should be made, after the widest possible discussion, in the light of the best scientific evidence available. That is one of the key roles of the Society. Whether it is the work of our Science Policy Centre, our journals, our discussion meetings, our work in education or our public events, we must be at the heart of helping policy makers and citizens make informed decisions.

E

But science isn't dogma. Its assertions are sometimes tentative, sometimes compelling; noisy controversy doesn't always connote balanced arguments; risks are never absolutely zero, even if they are hugely outweighed by potential benefits. In promoting an informed debate, the media are crucial. When reporting a scientific controversy, the aim should be neither to exaggerate risks and uncertainties, nor to gloss over them. This is indeed a challenge, particularly when institutional, political or commercial pressures distort the debate. Scientists often bemoan the public's weak grasp of science – without some 'feel' for the issues, public debate can't get beyond sloganising. But they protest too much: there are other issues where public debate is, to an equally disquieting degree, inhibited by ignorance. The Royal Society aims to sustain Britain's traditional strength in science, but also to ensure that wherever science impacts on people's lives, it is openly debated.

TEST 5 WRITING

Part 1

You **must** answer this question. Write your answer in **220–260** words in an appropriate style. In the exam, write your answer **on the separate answer sheet provided**.

1 You have listened to a radio discussion about how individuals can contribute to solving environmental problems. You have made the notes below.

What can individuals do to contribute to solving environmental problems?

- recycling
- campaigning
- using energy

Some opinions expressed in the discussion:

'Recycling anything is pretty pointless unless everyone does it.'

'Campaigning makes a real difference – it makes everyone aware of the issues.'

'We all need to save energy – I've got solar panels on my roof even though they're expensive.'

Write an essay discussing **two** of the ideas in your notes. You should **explain which idea enables individuals to make the biggest contribution** to solving environmental problems, **giving reasons** in support of your answer.

You may, if you wish, make use of the opinions expressed in the discussion, but you should use your own words as far as possible.

Part 2

Write an answer to **one** of the questions **2–4** in this part. Write your answer in **220–260** words. In the exam, write your answer **on the separate answer sheet provided**, and put the question number in the box at the top of the page.

2   You see the following announcement in a travel magazine.

> ### Have you been to a place you will never forget?
> ### We want to hear about it!
>
> We're compiling a list of the most memorable places in the world. Send us a review of a place that has stayed in your memory. What was so special about it? Why did it make such a lasting impression on you? Why should we put it on our list?

Write your **review**.

3   You see the following announcement in a consumer magazine.

> ### Shop till you drop?
>
> We're collecting information about young people's shopping habits across the world. Send us a report on your country. Your report should describe young people's shopping habits in your country, consider whether the way young people shop is changing, and suggest what might affect the kind of things young people buy in the future. We'll publish the most interesting reports.

Write your **report**.

4   You see this notice in the bus station of the town where you are studying English.

> The town council intends to spend money improving public transport in the area, and invites people who use it to send in proposals for improving the system. In your proposal you should outline any problems you have had with local transport, and make recommendations for improving the system in general.

Write your **proposal**.

TEST 5 LISTENING

Part 1

You will hear three different extracts. For questions **1–6**, choose the answer (**A**, **B** or **C**) which fits best according to what you hear. There are two questions for each extract.

In the exam, write your answers **on the separate answer sheet**.

Extract One

You hear two friends discussing a book.

1 What surprised the man about the book initially?

   A   the fact that it was a thriller

   B   the writer's underlying intention

   C   the way the characters interacted

2 The woman feels that the book has made her consider

   A   being more honest with people online.

   B   being more cautious with people online.

   C   choosing online contacts more carefully.

Extract Two

You hear part of a discussion about a jewellery designer.

3 What aspect of the designer's latest collection does the woman admire most?

   A   the flexibility it gives the wearer

   B   the diverse influences in the style

   C   the characteristic use of beadwork

4 She feels that the designer's next collection

   A   represents a brave change of direction.

   B   may turn out to be disappointing.

   C   promises to be very exciting.

Extract Three

You hear part of an interview with the owner of a shopping website.

5   When answering the interviewer's first question, he is

   A   justifying a rather hands-on approach.

   B   regretting that he lacks certain key skills.

   C   admitting that he needs to reconsider his priorities.

6   He feels the hardest part of being an entrepreneur is

   A   finding reliable people to work on a project.

   B   choosing the best time to launch a project.

   C   deciding which project to go with.

Part 2

You will hear a woman called Mara Styles telling a group of people about her holiday at an ecocamp in Patagonia. For questions **7–14**, complete the sentences with a word or short phrase.

In the exam, write your answers **on the separate answer sheet**.

ECOCAMP HOLIDAY

Mara uses the word **(7)** .... to describe her previous experiences of camping.

Mara says that traditional local buildings in the region were made out of **(8)** .... , skins and fur.

Like traditional buildings, good protection against **(9)** .... is a feature of the modern ecocamp domes.

Mara particularly appreciated the feeling of **(10)** .... in her dome.

In the communal areas, it was the quality of the **(11)** .... that impressed Mara most.

Something called a **(12)** .... helps to protect the ground on which the camp is sited.

Mara chose to go on hikes in the **(13)** .... category.

Mara is particularly proud of her photo of the **(14)** .... which she saw on a hike.

Part 3

You will hear part of an interview in which two racing cyclists called Greg Marton and Lina Derridge are talking about the different sports they have taken part in. For questions **15–20**, choose the answer (**A**, **B**, **C** or **D**) which fits best according to what you hear.

In the exam, write your answers **on the separate answer sheet**.

---

15 When talking about teenage ice hockey, Greg reveals that

    A he now wishes he'd trained harder.
    B he's sorry that he let his father down.
    C he resents the pressure he was put under.
    D he accepts that he lacked the drive to succeed.

16 What led Greg to take up rowing?

    A He followed up a suggestion made by friends.
    B He was frustrated by his performance as a runner.
    C He was told that he had the physical strength for it.
    D He was disappointed not to get on to a degree course.

17 What does Lina say about her initial failure to make the national rowing team?

    A She feels that she wasn't treated fairly.
    B She admits that she was mostly just unfortunate.
    C She disagrees with the way the selection process operated.
    D She recognises that she should have attended training camps.

18 What does Lina suggest about her move to California?

    A She saw it mainly as a way of furthering her career.
    B She was motivated by her desire to try a new activity.
    C She needed convincing that it was the right thing to do.
    D She wanted to concentrate her energies on work rather than sport.

19 Greg and Lina agree that cycling and rowing both require

    A a commitment to a team effort.
    B a tolerance of intense pain.
    C a willingness to take risks.
    D a good sense of timing.

20 According to Greg, why should cyclists include rowing as part of their training?

    A They might find it as enjoyable as he does.
    B They would develop a similar set of muscles.
    C It might help them to avoid injury in accidents.
    D It provides a break from the monotony of cycling.

Part 4

You will hear five short extracts in which actors are talking about performing in live theatre productions.

In the exam, write your answers **on the separate answer sheet**.

TASK ONE

For questions **21–25**, choose from the list (**A–H**) what each speaker usually does before a performance.

A gets some fresh air

B puts flowers in the dressing rooms　　Speaker 1 ☐ 21

C focuses on personal souvenirs　　　　Speaker 2 ☐ 22

D does some exercises　　　　　　　　Speaker 3 ☐ 23

E chats to the audience　　　　　　　　Speaker 4 ☐ 24

F leaves gifts for other cast members　　Speaker 5 ☐ 25

G has a rest

H checks everything is in place

TASK TWO

For questions **26–30**, choose from the list (**A–H**) what each speaker says went wrong on a recent production.

A being affected by illness

B getting a negative audience reaction　　Speaker 1 ☐ 26

C receiving poor reviews　　　　　　　　Speaker 2 ☐ 27

D being disturbed by noise　　　　　　　Speaker 3 ☐ 28

E having an accident　　　　　　　　　　Speaker 4 ☐ 29

F finding something unexpected on stage　Speaker 5 ☐ 30

G attracting a very small audience

H getting the words wrong

TEST 5 SPEAKING

PART 1

The interlocutor will ask you a few questions about yourself and on everyday topics such as work and study, travel, entertainment, daily life and routines. For example:

- What is your favourite way of travelling short distances? Why?
- Do you ever listen to the radio? Why/Why not?
- What do you prefer to do when you spend time with your friends?

PART 2

Feeling proud

Turn to pictures 1–3 on page 182, which show people feeling proud in different situations.

Candidate A, compare two of the pictures and say why the people might feel proud in these situations and how important the feeling might be to them.

Candidate B, who do you think will feel proud for the longest time? Why?

Weather conditions

Turn to pictures 1–3 on page 183, which show people experiencing different weather conditions.

Candidate B, compare two of the pictures and say what effect the weather conditions might have on the people's mood and how difficult it might be for them to deal with the conditions.

Candidate A, who do you think is most affected by the weather conditions? Why?

PART 3

Turn to the task on page 184, which shows some issues a travel company might take into account when designing a new website.

Talk to each other about why a travel company might have to take these issues into account when designing a new website.

Decide which issue would have the greatest positive or negative impact on consumers using the website.

PART 4

Answer these questions:

- What do you think are the advantages and disadvantages of buying a holiday online?
- In your opinion is working for a travel company a good job for young people? Why/Why not?
- Some people say that going away on holiday is a waste of money. What's your opinion?
- Why do you think some people prefer to travel independently while others prefer to travel in a group?
- How do you think people can benefit from travelling to other countries?
- In future, do you think people will travel more, or less? Why?

TEST 6 READING AND USE OF ENGLISH

Part 1

For questions **1–8**, read the text below and decide which answer (**A**, **B**, **C** or **D**) best fits each gap. There is an example at the beginning (**0**).

In the exam, mark your answers **on the separate answer sheet**.

Example:

0   A   capable   B   skilled   C   qualified   D   competent

0 A ■ B ☐ C ☐ D ☐

Mr Espresso

The idea that only an Italian is **(0)** …….. of making a truly great cup of coffee is actually a fairly recent phenomenon. Emilio Lavazza (1932–2010), can **(1)** …….. much of the credit. He taught the world not only how to make coffee, but also how to drink it.

Lavazza was a leading **(2)** …….. in the generation of Italian businessmen who **(3)** …….. their family firms in the 1950s. These began to expand rapidly, first around the country and then abroad as Italy **(4)** …….. its long post-war economic expansion. This was the generation that **(5)** …….. the seeds for what has **(6)** …….. to be known as 'Made in Italy', the **(7)** …….. of companies and brands that make high-quality household and consumer products, from fashion to food to furniture. These products are identified with a **(8)** …….. of craftsmanship on the one hand, and the elegant Italian lifestyle on the other. Emilio Lavazza ensured that coffee became an inextricable part of that heritage.

1   A   insist   B   claim   C   demand   D   uphold

2   A   figure   B   symbol   C   role   D   creature

3   A   enlisted   B   joined   C   enrolled   D   participated

4   A   entertained   B   appreciated   C   benefited   D   enjoyed

5   A   set   B   sowed   C   laid   D   buried

6   A   ended   B   come   C   finished   D   gone

7   A   cluster   B   pile   C   bundle   D   heap

8   A   range   B   connection   C   variety   D   combination

Part 2

For questions **9–16**, read the text below and think of the word which best fits each gap. Use only **one** word in each gap. There is an example at the beginning (**0**).

In the exam, write your answers **IN CAPITAL LETTERS on the separate answer sheet**.

Example: | 0 | W | H | O | | | | | | | | | | | | |

Drift Diving

Are you already an experienced diver (**0**) …….. fancies a change from splashing around a reef or a wreck? If (**9**) …….., then drift diving may be worth trying. Basically, drift diving (**10**) …….. use of the prevailing current in the ocean to propel you along underwater. Depending (**11**) …….. the speed of the current, drift diving can either be like flying underwater, (**12**) …….. simply the lazy person's approach to diving. A slow drift would involve travelling at the equivalent of just under two kilometres per hour, (**13**) …….. it feels much faster when you're down at depth.

With drift diving, of course, there's (**14**) …….. need to kick. You're being carried along, and can view all the local sealife as you float by. It feels quite surreal to begin with; you float along (**15**) …….. if you were on a conveyor belt. What's (**16**) …….., you often cover a much greater distance than on a conventional dive.

Part 3

For questions **17–24**, read the text below. Use the word given in capitals at the end of some of the lines to form a word that fits in the gap **in the same line**. There is an example at the beginning (**0**).

In the exam, write your answers **IN CAPITAL LETTERS on the separate answer sheet**.

Example: **0** I M P R E S S I O N

The Limits of Technology

There are certain moments when technology makes a big

(**0**) .... on you. One such revelatory moment occurred **IMPRESS**

while I was on a camel trek across the Sahara desert.

We were about fifty miles from the nearest human (**17**) .... **SETTLE**

Hardly any technological (**18**) .... had reached this corner **BREAK**

of the globe, or so it seemed. There were just sand dunes

as far as the eye could see. And yet, despite our (**19**) ...., **ISOLATE**

the silence was suddenly broken by the somewhat (**20**) .... **EXPECT**

noise of a frog. Ignoring for the moment the looks of distinct

(**21**) .... I got from my fellow travellers, I put my hand **APPROVAL**

in my pocket. The (**22**) .... frog was, of course, my ring tone. **ANNOY**

And when I pressed the button, there was my boss asking

me a simple work question, (**23**) .... of the fact that I was **REGARD**

thousands of miles away. We were beyond the limits of

civilisation, yet had not gone far enough to avoid an (**24**) .... **WELCOME**

work call from a colleague.

Part 4

For questions **25–30**, complete the second sentence so that it has a similar meaning to the first sentence, using the word given. **Do not change the word given.** You must use between **three** and **six** words, including the word given. Here is an example (**0**).

Example:

0 Chloe would only eat a pizza if she could have a mushroom topping.

ON

Chloe .... a mushroom topping when she ate a pizza.

The gap can be filled with the words 'insisted on having', so you write:

Example: | **0** | INSISTED ON HAVING

In the exam, write **only** the missing words **IN CAPITAL LETTERS on the separate answer sheet**.

---

25 Only time will tell whether Ella was right to change her training programme.

REMAINS

It .... whether Ella was right to change her training programme.

26 'Would you lend me your camera, Patrick?' asked John.

BORROW

John asked .... camera.

27 Ronan fully intends to write a blog about his round-the-world trip.

EVERY

Ronan .... a blog about his round-the-world trip.

28 If nobody objects, today's class will be held on the terrace outside.

UNLESS

Today's class will be held outside on the terrace .... objections.

29 Ursula's parents did not approve of her plan to visit a friend in the USA.

MET

Ursula's plan to visit a friend in the USA .... of her parents.

30 The big increase in hits on his website came as a surprise to Philip.

GOT

Much .... a big increase in hits on his website.

Part 5

You are going to read an article about children learning to cook. For questions **31–36**, choose the answer (**A**, **B**, **C** or **D**) which you think fits best according to the text.

In the exam, mark your answers **on the separate answer sheet**.

Cooking shouldn't be child's play

Take the fun out of cooking with your kids and there's a chance you'll have bred a chef with a great future. Television cook Nigella Lawson has revealed that her own mother put her and her sister 'to work' in the kitchen from the age of five. For the young Nigella, preparing food was certainly not recreational. Sounds intriguing. Will her new series feature her putting young ones through a blisteringly tough regime, sweating as they bone out chickens and being blasted when their souffle collapses? Apparently not, but she makes a good point. 'Parents sometimes feel that they have to get into children's TV presenter mode and make cooking all fun and recreational.' For the young Lawsons it was about getting a meal on the table. She and her sister took it in turns to cook their father's breakfast.

My mother took a similar view. She tutored us in cooking. We never made grey pastry in amusing shapes or had hilarious squirting sessions with icing bags. If we were going to cook, it was for a purpose. At first, the only aim was that it be edible. But my mother noticed the interest my sisters and I had in cooking (in her defence, she never forced us to do it) and set us some challenging tasks. My speciality was sweet pastry. She would look over my shoulder and suggest rolling it thinner 'so the light shines through it'.

Nowadays, this instructive style of upbringing is frowned upon. Learning to make things has to be all about play and each creation is greeted with exaggerated applause. Parents plaster their kitchen walls with their five-year-olds' paintings and poems; they tell their kids how clever and talented they are in the belief that if you do this often enough, clever and talented they will be. But experts say that overpraised children can, in fact, underachieve and that compliments should be limited and sincere. Analysis by researchers at Stanford University in California found that praising too much demotivates children – interestingly, more so with girls than boys.

Playschool cookery exists alongside another culinary crime – making funny faces on the plate. The idea goes that it's nothing but fun, fun and more fun to eat the cherry-tomato eyes, mangetout mouth and broccoli hair. Hmmm, is it? At some point, the cartoon stuff has to go. I have had dinner with grown men who, I suspect, have yet to get over the fact that their fish is not cut out in the shape of a whale. I'd love to meet the comic genius who decided it was somehow good to urge our children to eat food shaped like an endangered species. Nigella Lawson remembers making giraffe-shaped pizzas for her children, only to be asked why they couldn't have ordinary ones like their dad. Smart kids, those.

Sooner or later we have to chuck out all those books that tell you and the little ones what a laugh cooking is and tell the truth. Cooking is a chore – and not an easy one for busy people to keep up. Better to be honest than discover this disagreeable fact later. If my mother had not made cooking something to take seriously, I suspect I would have eaten far more convenience food.

But you can go too far with budding chefs. Nigella might say her early training 'just felt normal', but I am not sure that my childhood culinary regime was an ordinary part of growing up. Perhaps our families were too obsessed with food. We shouldn't be too didactic with our little ones, for children lose out if they never fool around with their parents.

The chef Mary Contini got it right, producing a great children's cookery book, *Easy Peasy*. The recipes were for real meals – Italian-inspired, common-sense food. Dishes have fun names – Knock-out Garlic Bread and Chocolate Mouse, but all the basics are there. The secret of getting children cooking is perhaps a step away from the intense tutorial given to Nigella and myself. My recipe would be two parts seriousness and one part creative fun. The result should be a youngster with a real passion for food.

31 In the first paragraph, the writer suggests that there is a connection between

  A parents' enthusiasm for cooking and children's ability to cook.
  B teaching children to cook and making a popular TV cookery series.
  C childhood experiences of cooking and success as a professional cook.
  D the effort children put into cooking and how much they enjoy doing it.

32 What does the writer say about her mother teaching her how to cook?

  A She sometimes resented her mother's demands on her.
  B Her mother's comments were intended to encourage her.
  C Her mother misunderstood her level of interest in cooking.
  D She wished that her mother would allow her to have more fun doing it.

33 In the third paragraph, the writer points out a contrast between

  A a belief about parental behaviour and the response of children to this behaviour.
  B public praise for children and private opinions of what they do.
  C the kind of praise given to boys and the kind given to girls.
  D what children are good at and what their parents would like them to be good at.

34 The writer mentions certain 'grown men' as an example of people who

  A grew up having a lot of fun while learning to cook.
  B have the wrong idea about how children view food.
  C pass bad ideas about cooking on to their children.
  D think that everything associated with food has to be fun.

35 What does the writer suggest about regarding cooking as 'a chore'?

  A It is something that children are not able to understand.
  B It is not necessary.
  C It can affect the kind of food that people cook and eat.
  D It is a lazy view.

36 The writer says that she differs from Nigella Lawson concerning

  A her aspirations as a cook.
  B her attitude to her family life as a child.
  C the way that children should be taught how to cook.
  D the amount of fun she thinks children should have at home.

Part 6

You are going to read four extracts from articles in which business trainers are talking about the issue of feedback on in-service training courses. For questions **37–40**, choose from the extracts **A–D**. The extracts may be chosen more than once.

Feedback in training: the issues

Four business trainers consider when and how to give feedback on in-service training courses.

A   Alec Jacobs
One of the hardest things for a business trainer providing in-service training courses to companies is dealing with the issue of evaluation. Each trainee needs feedback on how they're getting on as a course progresses and often need reassurance that they are meeting the targets set by trainers. Companies need feedback on how employees have performed on the course, and this has to be objective. But it doesn't end there. Some participants also seek to outdo their peers, which is not an atmosphere trainers will want to foster. For others, feedback can be threatening because if handled badly, it can colour how they feel about themselves, and affect confidence. So getting the process of evaluation right and presenting it in a positive way to trainees is a key skill that trainers need to master. This doesn't necessarily imply mincing words or avoiding criticisms, however, but rather focusing on transparency and clarity, and never losing sight of how an individual is likely to respond.

B   Brenda Evans
Training courses can be either an enjoyable break from routine or an added pressure for already stressed-out employees. Trainers have to take both attitudes in their stride, motivating the more laid-back types through games and other activities with clear winners and losers, whilst getting the stressheads to chill out and get things in perspective. Each trainee needs to know how they are getting on at regular intervals during the course, and this is the trainer's chance to address some of the individual needs of members of the group. Criticism that is softened by constructive comments may be beneficial, whilst focusing on failure can only create more of the same. Such verbal evaluation may be followed up in a written report to employers, but how much to include, and how it is worded, should be negotiated as part of the feedback discussion itself.

C   Carola Winstrup
Training courses can be a cause of anxiety for employees, and trainers have to accept that outcomes can have a profound effect on individual careers. To ignore the fact that some of the people in the room are vying for promotion or other perks is to miss an opportunity to manage group dynamics to the best effect. Feedback is important, but shouldn't interfere with the running of the training sessions themselves. The trainer needs to take notes against criteria agreed with companies, and make sure feedback on individuals doesn't become subjective – or open to manipulation by participants themselves. Any feedback given to trainees, therefore, should take the form of a summing up and be delivered after reports to employers have been completed. Such feedback needs to stress the outcomes of the training event by continually referencing agreed course aims and objectives.

D   Dario Pontini
There can be no effective training without properly calibrated courses, which means good pre-course design and thorough ongoing and post-course evaluation. But all the feedback in the world is pointless unless it is responded to in a meaningful and practical way. Trainers need to have a strategy for accurately measuring an individual's performance against the objectives originally set by their clients, and reporting back to companies clearly. Having a realistic idea of what can be achieved is crucial – many companies expect too much of trainers, or mistakenly see training as a way of seeing which employee will perform best. If the evaluation is objective, with measured outcomes expressed in a standard wording, the trainer avoids getting involved in one-to-one discussions with trainees about their performance. Vague and subjective feedback from trainers cannot be validated and/or acted upon, but managers and personnel departments can follow up on an objective report in a way that best suits the company's ethos.

Which trainer

shares Jacob's view about the value of personalised feedback to course participants? | 37 |

has a different view from Winstrup about how to approach feedback to employers? | 38 |

has the same opinion as Pontini about the desirability of getting participants to compete with each other? | 39 |

has a different opinion from the others about when trainers should give feedback to participants? | 40 |

Part 7

You are going to read an article about a British TV soap opera called *Coronation Street*. Six paragraphs have been removed from the article. Choose from the paragraphs **A–G** the one which fits each gap (**41–46**). There is one extra paragraph which you do not need to use.

In the exam, mark your answers **on the separate answer sheet**.

The birth of Coronation Street

Scriptwriter Daran Little has dramatised the beginnings of the first British soap.
He explains how sneers came before success.

I was 21 and fresh from university when I started work as an archivist on *Coronation Street*. My role was pretty simple: I had to memorise everything that had ever happened in the show and so help the writers with character histories.

41

Now my own dramatised version of how it all began, *The Road to Coronation Street*, is about to go on air. I moved on to become a writer on the show in the early 2000s. But those early black and white episodes will always be close to my heart, and so will the genius who created the show.

42

Last summer, I was sitting and chatting with colleagues about the latest plot twist in *Coronation Street*. While I was doing that, I suddenly realised what a compelling piece of television drama the creation of the programme itself would make.

43

Tony Warren was a one-time child actor with a passion for writing who turned up at the infant Granada Television with a vision for a new form of story-telling – a show about ordinary people and their everyday lives. It had never been done before.

44

It was that Granada had a condition, as part of its franchise, to create locally sourced programmes, an obligation it was not meeting at that time. One of the owners, Sidney Bernstein, was a showman who loved the entertainment business and was keen to develop it. He created Granada television in 1956 and shortly afterwards employed a Canadian producer, Harry Elton, to help nurture talent. It was Elton who employed Tony Warren, and it was these two men who would eventually change the face of British television.

45

It should have ended there. A script written and discarded by a broadcaster, Warren and Elton should have drowned their sorrows and moved on to the next project. But they didn't; they fought to change the bosses' minds. *The Road to Coronation Street* tells the story of how, against all the odds, a television phenomenon was born, and how a group of unknown actors became the first superstars of British television drama. On December 9, 1960, *Coronation Street* was first broadcast. With minutes to go before transmission, Warren was feeling sick, one of the lead actors was missing, and so was the cat for the opening shot.

46

It's a story I'm proud to have brought to the screen.

A Luckily, I wasn't the only one to be persuaded of this, and within a fortnight I had been commissioned to write a script. In a world of prolonged commissioning debates, this was highly unusual – but then the story of *Coronation Street* is also highly unusual.

B At that point, its creator Tony Warren had given it the title *Florizel Street*. The first episode was broadcast live and it was envisaged that there would be just 13 episodes of the show.

C Half a century later, that inauspicious beginning is a far cry from the ongoing success of one of Britain's most-watched soaps. My drama is more than a celebration of that event, it's a story of taking chances, believing in talent and following a dream.

D I first met that person, Tony Warren, as a student, after I wrote asking to interview him. We chatted about the show he had created when he was 23 – a show which broke new ground in television drama and brought soap opera to British television. I was fascinated by his story, and have remained so ever since.

E Tony Warren developed a show set around a Northern back street with a pub on the corner called the Rovers Return. Its characters were drawn from Warren's past. A script was written and sent 'upstairs' to management. He was told, in no uncertain terms, that this wasn't television. It had no drama, the characters were unsympathetic and if it was transmitted, the advertisers would withdraw their custom.

F At that stage, *Coronation Street* had been on air for 28 years and it took me three-and-a-half years to watch every episode that had been made. That's 14 episodes a day, which means that I went a bit stir crazy somewhere between 1969 and 1972 and was a gibbering wreck by the time a lorry crashed in the street in 1979.

G In fact, no original piece of television featuring regional actors had ever been broadcast. Television was ruled by Londoners who spoke with rounded vowels. The only Manchester accents on the screen were employed in a comic context. For broadcasters, the language of the North of England didn't translate to television drama. Besides, even if it did, no one in London would be able to understand it – so what was the point?

Part 8

You are going to read part of a brochure for visitors to Norway suggesting activities they could do during their visit. For questions **47–56**, choose from the sections of the article (**A–D**). The sections may be chosen more than once.

In the exam, mark your answers **on the separate answer sheet**.

In connection with which activity are the following mentioned?

a talk before visitors start doing this activity	47
the physical condition required to do this activity	48
people for whom the activity is essential	49
a belief that the activity no longer happens	50
the moments just before the activity starts	51
the length of time most visitors choose for the activity	52
a contrast with another activity	53
particular skills that are demonstrated to visitors	54
two benefits of doing the activity	55
something that may cause people a problem when learning how to do the activity	56

Activities for visitors to Norway

Norway offers some truly remarkable ways to explore the great outdoors.

A Ride a snowmobile

For many who live in Northern Norway, the snowmobile is an everyday means of transport – and nothing less than a lifeline for those in more remote areas. But these vehicles are also great fun to ride and snowmobile excursions are one of the most popular tourist experiences. It's a thrill indeed to roar in convoy through a landscape of wooded trails on the Arctic's answer to a Harley-Davidson motorbike. Anyone with a driving licence for a car may operate one and the basics are easily mastered. The only controls to worry about are a thumb-operated throttle and motorcycle-style brakes. All riders are kitted out with a helmet, warm waterproof overalls, boots and gloves, and given a comprehensive safety briefing. Scores of outfits throughout the region offer snowmobile excursions, from half-day taster sessions to expeditions of up to a week.

B Go fishing on a frozen surface

Fishing through a hole in the ice may seem like the ultimate Arctic cliché. Many people from Europe's warmer climes may think it is something that exists only in old footage of Eskimo living, but this isn't the case at all. Under the frozen surface, many of Norway's freshwater lakes and fjords are teeming with fish and there are plenty of enthusiasts who devote their days to catching them. Sign up for an excursion and you'll find out how the experts use the auger to drill through the ice, a skimming loop to keep the water from freezing over again and a familiar rod to catch the fish. There's something magical about seeing a tug on the line and a sparkling fish being suddenly whisked out of the icy depths. Some companies offer fishing trips lasting three days or more, involving snowmobile or dog-sled journeys up to remote mountain lakes.

C Go skiing or snowshoeing

Snowmobiling has high-octane attractions, but to appreciate fully the stillness and peace of the mountains, it's best to use your own feet to get around. There are several ways of doing this. Cross-country skiing is among the most popular Nordic pastimes and there are thousands of miles of trails. A few lessons are essential to pick up the rudiments of the technique. After that, you will discover that gliding around the snowy terrain is not just a great way of getting close to nature, but also fantastic aerobic exercise. Younger explorers will find plenty of opportunities for snowboarding fun. A more sedate manner of exploration (though still invigorating) is on snowshoes. The racquet-like footwear makes it possible to yomp over deep snow. A classic snowshoe safari involves a guided walk to a forest glade, where snacks are served.

D Try dog sledding

Before the invention of the petrol engine, dog sleds were vital to those who lived inside the Arctic circle, and a trip to a husky farm is something every visitor to northern Norway should experience. Half- or full-day sled safaris are most popular, although overnight and longer tours are also available. Norwegians treat dog sledding as a sport and regularly take part in prestigious races. It's difficult not to feel a frisson of excitement as a team of huskies is harnessed to your sledge. The instinct to run is so strongly bred into the dogs that whenever they realise an outing is imminent, they become as keyed up as domestic pets about to be taken for walkies – howling, leaping in the air and straining at their leashes. When the signal is given to depart, you may well be surprised at the speed that they can reach. Dog sledding is available through various companies at different locations in northern Norway and is suitable for novices, though you should be reasonably fit.

TEST 6 WRITING

Part 1

You **must** answer this question. Write your answer in **220–260** words in an appropriate style. In the exam, write your answer **on the separate answer sheet provided**.

1 You have listened to a discussion about the value of travelling to other countries. You have made the notes below.

What's the greatest benefit of travelling to other countries?

- education
- experience
- convenience

Some opinions expressed during the discussion:

'You learn so much when you travel, even if you're only in a place for a few hours.'

'There's no substitute for the feeling of actually being in a place.'

'It's so much cheaper and more convenient to watch TV at home – what's the point in the hassle of travelling?'

Write an essay discussing **two** of the points in your notes. You should **explain which is the greatest benefit of travelling** to other countries, **giving reasons** in support of your answer.

You may, if you wish, make use of the opinions expressed in the discussion, but you should use your own words as far as possible.

Part 2

Write an answer to **one** of the questions **2–4** in this part. Write your answer in **220–260** words. In the exam, write your answer **on the separate answer sheet provided**, and put the question number in the box at the top of the page.

2 Your new college careers advisor wants to provide more help for students leaving the college, and has asked older students for their suggestions. Write a report explaining the facilities currently available, describe those that have been most useful to you and suggest any improvements that could be made in providing information and access to work experience.

Write your **report**.

3 You have just returned from a holiday with an English-speaking tour company. You spent two weeks travelling by coach but were unsatisfied with the arrangements, the itinerary and the accommodation. Write a letter to the tour company, outlining your complaints with examples and explaining what you would like the company to do about the situation.

Write your **letter**. You do not need to include postal addresses.

4 You see this announcement in your local paper.

> ### Let's make next year's drama festival an even bigger success!
>
> We want to attract people of all ages to our new drama festival next summer, and we want your help. Send us your proposals for what kind of drama and theatrical events we should include in order to attract people of different ages, and what extra facilities the town might need to provide. Make suggestions for dealing with transport and accommodation issues.

Write your **proposal**.

TEST 6 LISTENING

Part 1

You will hear three different extracts. For questions **1–6**, choose the answer (**A**, **B** or **C**) which fits best according to what you hear. There are two questions for each extract.

In the exam, write your answers **on the separate answer sheet**.

Extract One

You hear two friends discussing a rock concert they both went to.

1 How does the boy feel about the main band?

    A disappointed by their performance

    B confused by all the advanced publicity

    C unsure whether he got value for money or not

2 What is the woman doing in her reply?

    A criticising the support band

    B defending the approach of the media

    C agreeing with comments about the main band

Extract Two

You hear part of a sports report about a football club manager.

3 What is the male presenter doing?

    A praising changes that the manager has made

    B suggesting that rumours about the manager are unfounded

    C describing a growing sense of dissatisfaction with the manager's performance

4 In the female presenter's opinion,

    A the manager's strategy is the correct one.

    B the real problem is a lack of talented players.

    C the pressure on the manager is likely to increase.

Extract Three

You hear two friends discussing an exhibition of modern sculpture.

5   What does the woman particularly admire about the artist?

    A   the originality of his work

    B   the way his art has developed

    C   the issues that his sculptures raise

6   What disappointed them both about the exhibition?

    A   the pieces of work that had been chosen

    B   the information provided for visitors

    C   the way it had been laid out

Part 2

You will hear a man called Carl Pitman, giving a group of tourists practical advice about learning the sport of surfing. For questions **7–14**, complete the sentences with a word or short phrase.

In the exam, write your answers **on the separate answer sheet**.

LEARNING THE SPORT OF SURFING

Carl recommends the **(7)** .... as the best place for learning to surf in his area.

Carl uses the term **(8)** .... to describe the distance between waves.

Carl advises getting a wetsuit that has a **(9)** .... fit.

Carl says it's important to check the quantity of material beneath the **(10)** .... of a new wetsuit.

Carl says that the wetsuit, **(11)** .... and footwear all need washing regularly.

According to Carl, a hanger made of **(12)** .... is best for storing wetsuits.

Beginners most often damage surfboards through contact with **(13)** ....

Carl suggests using a **(14)** .... as the first step in removing wax from a surfboard.

TEST 6: LISTENING

Part 3

You will hear an interview with a writer called Barry Pagham, who writes crime novels. For questions **15–20**, choose the answer (**A**, **B**, **C** or **D**) which fits best according to what you hear.

In the exam, write your answers **on the separate answer sheet**.

---

15 What does Barry say about his first two published novels?

    A They were more successful than he anticipated.
    B They were useful in proving that he could write.
    C It's a shame that they're no longer available to buy.
    D It was a mistake to write an unfashionable type of novel.

16 Barry admits that when he wrote the novel *Transgression*,

    A he only did it to please his publishers.
    B he didn't expect it to be so well received.
    C he didn't intend to produce any more like it.
    D he never meant it to be sold as a horror story.

17 Looking back, how does Barry view his decision to write his first crime novel?

    A He accepts that he took a big risk.
    B He wishes that he hadn't upset his publishers.
    C He recognises that he behaved unprofessionally.
    D He regrets putting himself under so much stress.

18 Barry tells the story of the arrest of an armed robber to illustrate

    A how true to life his novels are.
    B how dangerous his research can be.
    C how seriously the police take his work.
    D how unpredictably criminals can sometimes behave.

19 What does Barry say about the city where his novels are based?

    A He makes it sound more exciting than it actually is.
    B He regards it as an important element in the stories.
    C He doesn't attempt to create a realistic picture of it.
    D He's surprised that foreign readers want to visit it.

20 How would Barry feel about becoming a policeman?

    A He suspects that he wouldn't be brave enough.
    B He doubts whether he would have the patience.
    C He's sure someone of his age wouldn't be accepted.
    D He suggests that he wouldn't reject the idea completely.

Part 4

You will hear five short extracts in which people are talking about their experiences of travelling.

In the exam, write your answers **on the separate answer sheet**.

TASK ONE

For questions **21–25**, choose from the list (**A–H**) what advice each speaker gives about travelling.

A plan what you need to take carefully

B explore a range of booking methods   Speaker 1 [21]

C participate in local cultural events   Speaker 2 [22]

D sample as much local produce as possible   Speaker 3 [23]

E learn some of the language   Speaker 4 [24]

F consider how belongings should be packed   Speaker 5 [25]

G keep a diary of travel experiences

H carry sufficient funds with you

TASK TWO

For questions **26–30**, choose from the list (**A–H**) what mistakes each speaker has made about travelling.

A failing to check documents

B booking a hotel in an unattractive area   Speaker 1 [26]

C failing to research a destination   Speaker 2 [27]

D forgetting some pieces of luggage   Speaker 3 [28]

E making a poorly-considered purchase   Speaker 4 [29]

F not allowing enough preparation time   Speaker 5 [30]

G turning down a travel opportunity

H buying overpriced goods

TEST 6: LISTENING

TEST 6
SPEAKING

PART 1

The interlocutor will ask you a few questions about yourself and on everyday topics such as work and study, travel, entertainment, daily life and routines. For example:

- Is there something you would really like to study in the future? Why/Why not?
- What do you enjoy about travelling? Why?
- Do you read many books? Why/Why not?

PART 2

Working together

Turn to pictures 1–3 on page 185, which show people working together in different situations.

Candidate A, compare two of the pictures and say how important it might be for the people to work together in these situations and how difficult it might be for them to do the work alone.

Candidate B, who do you think benefits most from working with other people? Why?

Travelling

Turn to pictures 1–3 on page 186, which show people travelling in different ways.

Candidate B, compare two of the pictures and say why the people might have chosen to travel in these different ways, and how they might be feeling.

Candidate A, who do you think is having the easiest journey? Why?

PART 3

Turn to the task on page 187, which shows some aspects of life that could be preserved for the future.

Talk to each other about why it might be important to preserve these aspects of life for the future.

Decide which two things are most important to preserve for future generations.

PART 4

Answer these questions:

- Do you think that individuals can do very much on their own to protect things like these? Why/Why not?
- Do you think that children should be taught about conservation at school? Why/Why not?
- Some people say that it's better to spend money on preserving what we've got than on inventing new things. What's your opinion?
- Many young people feel that traditions are old-fashioned and not relevant to them. Do you agree with that view? Why/Why not?
- Do you think governments should work together to protect the environment? Why/Why not?
- Do you agree that in order to prepare for the future, we have to understand the past? Why/Why not?

TEST 7 READING AND USE OF ENGLISH

Part 1

For questions **1–8**, read the text below and decide which answer (**A, B, C** or **D**) best fits each gap. There is an example at the beginning (**0**).

In the exam, mark your answers **on the separate answer sheet**.

Example:

0 A term   B title   C caption   D label

0	A	B	C	D
	▬	▭	▭	▭

Renewable Energy Comes of Age

The **(0)** …….. 'alternative energy' was once used to describe the generation of wind, water and solar power. These days, we tend to **(1)** …….. to them as 'renewable energy' and the use of this name **(2)** …….. a real change in their status. These sources of energy, have now become mainstream and are **(3)** …….. to make a significant contribution to energy needs in the future.

Two closely linked developments **(4)** …….. behind this change in status. Firstly, the price of oil and gas has been rising **(5)** …….., reflecting the extent to which reserves of these fossil fuels are becoming **(6)** ………. . Equally important is the growing consensus that carbon emissions must be curbed. The scientific evidence for climate change is now irrefutable, and both policy makers and the **(7)** …….. public are finally in agreement that doing nothing about the prospect of global warming is no longer a viable option. Renewable energy represents one real way of **(8)** …….. both issues.

1 A consider   B refer   C mention   D regard

2 A regards   B reproduces   C reminds   D reflects

3 A set   B held   C put   D stood

4 A sit   B reside   C lie   D recline

5 A equably   B serenely   C habitually   D steadily

6 A depleted   B decreased   C depressed   D debased

7 A deeper   B greater   C larger   D wider

8 A coping   B engaging   C addressing   D dealing

Part 2

For questions **9–16**, read the text below and think of the word which best fits each gap. Use only **one** word in each gap. There is an example at the beginning (**0**).

In the exam, write your answers **IN CAPITAL LETTERS on the separate answer sheet**.

Example: | 0 | B | Y | | | | | | | | | | | | | |

The Demise of the Motor Car

Henry Ford's invention of the mass-produced car transformed Western civilisation. It changed the shape of our cities **(0)** .... accelerating migration to the suburbs. It **(9)** .... rise to vast new factory-based industries making vehicles and their components. It opened **(10)** .... unprecedented leisure and holiday opportunities by letting people travel wherever they wanted. What's **(11)** ...., it gave us shopping malls, theme parks, motels and fast-food outlets.

(12) .... a long time, people loved their cars. Many still **(13)** .... For some, they are a status symbol – a very visible, and mobile, demonstration of their wealth. For **(14)** ...., they are an extension of their personality, or of the one they would most like to project. Many more derive **(15)** .... a powerful feeling of independence from having a car parked outside the door that, paradoxically, they become dependent on it.

But car ownership is not **(16)** .... it was. Ever worsening traffic congestion means that mobility is correspondingly reduced, and the advantages of owning a car diminish.

Part 3

For questions **17–24**, read the text below. Use the word given in capitals at the end of some of the lines to form a word that fits in the gap **in the same line**. There is an example at the beginning (**0**).

In the exam, write your answers **IN CAPITAL LETTERS** on the separate answer sheet.

Example: **0** E N T I T L E D

Do Green Products Make us Better People?

A recent report in the journal *Psychological Science* was **(0)** .... **TITLE**
Do Green Products Make us Better People? After conducting
a series of experiments, psychologists reached the conclusion
that those who buy **(17)** .... ethical products were just as **SUPPOSE**
likely to be cheats and **(18)** .... as those who did not. In other **CRIME**
words, there was no direct correlation between a social or ethical
conscience about one aspect of life, and **(19)** .... in another. **BEHAVE**

Despite being an occasional buyer of organic vegetables, I myself
take great **(20)** .... from the study because it fits in with a **SATISFY**
long-held hypothesis of my own. It is what I call the theory of
finite niceness. We use the word 'nice' to describe those people
we encounter who seem **(21)** .... and kind. Yet, it is not a word **CHARM**
we use often to describe those to whom we are closest, because
we know that there is a **(22)** .... in their characters. We **COMPLEX**
understand them and realise that they are people who **(23)** .... **DOUBT**
have both faults and virtues, and that these do **(24)** .... come **VARIABLE**
out in different ways.

Part 4

For questions **25–30**, complete the second sentence so that it has a similar meaning to the first sentence, using the word given. **Do not change the word given.** You must use between **three** and **six** words, including the word given. Here is an example (**0**).

Example:

0 Chloe would only eat a pizza if she could have a mushroom topping.

ON

Chloe .... a mushroom topping when she ate a pizza.

The gap can be filled with the words 'insisted on having', so you write:

Example:	**0**	INSISTED ON HAVING

In the exam, write **only** the missing words **IN CAPITAL LETTERS on the separate answer sheet**.

---

25 The new computer game was every bit as good as Caroline had expected.

UP

The new computer game .... expectations.

26 Because he thought it might break down, Dan always kept a mobile phone in his car.

CASE

Dan kept a mobile phone in his car .... down.

27 Should you see Jack this evening, give him my regards.

HAPPEN

If you .... into Jack this evening, give him my regards.

28 Although the manager refused to buy us a new photocopier, she was still popular.

HER

The manager was still popular .... to buy us a new photocopier.

29 Paul wishes that he hadn't started arguing with his best friend.

HAD

Paul regrets .... with his best friend.

30 Lots more people have been shopping online this year.

SHARP

There .... the number of people shopping online this year.

Part 5

You are going to read an extract from a novel. For questions **31–36**, choose the answer (**A, B, C** or **D**) which you think fits best according to the text.

In the exam, mark your answers **on the separate answer sheet**.

My first day with the family replayed itself in my mind, but in black and white, and the reel grainy and distorted in places. I was seated with the family, nervous, pretending to follow Carl Sagan on TV, covertly assessing their movements and utterances. Peju, seated next to me, suddenly turned and asked casually, 'Lomba, what is the capital of Iceland?'

I discovered later she was going to read journalism at the university and ultimately become a presenter on CNN. She had stacks of cassette recordings of herself reading the news in a cool, assured voice. I looked at her blankly. She was seventeen, and her beauty was just starting to extricate itself from the awkward, pimply encumbrances of adolescence. Her eyes were polite but unrelentingly expectant. Surprised at the question, not knowing the answer, I turned to Bola for help – but he was lost in a loud and argumentative game of Ludo with his mum on the carpet. I shrugged and smiled. 'Why would I know what the capital of Iceland is?'

'Good answer, Lomba,' came the father's voice from behind the *Sunday Guardian*. He was lying on the sofa; he had been listening to us all along.

'Stay out, Daddy,' Peju pleaded, and turning back to me, she proceeded to lecture me on the name and geographical peculiarities of Reykjavik. The next salvo came from Lola, who was going to be a fashion designer. She was twelve and intimidatingly precocious. She had sidled up to me and sat on the arm of my seat, listening innocently to Peju's lecture; but as soon as it was over she took my arm and gave me a cherubic smile. 'Do you know how a bolero jacket looks?'

When I replied, naturally, in the negative, she jumped up gleefully and ran to their room and back with her sketchbook and pencil. She dragged me down to the carpet and quickly sketched a bolero jacket for me. I stared in silence at the tiny hand so sure behind the pencil, and the wispy but exact strokes slowly arranging themselves into a distinct shape.

'The tailor is making one for me. You'll see it when it is ready,' she promised.

'What do you use it for?'

'To dance the bolero – it is a Spanish dance.'

'Can you dance it?'

'No, but I'll learn.'

'You'll wear him out with your nonsense, girls,' the father said, standing up and stretching. He yawned. 'Time for my siesta.' He left.

At first, I was discomfited by his taciturnity, which I mistook for moodiness; but in close-up I saw the laughter kinks behind the eyes, the lips twitching, ready to part and reveal the white teeth beneath. I came to discover his playful side, his pranks on the girls, his comradely solidarity with Bola against the others. Apart from his work, his family was his entire life. Now I saw him – in black and white – after work, at home, seated on his favourite sofas, watching CNN or reading the papers, occasionally turning to answer Lola's persistent, needling questions, or to explain patiently to Bola why he couldn't afford to buy him a new pair of sneakers just now. Big, gentle, quiet, speaking only when spoken to. Remember him: conscientious doctor, dutiful father, loving husband and, to me, perfect role model.

But Ma Bola was my favourite, perhaps because she was so different from my mother, who was, coincidentally, the same age as her. Ma Bola was slim, her figure unaltered by years of childbirth.

'Your sister?' people often asked Bola, and he'd look at his mother and they'd laugh before correcting the mistake. Ma Bola was a secretary at the Ministry of Finance – she called her husband 'darling', like white people. Her children were 'dear' and 'honey'. The first time she called me that, I turned round to see if there was someone else behind me. She had laughed and patted me on the cheek. 'Don't worry, you'll get used to our silly ways.' ... Her greatest charm was her ease with people. She laughed so easily; she listened with so much empathy, patting you on the arm to make a point. After a minute with her, you were a captive for life.

'Take care of my husband for me,' she told me often. That was how she sometimes fondly referred to Bola, 'my husband'. 'He can be so impulsive, so exasperatingly headstrong.'

'I will,' I promised.

She went on to tell me how, in traditional society, parents used to select friends for their children. We were alone in the kitchen. She was teaching me how to make pancakes. 'Cousins, usually. They'd select someone of opposite temperament – someone quiet if theirs was garrulous, someone level-headed (like you) if their own was impulsive. They'd make them sworn friends for life, to check each other's excesses. Very wise, don't you think?'

'Very.'

'If I was to select a friend for Bola, it'd be you. But Providence has already done it for me.'

31 Lomba says that he later discovered that Peju

  A was older than he had first thought.
  B frequently asked people surprising questions.
  C was already preparing for her future career.
  D quickly made progress in her career.

32 When Lomba answered Peju's question,

  A she tried to stop her father from giving Lomba the answer.
  B she indicated that she was glad that Lomba did not know the answer.
  C Lomba knew that Bola would not have been able to give him the answer.
  D she supplied him with information he did not know.

33 What does Lomba say about Lola?

  A She was pleased that he didn't know the answer to her question.
  B She seemed younger than she really was.
  C She made him feel much more comfortable than Peju did.
  D He thought at first that she was playing a trick on him.

34 Lomba says that he found out that he was wrong about

  A how the father spent most of his time.
  B what the children thought of their father.
  C the father's priorities in life.
  D the father's sense of humour.

35 When describing Ma Bola, Lomba makes it clear that

  A he got on better with her than with his own mother.
  B he was not familiar with being addressed with the words she used.
  C her physical appearance made him feel comfortable with her.
  D he was envious of her children's relationship with her.

36 When she was talking to Lomba in the kitchen, Ma Bola said that

  A she thought he would be a good influence on Bola.
  B she was becoming increasingly worried about Bola.
  C she wanted him to take on a role he might not want.
  D she realised that a certain tradition was dying out.

Part 6

You are going to read the views of four economists on the subject of large-scale human migration. For questions **37–40**, choose from the extracts **A–D**. The extracts may be chosen more than once.

The winners and losers in mass migration

Four economists give their views on the economic consequences of large-scale migration.

A

Large-scale human migration between continents is often erroneously regarded as a recent phenomenon. It is remarkable, however, that a process that once took thousands of years now takes a few generations, as the history of countries like Australia and Canada bears witness. Most developed nations have seen migration from less developed areas this century, a trend that seems set to gather pace in years to come. Put simply, there's excess demand for labour in rich countries, and people from poorer countries arrive to plug the gap, thereby helping to keep the economies of the developed nations functioning smoothly. Although they tend to do lowly-paid work initially, such people are clearly much better off financially than they would be had they stayed where they were. What's more, because they often lend financial support to family members back home, the wealth of developed nations is effectively invested in the economies of less-developed areas, and everyone benefits.

B

In developed countries, each generation tends to gain improved access to education and employment opportunities, until eventually a shortage of unskilled labour, especially in the service sector, provides opportunities for incoming migrants, and in order to maintain levels of growth and development, rich societies need to attract such people. Given that economic growth is the aim of most western governments, it is hard to see this changing anytime soon. Sadly, however, it is often the most able and industrious individuals who leave poor countries to the detriment of the local economy. The potential benefits of migration can be overstated, however. Indeed, being by nature energetic and intelligent, some would-be migrants might actually be well advised to stay at home, where they are best placed to fuel economic growth and reap the benefits. Instead, these people often end up doing low-paid menial work in the developed world. Although some funds may be channelled back to their country of origin, the overall economic effect is negligible.

C

Economic growth is the aim of most democratic western governments, as it keeps voters in work and allows them to enjoy an increasingly sophisticated lifestyle based on consumption of goods and services. Part of this equation is population growth, which especially in the case of service industries, tends to fuel economic development. Low birth rates in developed countries mean that migrant labour needs to be recruited if targets for economic growth are to be achieved. It seems an irreversible trend. Migrants tend to come from less-developed parts of the world. Individuals are attracted by the opportunity to earn much more than they could back home, although this could be a false impression given the realities of living on a low income in a country with a high cost of living. Meanwhile, poorer economies may be denied the contribution of some of their most able members.

D

Clearly, economic growth in the USA was fuelled in the nineteenth century by a steady influx of labour from other parts of the world. Some argue that the same process that produced economic growth in that infant economy will have the same effect on modern post-industrial ones. But the issues are much more complex. Indeed, although migrants arrive in European countries in response to labour shortages, these do not exist in a free market, and I would question the assumption that the current level of economic migration across continents will be sustained. The existence of minimum wage legislation and other social initiatives, unimaginable in the nineteenth century, serve to distort the picture and make it difficult to say whether immigration is serving the needs of a growing economy effectively or not. It is certainly depleting the pool of talent in poorer nations, for although materially better off, migrants rarely return to channel their new found wealth or skills into the local economy.

Which economist

doesn't have the same opinion as Economist A regarding the impact of migration on the economy of the host country?

37

holds a different view to Economist C regarding how migration can affect a migrants' country of origin?

38

shares Economist B's view regarding the financial benefits of migration to the individual migrant?

39

has a different opinion from the others regarding how likely current migration patterns are to continue?

40

Part 7

You are going to read an article about the hobby of cloudwatching. Six paragraphs have been removed from the article. Choose from the paragraphs **A–G** the one which fits each gap (**41–46**). There is one extra paragraph which you do not need to use.

In the exam, mark your answers **on the separate answer sheet**.

The sky's the limit for cloudwatchers

Christopher Middleton learns to distinguish an altostratus from a cirrus at Britain's first Cloud Bar.

High above the Lincolnshire coastline, a swirl of small white clouds moves slowly across a clear blue sky. In normal circumstances, you'd describe them as wispy and feathery. But because we're standing on the roof of Britain's first Cloud Bar, and it's decked out with wall charts, we assembled skygazers can identify the above-mentioned phenomena as *Cirrus fibratus*. For the moment anyway, since clouds only live for ten minutes (it says on the chart).

41

'It's a fantastic idea, this place,' says off-duty fireman Peter Ward, who's brought his young family here. 'Really inspiring.'

42

At the last count, membership of the Cloud Appreciation Society stood at 23,066, covering 82 nations and all kinds of skywatchers from hillwalkers to airline pilots. 'We think that clouds are nature's poetry,' says the society's founder Gavin Pretor-Pinney, author of *The Cloudspotter's Guide* (sales of 200,000 and still rising). 'Clouds are for dreamers and their contemplation benefits the soul.'

43

'In fact, you don't really need to travel at all to see interesting clouds. You can just lie in your back garden and look upwards,' he says. For many cloudwatchers, the most important factor is not so much geographical location, as your philosophical disposition.

44

'That said, clouds can be tremendously exciting too,' he adds. 'The first cloud I noticed was at the age of four and a half. I saw this magnificent *Cumulonimbus*, with rays of sunshine sprouting out from behind. Even now, I love to see those towering great formations. In my mind, clouds are the last great wilderness available to us.'

45

Cloudspotters in search of similar experiences flock each autumn to North Queensland in Australia for the tube-shaped phenomenon knows as Morning Glory. 'You go up and surf the wave of air it creates,' says Gavin Pretor-Pinney, whose follow-up book is *The Wavewatcher's Companion*. 'Even more thrilling is to travel through clouds on a hang-glider. The strange thing is, you put your hand inside a cloud, but although it's wet and chilly, there's no actual substance to it.'

46

There's something about clouds which appeals to the soul, Ian Loxley says. 'The line I like best is the one that goes, "Life is not measured by the number of breaths you take, but by the moments that take your breath away."'

A Gavin Pretor-Pinney explains why this is: 'Because of the stately way in which clouds move and the gradual rate at which they develop, contemplating them is akin to meditation,' he says. 'The mere act of sitting, watching and observing slows you down to their pace.'

B Absolutely. And as well as stimulating the imagination, clouds get you out and about. The keeper of the Society's photo gallery, Ian Loxley, has been on cloud-seeking expeditions in places as far afield as Cornwall and Canada, though his favourite location is around his home in the Lincolnshire Wolds.

C The Cloud Appreciation Society website is full of reports of such encounters. Some, like that one, are in mid-air at close quarters, while others are miles below on the ground.

D *Alto* clouds are a good example. They are primarily made up of water droplets, making them appear as grey puffy masses. If you see these on a humid summer morning, watch out for a potential thunderstorm later.

E Yes, spend an hour here and you become an instant expert on telling your *altos* (four to six miles high) from your *cumulos* (anything lower). As for these, they don't start until eight miles up, and they're identifiable because of their long, thin, shape (the name in Latin means a strand of hair).

F And, like all such places, humans want to explore them. Glider pilot Mike Rubin not only flies inside clouds but rides on them. 'You fly underneath, find the thermal lift that is generating this cloud, and climb up by circling inside it,' he says. 'Use the thermals, and on a good day, you can travel hundreds of kilometres.'

G Other beachgoers aren't as convinced that the country has been crying out for a purpose-built pavilion like this, equipped with adjustable mirrors so that you don't even have to look up at the sky. But the world's nephophile community (that's cloud enthusiasts) would beg to differ, especially now that more changeable autumn weather offers fewer cloudless blue-sky scenarios, and lots more action of the scudding and billowing kind.

Part 8

You are going to read an article about sea creatures. For questions **47–56**, choose from the sections of the article (**A–D**). The sections may be chosen more than once.

In the exam, mark your answers **on the separate answer sheet**.

In which section of the article are the following mentioned?

the kind of sea creature that people in general find appealing	47
how certain creatures reached the sea where they are currently found	48
the replacement of various kinds of sea creature by other kinds	49
the likelihood that only a small proportion of all sea creatures is included in the Census	50
a situation that is not immediately apparent in the Census	51
a doubt about the accuracy of existing information about sea creatures	52
the basis on which sea creatures are included in the Census	53
an informal term to describe a large proportion of all sea creatures	54
a task that would be very difficult to carry out	55
the aim of the people carrying out the Census	56

What lies beneath

Marine scientists have discovered strange new species, but their census also reminds us how little we know about sea creatures, says Tim Ecott.

A In the latest Census of Marine Life, the Mediterranean has been identified as one of the world's top five areas for marine biodiversity. The others are the oceans off Australia, Japan, China and the Gulf of Mexico, each containing as many as 33,000 individual forms of life that can be scientifically classified as species. In total, the Census now estimates that there are more than 230,000 known marine species, but that this is probably less than a quarter of what lives in the sea. The Census has involved scientists in more than 80 countries, working over a decade. They hope that by creating the first catalogue of the world's oceans, we can begin to understand the great ecological questions about habitat loss, pollution, over-fishing and all the other man-made plagues that are being visited upon the sea. The truth is that, at present, much of what passes for scientific 'facts' about the sea and what lives in it are still based on guesswork.

B So far, the Census tells us that fish account for about 12 percent of sea life, and that other easily recognisable vertebrates – whales, turtles, seals and so on – are just two percent of what lives beneath the waves. It is the creepy-crawlies that are out there in really big numbers. Almost 40 percent of identified marine species are crustaceans and molluscs – things like crabs, shrimp, squid and sea-snails. The Census continues to add images and data relating to a myriad range of creatures that could have slithered out of the pages of science fiction. For example, there is something enchanting about the 'Yeti crab' (*Kiwa hirsuta*), another new discovery from the Pacific, with a delicate, porcelain-smooth carapace and arms longer than its body, encased in 'sleeves' of what look like ginger fur.

C In shallower waters, the iridescent pink fronds of *Platoma algae* from Australia resemble the sheen of a pair of pink stockings. Juvenile Antarctic octopuses, speckled brown, mauve and orange, look like exquisitely carved netsuke ornaments, perfectly proportioned and endearing for their donnish domed heads. For its bizarre variety and for its enduring mystery, we must learn to treasure the sea. It is easy to be captivated by intelligent, seemingly friendly sea creatures such as dolphins, or even by the hunting prowess of the more sinister sharks. The Marine Census helps us understand that it is the less glamorous, less appealing and less dramatic creatures that are the great bedrock of life on which the oceans depend. As Nancy Knowlton, one of the Census scientists, observes, 'Most ocean organisms still remain nameless and unknown' – and how would we begin to start naming the 20,000 types of bacteria found in just one litre of seawater trawled from around a Pacific seamount?

D Hidden within the Marine Census results is a dark message. Maps showing the density of large fish populations in tropical waters reveal that numbers of many of the biggest open ocean species have declined by more than 50 percent since the 1960s and specific species, including many of the sharks, by as much as 90 percent. The Census also points to the effect of the so-called 'alien species' being found in many of the world's marine ecosystems. The Mediterranean has the largest number of invasive species – most of them having migrated through the Suez Canal from the Red Sea. So far, more than 600 invasive species have been counted, almost 5 percent of the total marine creatures in the Mediterranean. There is evidence that a global jellyfish invasion is gathering pace. As Mediterranean turtles lose their nesting sites to beach developments, or die in fishing nets, and the vanishing population of other large predators such as bluefish tuna are fished out, their prey is doing what nature does best; filling a void. Smaller, more numerous species like jellyfish are flourishing and plugging the gap left by animals higher up the food chain. In the not too distant future, they may be the most plentiful marine species around.

Part 1

TEST 7 WRITING

You **must** answer this question. Write your answer in **220–260** words in an appropriate style. In the exam, write your answer **on the separate answer sheet provided**.

1   Your class has had a discussion on the best ways of improving the general health of people in today's world. You have made the notes below.

> **What's the best way of encouraging people to lead healthier lifestyles?**
>
> - television advertising
> - government campaigns
> - education in schools
>
> Some opinions expressed in the discussion:
>
> 'There's so much TV advertising of junk food – no wonder everyone's overweight.'
>
> 'It's up to individuals to decide how they live, not the government.'
>
> 'If children understand the importance of good health, there won't be a problem in the future.'

Write an essay discussing **two** of the ways in your notes. You should **explain which is the best way of encouraging people** to lead healthier lifestyles, **giving reasons** in support of your answer.

You may, if you wish, make use of the opinions expressed in the discussion, but you should use your own words as far as possible.

Part 2

Write an answer to **one** of the questions **2–4** in this part. Write your answer in **220–260** words. In the exam, write your answer **on the separate answer sheet provided**, and put the question number in the box at the top of the page.

2 You have received a letter from a younger friend asking for your advice.

> I'm really worried – I've got to decide whether to go to university miles away from all my mates and family, or not bother and take a job locally working for a computer company (you know I love anything technical!). It might possibly lead to promotion in the long-term but I know that university has loads of benefits. Have you ever regretted going to university? What did you gain or lose from it? What should I do?

Write a **letter** in reply. You do not need to include postal addresses.

3 You see the following announcement on a website, *Books and films of our time*.

> ### It speaks to us now!
> Send us a review of a book or film with a theme you feel is particularly important or relevant in society today.
>
> Did the book or film give a particular message to readers or viewers? What did you learn from it? Did it help you to understand more about society today in a useful or meaningful way?

Write your **review**.

4 You see the following announcement in an international travel magazine.

> ### Do you use buses or trains?
> We are running a survey on facilities and services provided at bus and train stations around the world, and would like to find the best and the worst. Send us a report on a bus or train station you have used.
>
> We'd really like to know what was good or bad about the bus or train station and any problems you have experienced. We'd also like your suggestions for ways in which the bus or train station could be improved.

Write your **report**.

TEST 7 LISTENING

Part 1

You will hear three different extracts. For questions **1–6**, choose the answer (**A**, **B** or **C**) which fits best according to what you hear. There are two questions for each extract.

In the exam, write your answers **on the separate answer sheet**.

Extract One

You hear two students discussing a part-time design course they are doing.

1 What aspect of the course do they appreciate most?

  A the way it is delivered

  B the attitude of the staff

  C the content of the sessions

2 Which aspect does the woman feel could be improved?

  A feedback on assignments

  B access to certain resources

  C pre-course information for students

Extract Two

You hear part of an interview with a young man who has been travelling in many remote parts of the world.

3 What does he say about his luggage?

  A He's yet to find the best way of carrying things.

  B He's learnt to leave out unnecessary pieces of equipment.

  C He's become very good at packing the absolute minimum.

4 When asked what he's learnt from travelling, he says that

  A he now longs for his comfortable lifestyle at home more.

  B he appreciates why others don't feel able to do what he's done.

  C he regrets visiting places where people are less fortunate than him.

Extract Three

You hear part of an interview with the lead singer in a rock band.

5   How does he feel about the criticism of his band's latest album cover?

   A   He thinks it's been exaggerated.

   B   He admits it's the reaction he wanted.

   C   He resents the suggestion that the cover was unoriginal.

6   He thinks much of the criticism was due to

   A   a lack of respect for his band in the music business.

   B   a foolish comment he made to a journalist.

   C   a misunderstanding of his real intentions.

Part 2

You will hear a student called Kerry giving a class presentation about a type of bird called the swift. For questions **7–14**, complete the sentences with a word or short phrase.

In the exam, write your answers **on the separate answer sheet**.

THE SWIFT

Kerry says that the Latin name for the swift translates to the words **(7)** .... in English.

Kerry describes the noise made by swifts as a **(8)** ....

Kerry says many people think that the bird's shape most resembles a **(9)** ....

Kerry thinks that the swifts' natural nesting site is on **(10)** ....

Kerry was surprised to learn that **(11)** .... is a common material found in swifts' nests.

Kerry has observed swifts flying fast to avoid **(12)** ....

Kerry says that swifts tend to be strangely **(13)** .... when they are in Africa.

In the past, a rich family's **(14)** .... often used the swift as a symbol.

Part 3

You will hear an interview in which two professional kayakers called Glenda Beachley and Declan Speight are talking about their sport. For questions **15–20**, choose the answer (**A**, **B**, **C** or **D**) which fits best according to what you hear.

In the exam, write your answers **on the separate answer sheet**.

15 What does Glenda find most enjoyable about kayaking?

    A It requires a range of skills.
    B It is a test of physical strength.
    C It requires her to work out problems.
    D It gives her a feeling of independence.

16 Glenda advises young novice kayakers to

    A vary their training routine.
    B choose a club very carefully.
    C concentrate on enjoying the sport.
    D keep trying to beat their friends in races.

17 When Declan talks about what's called 'wild-water' racing, he suggests that

    A he sees it as more a test of stamina than speed.
    B the hardest part is keeping to the prescribed route.
    C his chances of success in races depends on the weather.
    D his main motivation comes from entering competitions.

18 When asked about the dangers of kayaking, Glenda says that

    A a certain level of fear is desirable.
    B you have to learn from your mistakes.
    C a calm assessment of the risks is essential.
    D over-confidence can get you into difficulties.

19 What advice does Declan have about equipment?

    A Only the most expensive equipment is likely to be durable.
    B Expert help is needed to make the right decisions.
    C People should get whatever looks most comfortable.
    D Doing research is important to get the best value for money.

20 Glenda and Declan agree that their best kayaking memories involve

    A exploring new places with friends.
    B performing well in international events.
    C meeting people from a variety of backgrounds.
    D finding unexpectedly good stretches of river to run.

Part 4

You will hear five short extracts in which people are talking about leaving their own country to study abroad.

In the exam, write your answers **on the separate answer sheet**.

TASK ONE

For questions **21–25**, choose from the list (**A–H**) why each speaker decided to study in another country.

A to explore an alternative career

B to extend skills already acquired   Speaker 1   [21]

C to satisfy family expectations   Speaker 2   [22]

D to turn a dream into reality   Speaker 3   [23]

E to learn another language   Speaker 4   [24]

F to be nearer to places of historical interest Speaker 5   [25]

G to escape from a dead-end job

H to pursue a simpler lifestyle

TASK TWO

For questions **26–30**, choose from the list (**A–H**) what each speaker says they gained from the experience.

A a feeling of being at home

B a new attitude towards money   Speaker 1   [26]

C a completely new interest   Speaker 2   [27]

D the opportunity to make useful contacts   Speaker 3   [28]

E a more relaxed attitude towards other people Speaker 4   [29]

F a greater sense of motivation   Speaker 5   [30]

G friends with the same interests

H a new sense of independence

TEST 7
SPEAKING

PART 1

The interlocutor will ask you a few questions about yourself and on everyday topics such as work and study, travel, entertainment, daily life and routines. For example:

- If you could do any job, what would it be? Why?
- Do you prefer having one long holiday or several short breaks? Why?
- Do you watch the same kind of television programmes now as you did in the past? Why/Why not?

PART 2

Learning

Turn to pictures 1–3 on page 188, which show people learning in different situations.

Candidate A, compare two of the pictures and say what the benefits are of learning in these different situations and how enjoyable the learning process might be.

Candidate B, which situation do you think is best for learning something quickly? Why?

Making choices

Turn to pictures 1–3 on page 189, which show people making choices in different situations.

Candidate B, compare two of the pictures and say how easy it might be for the people to make a choice in these situations and how important it might be for them to make the right choice.

Candidate A, which choice do you think is most difficult for the people to make? Why?

PART 3

Turn to the task on page 190, which shows some reasons people give for choosing to do different kinds of work.

Talk to each other about how important these reasons are when people are choosing what kind of work to do.

Decide which reason is least important for people to consider when taking a new job.

PART 4

Answer these questions:

- What's the best way to find out what a job is really like?
- Do you think the media often gives a false impression of how glamorous some jobs are? Why/Why not?
- Do you think that some kinds of work are under-paid? Why/Why not?
- Some people say there's no point in getting a university qualification nowadays because it's better to get training while you work. Do you agree?
- How easy do you think it is to achieve a good work/life balance nowadays? Why?
- Is it a good thing to be ambitious? Why/Why not?

GENERAL MARK SCHEME FOR SPEAKING

Assessment scales

Throughout the test, candidates are assessed on their own individual performance and not in relation to each other. They are awarded marks by two examiners: the assessor and the interlocutor. The assessor awards marks by applying performance descriptors from the analytical assessment scales for the following criteria:

- Grammatical resource
- Lexical resource
- Discourse management
- Pronunciation
- Interactive communication.

The interlocutor awards a mark for Global Achievement using the Global Achievement scale.

Assessment for *Cambridge English: Advanced* is based on performance across all parts of the test, and is achieved by applying the relevant descriptors in the assessment scales.

Grammatical Resource

This refers to the accurate and appropriate use of a range of both simple and complex grammatical forms. Performance is viewed in terms of the overall effectiveness of the language used in spoken interaction.

Lexical Resource

This refers to the candidate's ability to use a range of vocabulary to meet task requirements. At the Advanced level, the tasks require candidates to speculate and exchange views on unfamiliar topics. Performance is viewed in terms of the overall effectiveness of the language used in spoken interaction.

Discourse Management

This refers to the candidate's ability to link extended utterances together to form coherent speech, without undue hesitation. The utterances should be relevant to the tasks and should be arranged clearly and logically to develop the themes or arguments required by the tasks.

Pronunciation

This refers to the candidate's ability to produce intelligible utterances to fulfil the task requirements. This includes stress and intonation, as well as individual sounds. Examiners put themselves in the position of a non-ESOL specialist and assess the overall impact of the pronunciation on the listener and the degree of effort required to understand the candidate.

Interactive Communication

This refers to the candidate's ability to take an active part in the development of the discourse. This requires an ability to participate in the range of interactive situations in the test, and to develop discussions on a range of topics by initiating and responding appropriately. This also refers to the deployment of strategies to maintain interaction at an appropriate level throughout the test so that the tasks can be fulfilled.

Global Achievement

This refers to the candidate's overall effectiveness in dealing with the tasks in the four separate parts of the Advanced Speaking test. The global mark is an independent impression mark which reflects the assessment of the candidate's performance from the interlocutor's perspective.

Part 1

In Part 1, you answer questions on personal topics such as likes, dislikes, routines, work, holidays, and so on for about two minutes.

Watch the full test online.

Exam help

- Only answer your own questions. Don't contribute to your partner's answers.
- Give answers that are interesting, but not too long.
- Don't answer just *yes* or *no* – always give a reason for your answer.
- Imagine that you are in a social situation and meeting someone for the first time. Think about how you might answer general social questions such as:
    - What kind of magazines or newspapers do you read regularly? Why?
    - Do you ever listen to the radio? Why/Why not?
    - What time of day do you find best for studying? Why?
    - What do you like to do when you go out with your friends?
    - Do you have a particularly busy life generally? Why/Why not?
    - Do you think that it's useful to have a daily routine? Why/Why not?

Useful language

Responding to questions

I really enjoy … because …

I'm afraid I don't really like … because …

My favourite … is … because …

In the future, I'd really like to …

My family consists of …

I think my friends might say … but in my opinion …

I don't know what to say – it's a difficult question, but probably I'd say that …

I don't think I really have a preference, although if I had to choose …

Part 2

In Part 2, you compare two pictures and say something else about them. You have to speak for about a minute.

Watch the full test online.

Exam help

- Listen to the interlocutor's instructions, and only ask for them to be repeated if you really didn't understand. Remember that the questions are written on the paper to help you.
- Look at the questions written at the top of the page so that you don't forget the last two parts of the task. These give you the chance to speculate and show a range of language.
- Spend about 20 seconds comparing the pictures and the remaining time dealing with the rest of the task. This will help you to organise your talk.
- Only compare two of the pictures, otherwise you will run out of time and not complete the task.
- Don't describe what you can see. Don't repeat the question in your answer as you will lose time.

Useful language

Comparing the pictures

Whereas the people in the first picture are very busy, those in the second picture are …

The first picture shows a workplace. **Conversely**, the second …

The people in the second picture are enjoying themselves more than …

There's a big difference in how the people are feeling …

Expressing opinions

I think that …

It seems to me that …

What I think is …

I think it's quite clear that …

I feel quite strongly that …

Speculating

What I would probably say about the people is that …

The people seem to me to be …

Perhaps they are feeling … because …

It's possible that they are … since …

I'm really not sure, but I think that …

Organising your talk

Both pictures show people who are …

To find similarities and differences, I'd say that …

To add to what I said about …

On top of that, I'd say …

Against that is the fact that …

Part 3

In Part 3, you discuss a task with your partner. You have to respond appropriately to what your partner says, and discuss the written prompts in as much detail as you can.

Watch the full test online.

Exam help

- Concentrate on saying as much as you can about each prompt before moving on to the next.
- Make sure that you and your partner take it in turns to initiate discussion.
- Respond to what your partner says before moving the discussion on to the next idea.
- Don't worry if you can't talk about all the prompts in two minutes; it's more important to have a detailed discussion.
- When you are asked to make a decision, use the whole minute to discuss your ideas.

Useful language

Agreeing/disagreeing

You made a good point when you said …

That's an interesting point.

I take your point.

You said … but I'm afraid I can't agree with you.

I can't see how that's relevant to the question.

I can't see what you're getting at really.

Suggesting

Why don't we think about …?

This seems to me to be a good idea.

We could link this to …

Let's move on to …

Justifying and clarifying

I'm sure that's right, because …

What I meant by that is …

What I said was …

So what you really mean is …

So when you said …, you meant …

Initiating and moving on to another prompt

I'm not sure what to say about this. What do you think?

What do you think about …?

What does this add?

How about considering this one?

Shall we go on to the next prompt?

I think this is similar to … . In fact, we could link the ideas together.

Asking for opinions

What do you think?

Are you with me on that one?

Anything to add?

Do you feel the same?

SPEAKING FILE: PART 3

Part 4

In Part 4, you discuss abstract questions related to Part 3. You should give fuller answers than in Part 1, and you can discuss ideas with your partner if you want.

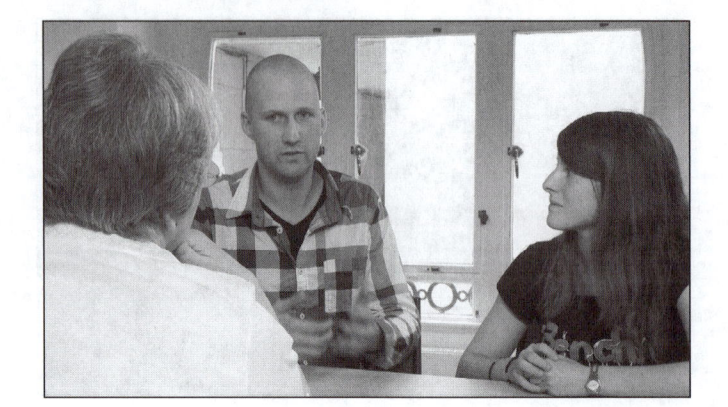

Watch the full test online.

Exam help

- The interlocutor may ask you a direct question or may ask a question to you both. Even if the interlocutor asks your partner a question, you can still add your own ideas once your partner has answered. You don't have to agree with your partner.

- If you're not sure of the answer to your own question or have no ideas, use fillers to gain time to think, or ask your partner what they think.
- There are no 'right' answers to these questions – you are simply being asked to express your opinions.

Useful language

Using 'fillers' to have time to think

Let me think about that …

That's a good question! Just a minute. … What I think is …

I've never really thought about it before, but what I would say is …

That's an interesting question!

Responding to a question

What I think about that is …

It seems to me that …

This question is really interesting because …

I've actually thought about this before, and I feel that …

Developing an answer

So if I really think about it, I could also say that …

It also occurs to me that …

What I said doesn't mean that …

To add to what I've already said …

It's true that …, but I think that …

To go into it a bit further, I'd say that …

GENERAL MARK SCHEME FOR WRITING

GENERAL IMPRESSION MARK SCHEME

BAND 5

For a Band 5 to be awarded, the candidate's writing has a very positive effect on the target reader. The content is relevant* and the topic is fully developed. Information and ideas are skilfully organised through a range of cohesive devices, which are used to good effect. A wide range of complex structures and vocabulary is used effectively. Errors are minimal, and inaccuracies which do occur have no impact on communication. Register and format are consistently appropriate to the purpose of the task and the audience.

BAND 4

For a Band 4 to be awarded, the candidate's writing has a positive effect on the target reader. The content is relevant* and the topic is developed. Information and ideas are clearly organised through the use of a variety of cohesive devices. A good range of complex structures and vocabulary is used. Some errors may occur with vocabulary and when complex language is attempted, but these do not cause difficulty for the reader. Register and format are usually appropriate to the purpose of the task and the audience.

BAND 3

For a Band 3 to be awarded, the candidate's writing has a satisfactory effect on the target reader. The content is relevant* with some development of the topic. Information and ideas are generally organised logically, though cohesive devices may not always be used appropriately. A satisfactory range of structures and vocabulary is used, though word choice may lack precision. Errors which do occur do not cause difficulty for the reader. Register and format are reasonably appropriate to the purpose of the task and the audience.

BAND 2

For a Band 2 to be awarded, the candidate's writing has a negative effect on the target reader. The content is not always relevant. Information and ideas are inadequately organised and sometimes incoherent, with inaccurate use of cohesive devices. The range of structures and vocabulary is limited and/or repetitive, and errors may be basic or cause difficulty for the reader. Register and format are sometimes inappropriate to the purpose of the task and the audience.

BAND 1

For a Band 1 to be awarded, the candidate's writing has a very negative effect on the target reader. The content is often irrelevant. Information and ideas are poorly organised, often incoherent, and there is minimal use of cohesive devices. The range of structures and vocabulary is severely limited, and errors frequently cause considerable difficulty for the reader. Register and format are inappropriate to the purpose of the task and the audience.

BAND 0

For a Band 0 to be awarded, there is either too little language for assessment or the candidate's writing is totally irrelevant or illegible.

*Candidates who do not address all the content points will be penalised for dealing inadequately with the requirements of the task.

Candidates who fully satisfy the Band 3 descriptor will demonstrate an adequate performance in writing at Advanced level.

Essay (Part 1)

Test 1, Part 1, Question 1

You **must** answer this question. Write your answer in **220–260** words in an appropriate style. In the exam, you write your answer **on the separate answer sheet provided**.

1   Following a class discussion on how technology has affected the way we live today, you have made the notes below.

> **Which aspect of our daily lives has been affected most by technology?**
>
> - communication
> - relationships
> - working life
>
> Some opinions expressed in the discussion:
>
> 'It's great to be able to communicate with people 24 hours a day.'
>
> 'It's so hard to make personal relationships – everyone's online all the time.'
>
> 'People have an easier working life because they can work from home.'

Write an essay discussing **two** of the points in your notes. You should **explain which aspect of daily life you think has been most affected** by technology, **giving reasons** in support of your answer.

You may, if you wish, make use of the opinions expressed in the discussion, but you should use your own words as far as possible.

Exam help

Part 1

- Make sure that you have enough ideas about the topic to write 220-260 words. The point of an essay is to present an argument clearly and provide evidence for your point of view. You may be asked to agree or disagree with a statement, or write about issues on a given topic.
- Read the question carefully, choose the two points you want to discuss, and then plan your answer in paragraphs. It is easy to organise your essay if these paragraphs are the points you have chosen from the task. You are presenting an argument, so you need to explain your ideas clearly and justify them. This means you should use suitable connectors.
- Use a formal or semi-formal style. It may be appropriate to use rhetorical questions to lead into your argument or ideas.
- Use a range of vocabulary and try to think of interesting details to support your ideas.
- Try to present a balanced argument, showing that you are aware of all the possible issues.
- Don't begin your essay giving your opinion, but finish with a conclusion summarising your own point of view. This should be the one you have argued for in your essay.

Essay

- The purpose of an essay is to present an argument. It should highlight and discuss important points or issues on a topic, supporting and developing the argument with extra points which are clarified through reasons and examples. The reader should understand the opinion of the writer through the argument presented in the essay.
- An essay should be well-organised with an introduction, clear development of ideas and an appropriate conclusion to round off the argument. It should use appropriate connectors and range of language.
- It may be written as a result of an activity like taking part in a class discussion, listening to a radio programme or watching a film.
- The style is usually formal or semi-formal.

Sample answer

Technology is such a feature of everyday life that it is difficult to remember what we did without it. It impacts on almost every aspect of our daily lives. But where has technology's greatest impact been?

Firstly, technology has affected the way we make relationships and our expectations of them. It is increasingly common to find people with more friends on the internet than in real life, and they spend more time chatting to cyber friends than they do to real world friends. Although feeling part of a wider community like this can be positive, it could also have a negative effect on people's ability to relate to others on a personal level. In turn, this could make it hard not only to establish relationships initially but to maintain them. The impact of this development on society is clearly enormous.

Another area in which technology has affected people's lives is in the workplace. Sitting in open-plan offices working at computer screens creates an unsatisfying and unsupportive environment. On the plus side, technology also enables people to work from home, which can lead to a healthier work/life balance. Of course, people may also find this difficult as it can lead to isolation.

To sum up, it appears that the impact of technology has been greatest on the way we form relationships, because this affects people emotionally as well as practically. However, given that it is impossible to return to a world without technology, we must accept its increasing impact on our lives in as many areas as we can.

- Use suitable connectors to link points.
- Support your ideas with examples.
- Use clear paragraphs for each discussion point or issue.
- Show that you appreciate other points of view as it strengthens your argument.

- Introduce the topic in general terms, using rhetorical questions to lead in to the discussion.
- Don't give your own opinion until the final paragraph. Make sure your conclusion follows your argument clearly.

Useful language

Introduction
It is often said that …
This is a hotly-debated topic.
This is a topic that is often discussed but rarely solved.
Many people feel that …

Linking ideas
While many may agree with this, it may still be a mistake.
Conversely, it may be inappropriate for this situation.
On the contrary, it is seen by many as an excellent solution to the problem.
While I can see some benefits, these may be outweighed by the disadvantages.

Giving opinions
It seems to me that …
In my opinion, this is …
From my perspective, this seems to be …
To be honest, I feel that …

Conclusion
To sum up, it seems to me that …
On balance, I feel that …
Taking all the arguments into account, I would say that …

Proposal (Part 2)

Test 1, Part 2, Question 2

You are on the social committee of your college. You have been asked to write a proposal for your college principal on the kind of social and sporting activities the college should provide for new students. You should assess the current situation, describe the needs of new students and suggest activities the college should provide.

Write your **proposal**. Write your answer in **220–260** words in an appropriate style.

Sample answer

Introduction
Starting at a new college can be daunting for new students. The purpose of this proposal is to evaluate the social and sporting activities already on offer, describe the needs of new students and suggest further activities the college should provide.

The style is formal because it is for a proposal. An introduction stating the aims of the proposal is important for clarity.

It is useful to state the purpose of the proposal in the introduction.

Current social and sporting activities
There are football and tennis clubs in college, where new students can make friends. However, if they are not particularly interested or talented, these may not be of interest to them. On the social side there are meeting places like the café, but they are not particularly welcoming. Finally, there are two music clubs which are generally popular, but they only meet weekly and the type of music is limited to jazz and pop. The worst thing is that accessing information about social activities can be difficult.

Headings make the proposal easy to read.

Needs of new students
New students must establish social contacts otherwise they can be lonely. Apart from finding out about activities on offer, they may be unaware of existing facilities.

Recommendations
Support your recommendations with reasons.

- The range of social opportunities should be extended to include a dance club and a debating club. The latter would be particularly effective as it would also develop life skills.
- Music clubs should meet more frequently and include types of music like classical and choral. Singing has been proved to be effective in bringing people together.
- I would recommend displaying information in the Student Union and on the college intranet.
- The café should be refurbished to improve the atmosphere.

Conclusion
Include an appropriate conclusion.

The recommendations above would be simple to implement, and would not only improve the lives of new students, but current ones too.

Exam help

Part 2
- Read through all the questions before choosing which one to answer. You should think about what type of writing you are best at, and then any ideas you have for each topic.

Proposal
- The purpose of a proposal is to give information and not engage the reader, so techniques like rhetorical questions are not appropriate.
- A proposal is usually for the future, and recommendations may be expressed using modal verbs.
- The style is usually semi-formal or formal.
- It's a good idea to use headings so that you present information clearly.
- Don't use too many bullet-points as you need to show a range of language. Bullet points are useful for recommendations because they are clear and easy to find in the proposal.
- Support your recommendations with reasons.

Useful language

Making formal recommendations
It would be a good idea to …
One suggestion would be to …
It would be useful to …
I would recommend that …
It might be possible to …

Providing useful information
We hope to …
High among our future plans is …
One of our future priorities is …
One key aspect of our future is …
Our future plans include …

Giving reasons
This would mean that …
This would not only … but also …
In this way …
This addresses the issue of …
This would enable … to …

Conclusion
In the light of …
If these recommendations were to be implemented …
While there may be issues still to resolve, following these suggestions would mean …

Review (Part 2)

Test 1, Part 2, Question 3

Reviews wanted: best film ever!

We are planning to produce a set of DVDs of the ten best films of all time. Send us a review of your favourite film. What was it about? What made it so good? Why should we include it in the set of DVDs? The best reviews will be included with the set of DVDs.

Write your **review**. Write your answer in **220–260** words in an appropriate style.

Sample answer

This introduction gets the reader interested before revealing what the film is.

I am a great fan of science fiction films, and although I know these particular films are now old, the original trilogy is so iconic that I don't see how any set of the best DVDs ever could fail to include them. Of course, I'm talking about *Star Wars*.

Don't give too much detail about the plot – just enough to give an idea of what happens.

Who doesn't know the plot? Evil Darth Vader is building the massive Death Star space station to help the Empire overcome the Rebel Alliance, which has been formed to fight back against tyranny. Vader captures Princess Leia, who has stolen the plans to the Death Star and hidden them in the robot R2-D2, who is later bought by Luke Skywalker. Luke accidentally triggers a message put into the droid by Leia, asking for assistance. Luke later trains to be a Jedi and with his friends sets out to crush the Empire. What follows is an action-packed roller coaster, crammed with special effects and enthralling plot twists.

Use interesting and dramatic language to support your points.

The film has to be included in the set of DVDs because everything about it was fresh and new at the time, the special effects were totally spectacular and, amazingly, it still has the power to thrill the audience today. The music is instantly recognisable, and still sends a shiver down my spine. The characters are powerful and interesting and have made stars of some of the actors. The technical effects were well ahead of their time and have influenced many films since they were first seen on screens all over the world.

This rhetorical question in the conclusion is effective in reinforcing the writer's opinion.

Do you really think any set of 'The best films ever' would be complete without this trilogy?

Exam help

Review

- A review is often of a book or film, but it can also be about an exhibition, an event, etc.
- Plan your ideas carefully before you start to write and remember that the focus of a review is usually to interest or inform the reader, and to give your opinion of whatever you are reviewing.
- Try to involve the reader by using techniques such as rhetorical questions, though don't use too many as they can become boring. You can talk to the reader directly.
- The style of a review depends on the context, type of publication and who the reader is. It may be semi-formal or informal, but should use a range of language.
- Add examples to support your ideas.
- Try to finish in an interesting way, and remember to make your opinion clear.

Useful language

Making recommendations

I would recommend …
The … has to be included …
I can't see how … can be ignored
This is an iconic film/book …
It's well ahead of its time …
It's been very influential …

Using interesting and dramatic language

It's totally spectacular and amazing …
It still has the power to thrill …
It sends a shiver down my spine …
The music is instantly recognisable …

Talking directly to the reader

We're all supposed to hate reality shows but do we really?
I'm fairly sure that you will all agree with me when I say …
Why not think about it? You'll find that …
Have you ever seen anything like this?
So is this really true?
So what do I really think about the whole thing?

Concluding a review

For all the reasons given, I recommend …
It must be clear that this is the … to win the competition.
How could the … be considered complete without this …?

WRITING FILE: REVIEW

Letter (Part 2)

Test 1, Part 2, Question 4

You have received a letter from an English friend:

> Hi!
> I remember that you worked in a ski resort last winter, and I'm thinking of doing the same this year. Were there any drawbacks? Did you meet interesting people? What opportunities were there for skiing? Would I gain much from doing it for just four months? Should I apply for it?
> Thanks for your help
> Jack

Write your **letter**. Write your answer in **220–260** words in an appropriate style. You do not need to include postal addresses.

Exam help

Letter
- The style of a letter could be semi-formal, formal or informal depending on the purpose of the letter and the context. Make sure you read the instructions carefully, and identify the target reader and reason for writing. Keep the style consistent throughout.
- Use clear paragraphs and appropriate opening and closing phrases.

Useful language

Beginning an informal letter

Thanks so much for your email …

Sorry not to have contacted you earlier …

Thought it was time I dropped you a line …

Referring to a previous letter

You said in your letter that you want to …

Last time you wrote, you mentioned …

I remember that you spoke about …

Ending an informal letter

I think that's all for now. Do write soon!

Once again, thanks for contacting me.

Give my love to …

Speak to you soon.

Ending a formal letter

Yours sincerely (if beginning with the person's name)

Yours faithfully (if beginning with 'Dear Sir/Madam')

Sample answer

Hi Jack,

Great to hear from you. So you're thinking of applying for my old job – there are positive things about it, but there are loads of downsides.

I know how much you love skiing, but to be honest you'll be lucky to get more than a couple of days in all. And you have to buy your own ski pass, which is pricey – no freebies! I got pretty frustrated when snow conditions were good and I could've been on the slopes.

It can be stressful because you're dealing with clients the whole time, getting equipment sorted, stuff like that. They come from all over the world and lots of them are really interesting to talk to – like one was a professional singer, and another was a journalist who told fascinating stories. But when snow conditions are poor, you have to find entertainment for them, and they may not be thrilled about the situation! When I was there they complained a lot. It's true I got the chance to pick up a smattering of other languages but in four months you don't learn a whole lot! I guess I did improve my people skills, but I hated the paperwork, which was really time-consuming. Filing isn't my thing, and there was piles of it.

I don't really know what to advise. You won't get much skiing, it's stressful, but it's paid employment and learning to deal with people in difficult situations is a bonus.

It's your call! Let me know if I can do anything, or if you want any contact names.

All the best
Carlo

Annotations:
- Try to use interesting language and idioms.
- This is an informal letter, so use informal language.
- Add your own ideas to create interest.
- You have been asked for advice, so summarise your position.
- Finish with an appropriate phrase – in this case, it is an informal letter. If you were writing a formal letter you would finish with 'Yours sincerely' or 'Yours faithfully'.

Report (Part 2)

Test 2, Part 2, Question 4

> You have just finished a short period of work in a company abroad as part of your business course. You have now been asked to write a report for your course organiser.
>
> In your report you should explain what you did and how you benefited from the period of work, describe any problems you had and make recommendations for other students on the business course who will be working in the same company abroad later.
>
> Write your **report**. Write your answer in **220–260** words in an appropriate style.

Sample answer

You can use headings for clarity.

State the aim of the report and who it is for.

Introduction
The aim of this report for the course organiser is to outline my work experience abroad, identify the benefits and problems and make recommendations for students doing the same thing in the future.

Background information
I was assigned to a large office in the city centre in order to gain experience in management. My daily duties involved shadowing the office manager and learning different procedures. I also took part in a specific project aimed at building up new clientele, which was particularly interesting as it linked to my current course module.

Benefits and problems
Explain the benefits and problems, with examples.

I gained a great deal from seeing different management styles in action, which enabled me to put the theoretical aspects of the course into a practical context. It was also valuable in giving me independence and responsibility, and in a global world it is particularly useful to experience the working environment of another country.

I found a few problems in adapting to the cultural differences as I was only there a short time, and in being accepted as a full member of the office team. This may be inevitable, and I certainly did not feel unwelcome.

Recommendations
Give reasons to explain your recommendations.

I would suggest making contact with members of the office before joining them, and asking for an overview of the office culture. This would avoid the feeling of being an outsider, and create more of a feeling of teamwork.

If students were given a schedule before the period of work experience, they could prepare more thoroughly. This would make the secondment run smoothly.

Conclusion
Finish with an appropriate conclusion.

Overall it was a positive experience, which I recommend to other students.

Exam help

Report

- Read the context carefully to decide what style to use. It will probably be semi-formal.
- Try to think of interesting and appropriate details to support your ideas.
- Remember that the purpose of a report is to inform the reader about an existing situation in order for them to make some kind of decision. You should make recommendations, and give your own personal opinion in order to help the reader to their decision.
- Plan your report carefully, thinking about the best layout to use. You can use bullet points and headings, but the format and style should be appropriate for the context and the person you are writing the report for.
- Although you want to be clear, don't use language that is too simple. You still need to show a range of language.
- Include a conclusion, possibly with a final evaluation.

Useful language

Introducing the report
The aim of this report is to …
In this report, I will …
This report presents …
This report is for …

Making recommendations
In the light of … it seems to me that the best approach to take is …
I would recommend … as …
I would suggest …
I definitely recommend this book/film because …

Finishing the report
For the reasons stated, I feel that …
In conclusion, I feel that …
In short, I feel confident in recommending …

Candidate A

1

- What do you think the people might be enjoying about learning the new skill?
- How easy might it be for the people to master it?

Candidate B

2

- Why are the people entertaining others in these different places?
- How memorable might it be for the people watching?

TEST 1: SPEAKING   171

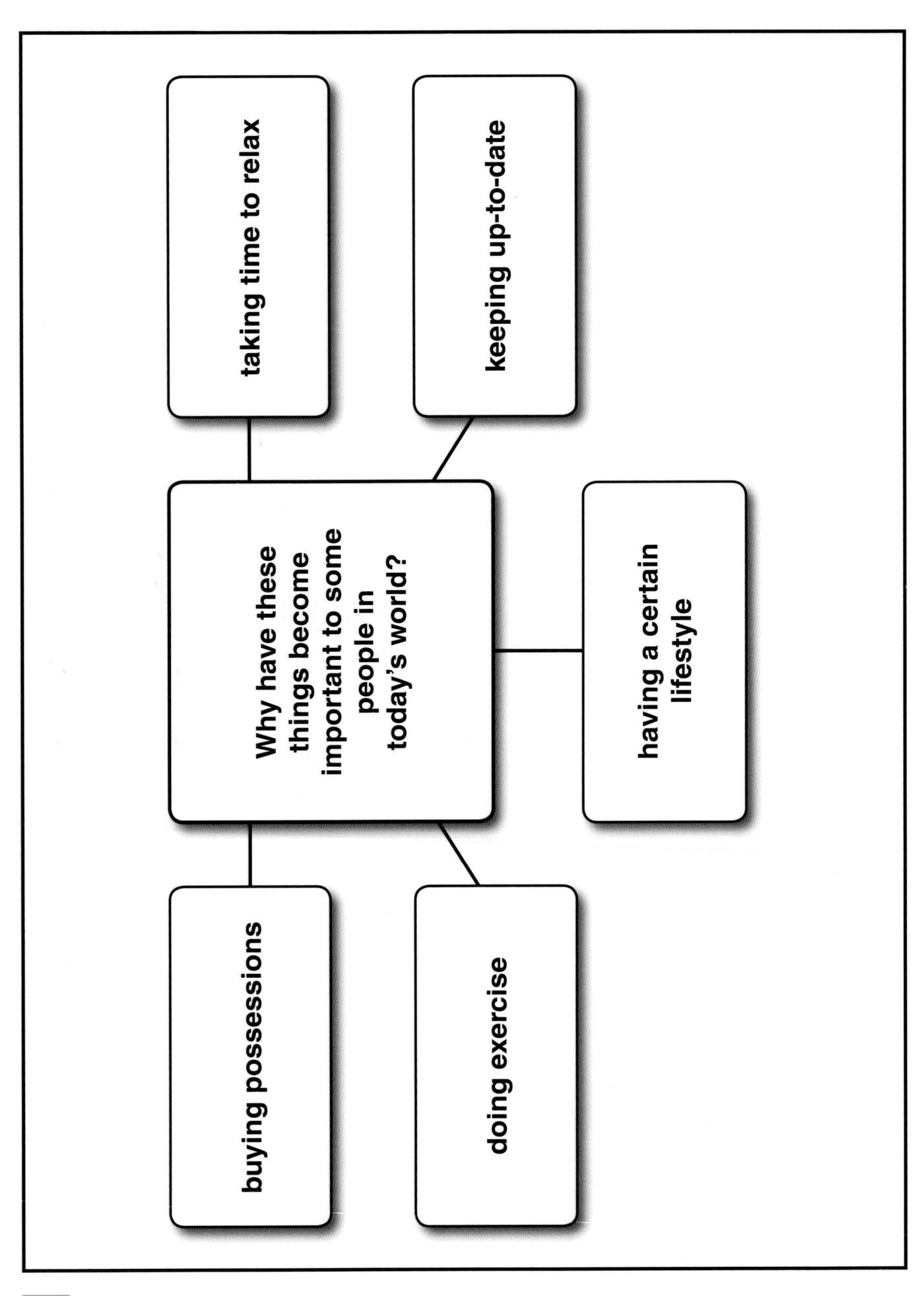

Why have these things become important to some people in today's world?

- taking time to relax
- keeping up-to-date
- having a certain lifestyle
- doing exercise
- buying possessions

Candidate A

1

- How might people benefit from playing games like these?
- How might the players be feeling?

TEST 2: SPEAKING 173

Candidate B

2

- Why might the people need to take a break?
- How relaxing might the situations actually be?

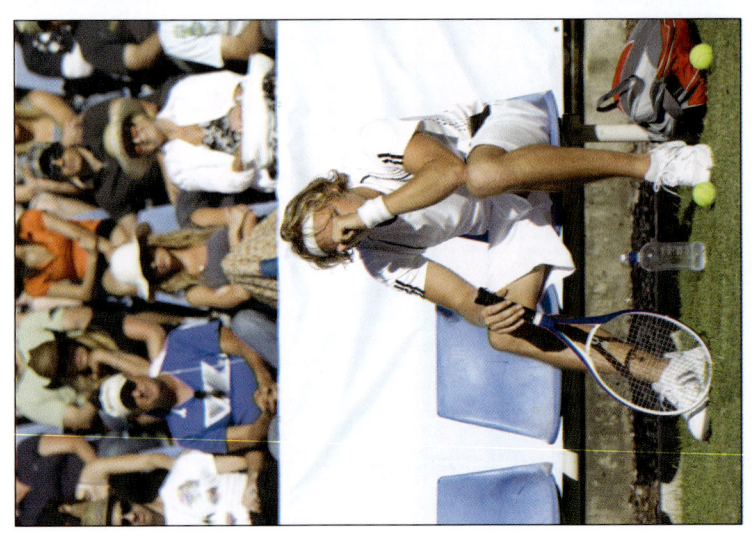

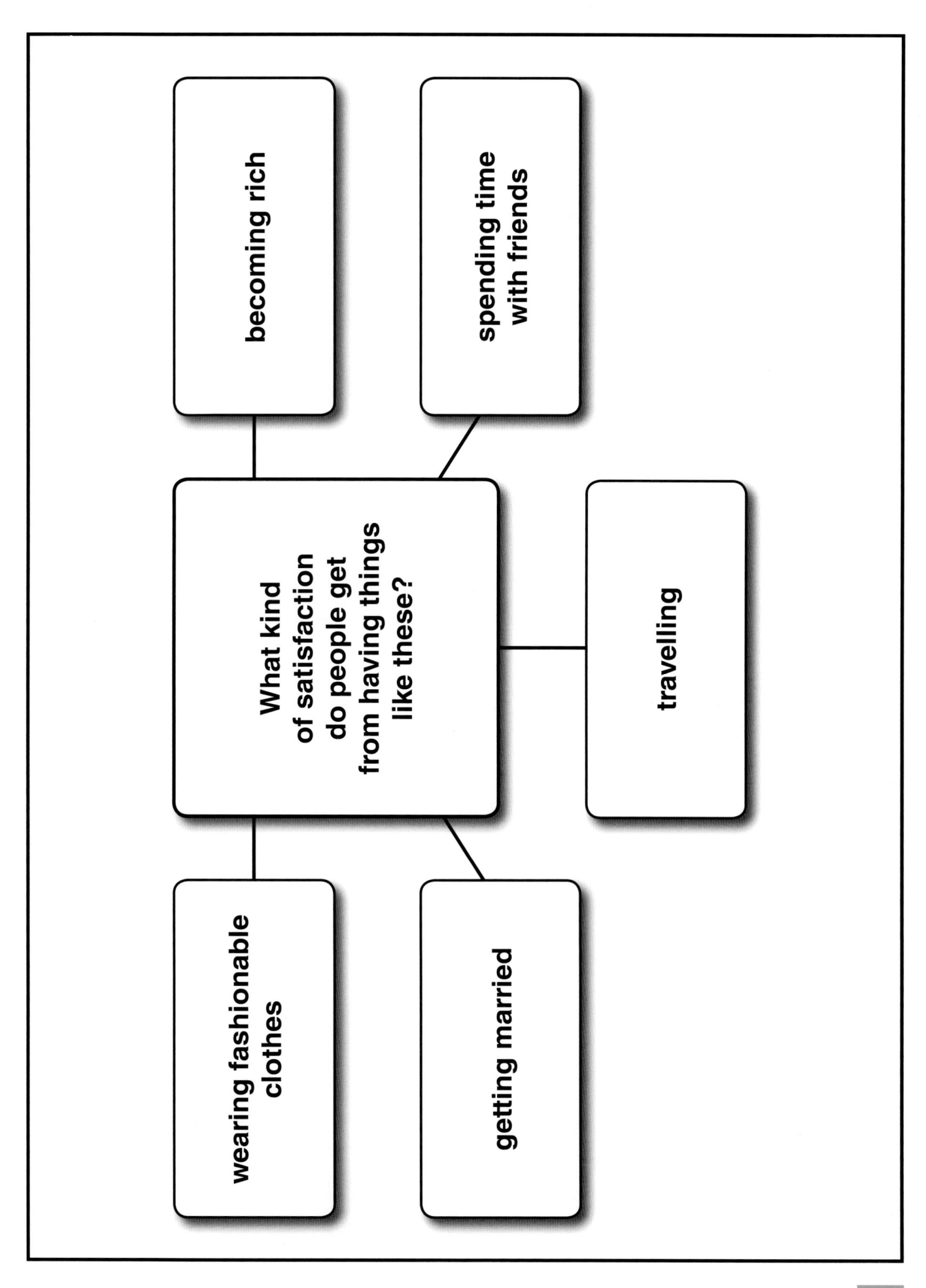

- becoming rich
- spending time with friends
- travelling
- getting married
- wearing fashionable clothes

What kind of satisfaction do people get from having things like these?

Candidate A

1
- Why might the people be feeling emotional in these situations?
- How long might the feeling last?

TEST 3: SPEAKING

Candidate B

2

- What might be difficult for the people to deal with in these situations?
- How important might it be for them to deal with the situations well?

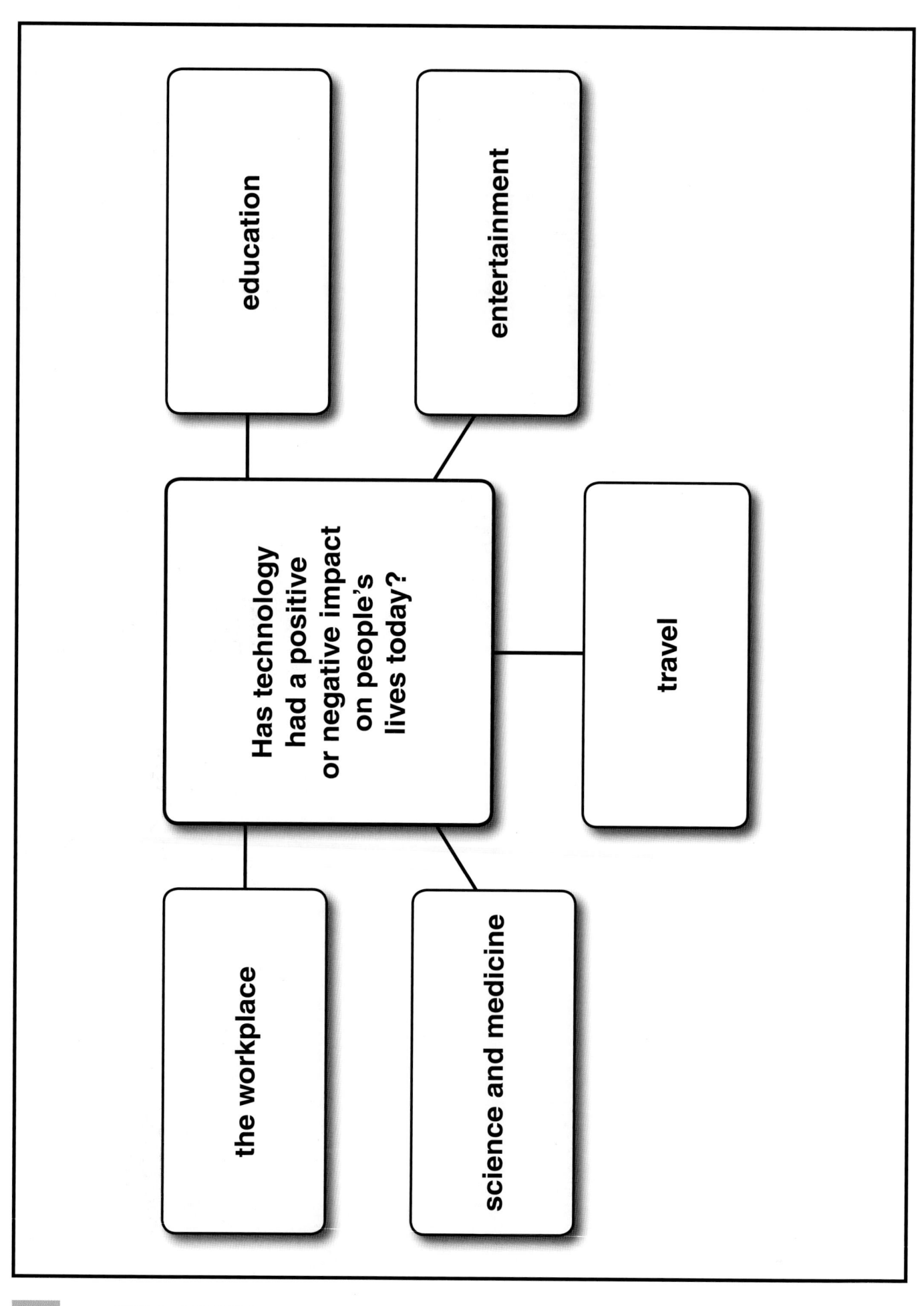

- education
- entertainment
- **Has technology had a positive or negative impact on people's lives today?**
- travel
- the workplace
- science and medicine

Candidate A

- Why might the people be finding these activities challenging?
- Which activity might give them the most satisfaction?

2

- What are the advantages of learning about the past in these ways?
- Who might actually learn most about the past?

Candidate B

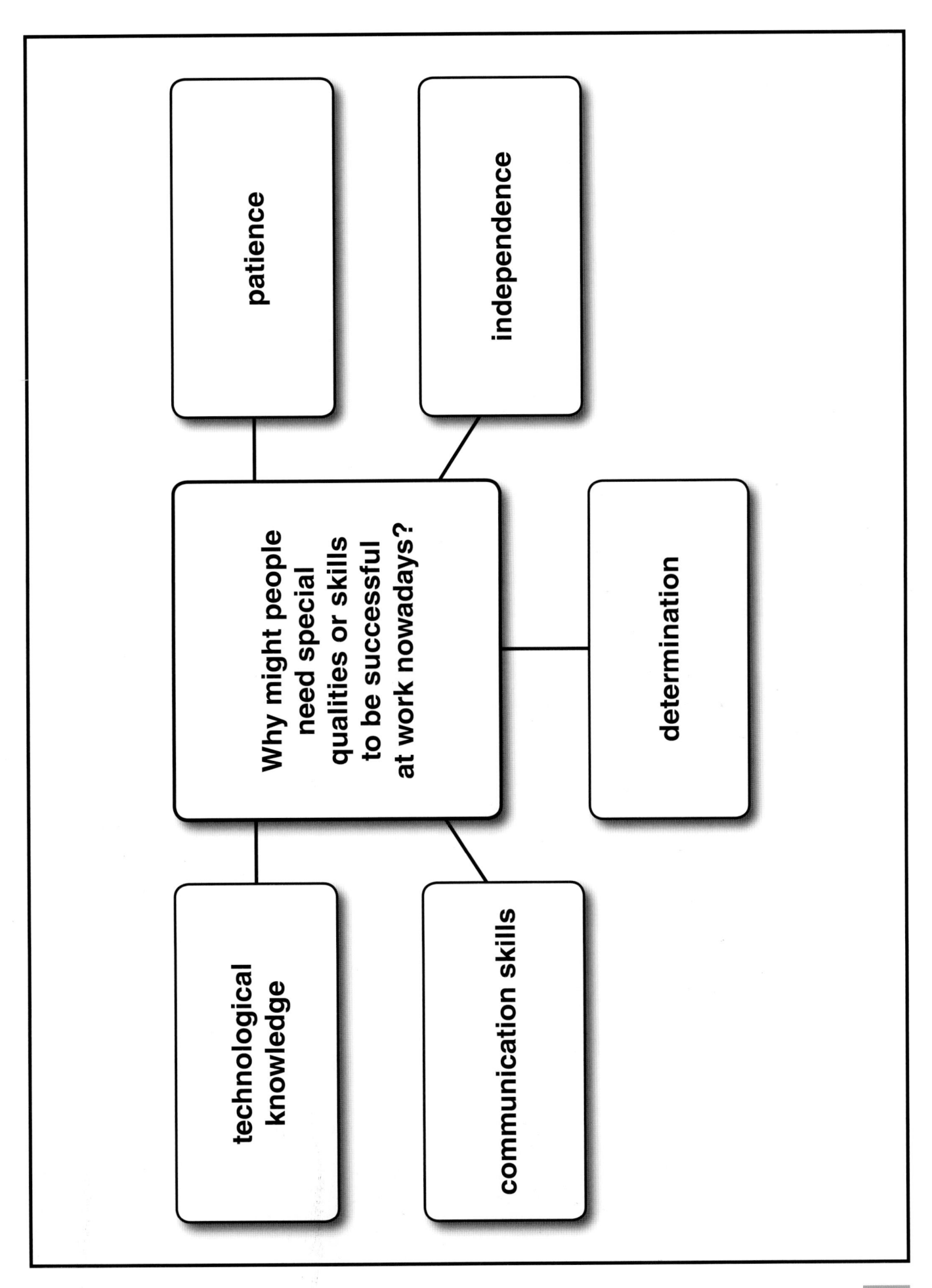

- patience
- independence
- determination
- communication skills
- technological knowledge

Why might people need special qualities or skills to be successful at work nowadays?

Candidate A

1

- Why might the people feel proud in these situations?
- How important might the feeling be to them?

TEST 5: SPEAKING

Candidate B

2

- What effect might the weather conditions have on the people's mood?
- How difficult might it be for them to deal with the conditions?

TEST 5: SPEAKING 183

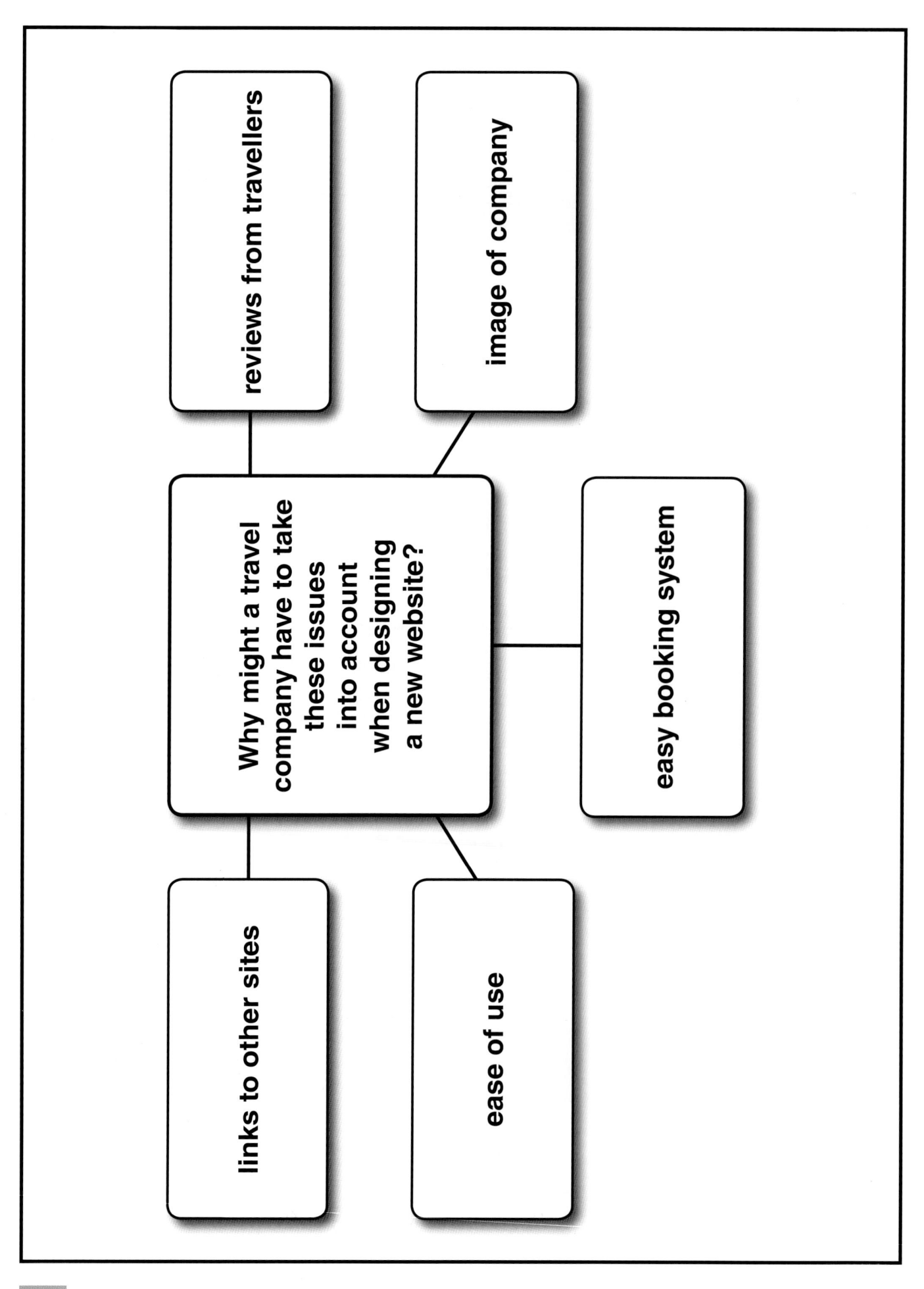

- reviews from travellers
- image of company
- **Why might a travel company have to take these issues into account when designing a new website?**
- easy booking system
- ease of use
- links to other sites

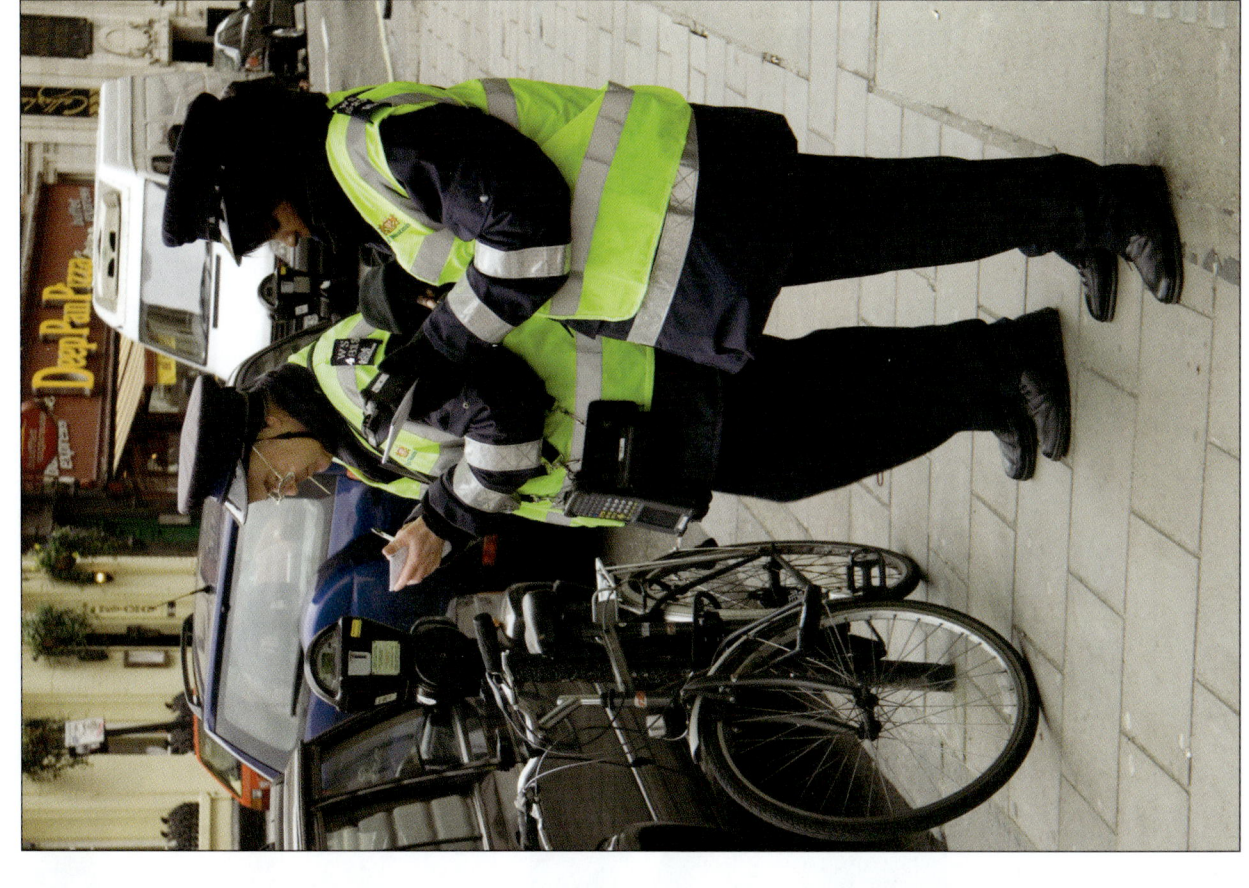

Candidate A

1
- How important might it be for the people to work together in these situations?
- How difficult might it be for them to do the work alone?

Candidate B

- Why might the people have chosen to travel in these different ways?
- How might they be feeling?

TEST 6: SPEAKING

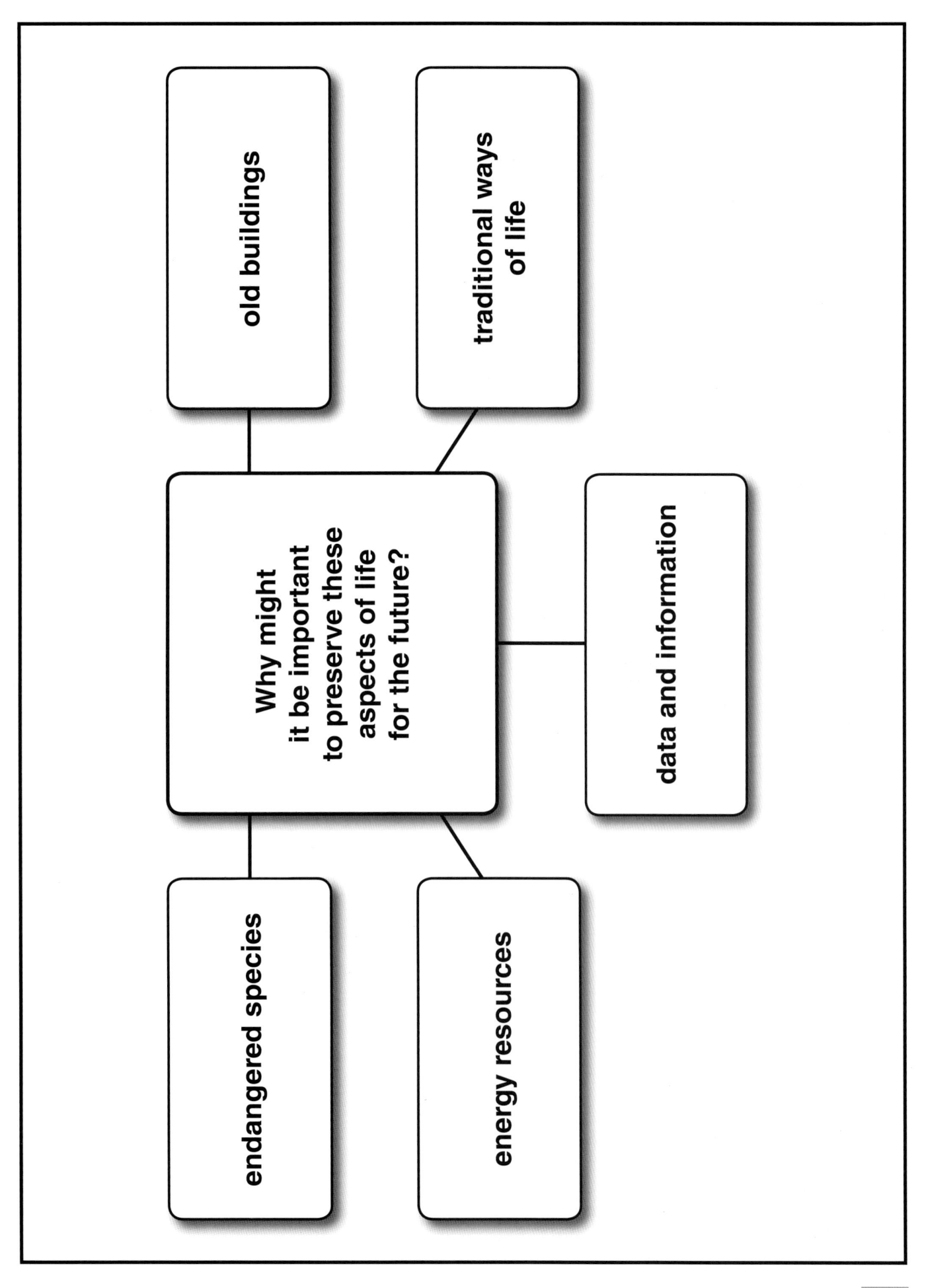

- old buildings
- traditional ways of life
- data and information
- energy resources
- endangered species

Why might it be important to preserve these aspects of life for the future?

Candidate A

1

- What are the benefits of learning in these different situations?
- How enjoyable might the learning process be?

TEST 7: SPEAKING

Candidate B

2

- How easy might it be for the people to make a choice in these situations?
- How important might it be for them to make the right choice?

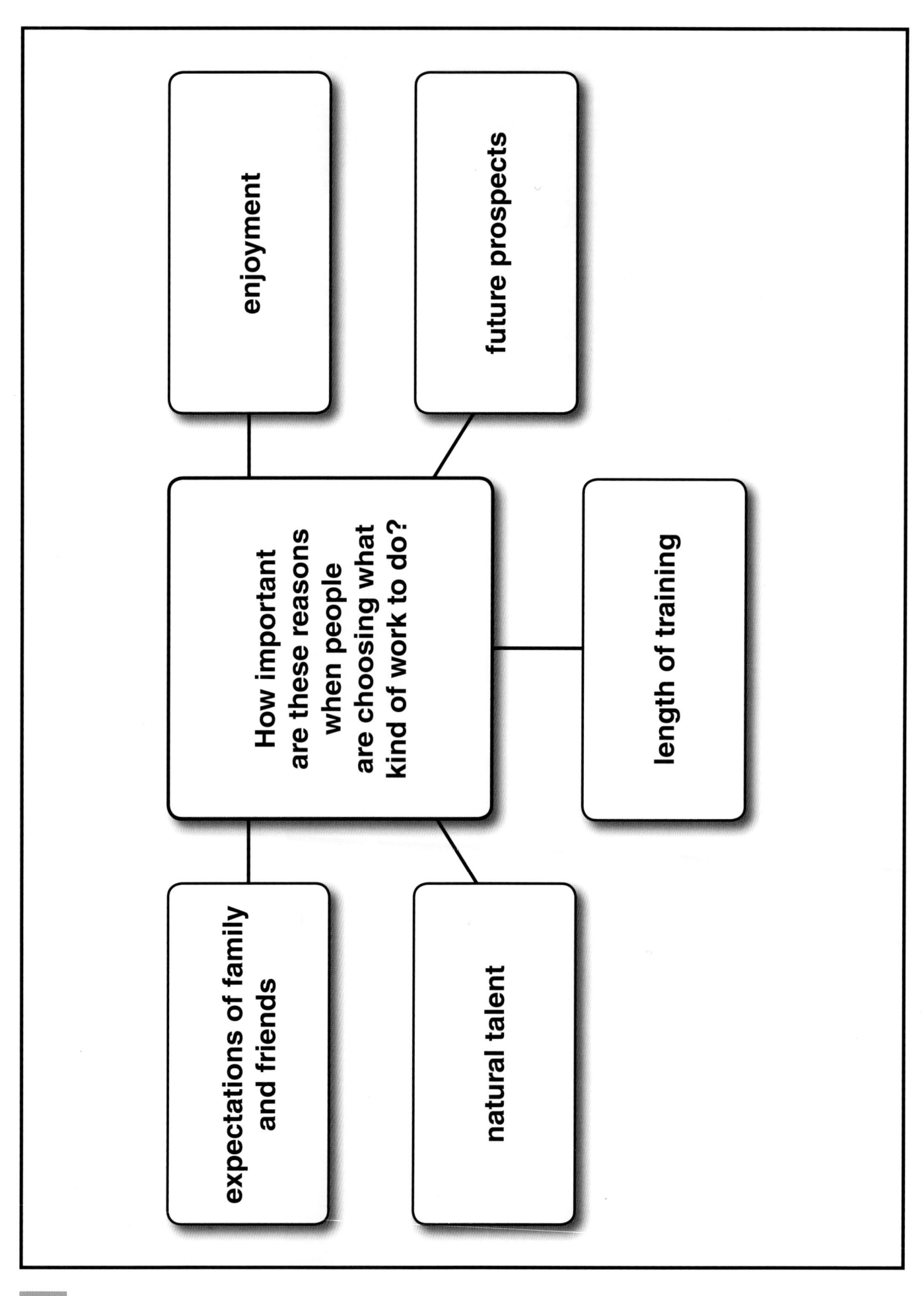

- enjoyment
- future prospects
- length of training
- natural talent
- expectations of family and friends

How important are these reasons when people are choosing what kind of work to do?

Answer Key

Test 1, Reading and Use of English (page 8)

Part 1: The Mysterious Isle

1. C: The other words do not complete the fixed phrase.
2. B: Only this answer creates the correct phrasal verb.
3. D: Only this word can be used in the context to mean 'the exact place'.
4. A: The other words cannot be followed with 'out of'.
5. C: Only this phrase indicates what's already been mentioned.
6. B: Although the meaning of the other words is similar, they do not collocate with 'intact'.
7. D: Only this word collocates with 'permanent' to describe an island.
8. D: Only this answer collocates with 'opportunity'.

Part 2: Choosing Binoculars

9. in (preposition) follows the verb 'invest'
10. it (pronoun) part of fixed expression
11. more (comparative) part of linking expression
12. their/his/her (possessive pronoun) refers to everyone
13. which (determiner) to indicate one of many possible
14. is (verb) part of a cleft sentence
15. give (verb) collocates with 'test run'
16. (Al)though/While(st) (linker) introduces a contrast

Part 3: The Inventor of the Bar Code

17. irregular (adjective to negative adjective)
18. length (adjective to noun)
19. outlets (verb to plural compound noun) part of common collocation
20. checkout (verb to compound noun)
21. encoded (verb to adjective) part of noun group
22. potentially (noun to adverb)
23. application(s) (verb to noun)
24. arrival (verb to noun)

Part 4

25. (already) started by the time: past perfect
26. had great/a good deal of/a great deal of/a lot of difficulty: adjective to noun phrase
27. gave a faultless performance: verb to noun
28. was on the point of calling: fixed expression
29. came as a disappointment: adjective to noun
30. feels the effects of: dependent preposition

Part 5: Is the internet making us stupid?

31. C: Patricia Greenfield 'reviewed dozens of studies on how different media technologies influence our cognitive abilities' and looked at the results of these studies as a whole.
32. B: The University experiment tested how well the students 'retained the lecture's content'; an earlier experiment showed that the more types of information are placed on a screen, the less people can remember.
33. B: Greenfield concluded that 'growing use of screen-based media' had resulted in 'new weaknesses in higher-order cognitive processes' and listed several mental processes that have been affected (abstract vocabulary, etc.).
34. C: It was expected that the people who did a lot of multitasking would 'have gained some mental advantages' from their experience of multitasking but this was not true. In fact, they 'weren't even good at multitasking' – contrary to the belief that people who do a lot of multitasking get good at it.
35. C: The writer says that the 'ill effects' are permanent and the structure of the brain is changed. He quotes someone who is very worried about this and regards the long-term effect as 'deadly'.
36. D: The writer uses Ap Dijksterhuis's research to support his point that 'not all distractions are bad' – if you are trying to solve a problem, it can be better to stop thinking about it for a while than to keep thinking about it all the time.

Part 6: The Pinnacle

37. B: 'the graceful structure blends in remarkably well' matches 'a tall elegant pyramid' in A.
38. A: 'the building seems set to become a mainstay on the itinerary of visitors to the city' matches 'There can be little doubt that visitors to the city will be drawn to the east bank by the building' in D.
39. A: 'the height and scale of the Pinnacle will take some beating' is the opposite idea to 'the building's inevitably short-lived reign as the city's tallest structure' in D.
40. C: 'how keen are the local residents on having this monstrous structure spring up literally on their doorstep? The central business district, already the site of other high-rise structures, could surely have accommodated the intrusion more easily.' The other articles all say positive things about the choice of location:
    A: 'Located in the unfashionable east of the city, the building will also bring work and development to an area that has long been in need of it.'
    B: 'Some have questioned the Pinnacle's location in an otherwise undeveloped quarter, dwarfing as it does the eighteenth-century houses below it. But I would disagree.'
    D: 'the decision to build the structure in a forgotten corner of the city, originally perceived as rather unwise, has proved a stroke of genius.'

Part 7: Learning to be an action hero

41. F: link between the fact that the writer 'can't reach much past my knees' and how difficult he is finding this and that belief that the reader will think 'this sounds a bit feeble' – that the writer is weak and incapable of doing the exercise well.
42. D: link between 'get there' in D and 'a very particular, very extreme kind of fitness' before the gap; 'get there' = achieve that kind of fitness.
43. A: link between 'it had all started so well' before the gap and the first thing they did in the session, which was 'a piece of cake' (very easy) for the writer.

44 E: link between 'a few' in E and the 'movements for building strength in your back and arms' on the chinning bar mentioned before the gap.
45 G: link between the bar mentioned before the gap and Steve jumping on to that bar at the beginning of G; link between 'from one to another' and the various bars mentioned in the paragraph before the gap.
46 B: link between the 'one comforting piece of knowledge' mentioned in B and what that piece of knowledge was – that the writer will 'never suffer from an anatomical anomaly'.

Part 8: The way we worked

47 B: 'Search your high street for a typewriter repairman and your chances of a result at all are ribbon-thin.'
48 C: 'In 1888, thousands of matchgirls at the Bryant and May factory in London famously went on strike to protest over conditions.'
49 B: They serve 'septuagenarian retirees', 'technophobes', 'novelists' and 'people weaned on digital keyboards who see typewriters as relics of a distant past'.
50 D: When warned that someone might steal his techniques, he says that 'no one wants to' copy him or learn to do what he does.
51 C: 'Over subsequent decades, the long hours, tiny pay packets and exposure to toxic chemicals were addressed'.
52 A: His father told him 'these things will come back' and 'the more technology comes into it, the more you'll be seen as a specialist' and his words showed 'a lot of foresight'.
53 C: 'The majority of staff are still female'; 'it's still mainly female'.
54 A: As his trade is a 'rare one', people employ him in all sorts of places.
55 B: 'It amazes us the price the old manual machines sell for on the internet'.
56 C: 'The industry largely relocated its production to other countries where labour was cheaper.'

Test 1, Writing (page 21)

Part 1

Question 1 (essay)
Style: Formal or semi-formal, and objective as you are writing for your teacher. You should discuss two of the points, giving reasons and/or evidence. Use clear paragraphs, one for each issue, and include an introduction that leads in to the topic and a conclusion that rounds off the argument. This should state your point of view.
Content: You should include discussion of the effect of technology on two of these points:
- communication, e.g. *it's quick and easy.*
- relationships, e.g. *it can be hard to make real relationships.*
- working life, e.g. *people can work from home.*

In your conclusion you should decide which aspect of daily life has been affected most by technology. You can use the opinions given in the task if you choose, and/or use your own ideas.

Part 2

Question 2 (proposal)
Style: Proposal format and formal or semi-formal language as the proposal is for the college principal. Your paragraphs must be very clearly divided. You can use headings, numbering or bullet points if you like, but remember that if you use bullet points in any section you must still show a range of language across the whole proposal.
Content: You should:
- state the purpose of the proposal.
- outline the current social and sporting activities provided by the college.
- describe the needs of new students.
- make recommendations for activities with reasons.

Question 3 (review)
Style: Semi-formal moving towards informal as this is a review in a column written by readers of the magazine. The purpose of the review is to tell people about the DVD, and say why it was so good. You need the language of description or narration, evaluation and justification. Use clear paragraphs: introduction, description, evaluation and conclusion with recommendations.
Content: Remember to
- describe the film briefly.
- give reasons why you think it was exceptional.
- explain why you would recommend it as part of the set of DVDs.

Question 4 (letter)
Style: Letter, informal language as Jack is a friend. You should use clear paragraphs, with an appropriate greeting and ending.
Content: Include the following points:
- what kind of people he would meet.
- any opportunities for skiing.
- what he would gain from the experience.
- whether he should apply for the job, with reasons.

Test 1, Listening (page 24)

Part 1

1 A: 'What companies want is people who can come up with ideas. I get a buzz from that side of it.'
2 C: M: 'Hours aren't fixed and can be long in relation to the salary.'
    F: 'The job's not the big earner that people assume it is.'
3 A: 'I've always been competitive, and I work harder than anyone else … I copy the person who beat me. I won't stop till I'm better than them.'
4 C: 'Although I'm not such an experienced cyclist … I jumped at the chance to try it'.
5 C: 'My own experience is much like that of other callers.'
6 B: 'Choose what you plant carefully.'

Part 2: The albatross

7 Arabic
8 21/twenty-one
9 (the) wind
10 shoulder(s)
11 smell
12 (little) mice
13 feathers
14 bottle caps/tops

Part 3

15 B: I naturally leaned towards rather athletic dance styles, and there wasn't much of a repertoire for that, so creating dances was the natural way forward.

16 A: Any choreographer worth her salt would pick up on that and call it a day.

17 C: It can be pretty experimental and almost random – like you might see a movement that really works by chance – if, say, a dancer slips and creates a particular shape – and you make something of it.

18 B: I want them to understand what I'm doing and the idea I'm trying to put across.

19 C: Working with students is more straightforward because they've got the basic training, they're desperate to learn, but they're not weighed down with expectations. I guess I like the idea of the blank canvas best.

20 D: I think I stay true to the spirit of the piece – and to my own instincts. ... but if you're talking about the essence – the choreographer's vision – her craft if you like – then for me there's hardly a gulf at all.

Part 4

21 B: 'sitting about in front of a screen…. (I) never really felt fit.'

22 F: 'it was the sort of people you had to work with … you needed a bit of light relief, but nobody there could see the funny side of my anecdotes.'

23 H: 'it was having to do everything by yesterday that got me down.'

24 E: 'We were all packed into this really small area.'

25 A: 'I'd no commitment to it anymore.'

26 B: 'I really feel that people who employ me are grateful – that's worth a lot to me.'

27 C: 'when I suggest a new style to a client.'

28 G: 'I'm actually a bit better off as a nurse …. because I had been expecting a cut in my standard of living'.

29 F: 'that makes me determined to do it as well as I can.'

30 D: 'People look up to you when you say you're a plumber … It means you can do things they can't.'

Test 2, Reading and Use of English (page 34)

Part 1: Seaside Artist

1 D: The right answer is a strong collocation that is a commonly used term.

2 A: Only the right answer creates a parallel meaning to 'like' earlier in the sentence.

3 C: Only the right answer can be followed by 'afield' to create the fixed expression.

4 D: Only the right answer can introduce this type of clause.

5 C: The other words cannot be preceded by the verb 'to be' and followed by the infinitive.

6 B: The other words do not follow the preposition 'by'.

7 A: The other words are not followed by the preposition 'with'.

8 B: The other words cannot be used after 'to get' without an article.

Part 2: Early Stone Tools

9 make (verb) collocates with the noun 'use'
10 than (preposition) links two parts of the comparison
11 after (adverb) time marker
12 back (preposition) phrasal verb
13 to (preposition) follows 'similar'
14 which/that (relative pronoun) introduces a defining relative clause
15 As (adverb) part of fixed phrase
16 in (preposition) part of fixed phrase

Part 3: Marathon Dreams

17 coverage (verb to noun)
18 endurance (verb to noun)
19 admiration (verb to noun)
20 exhaustion (verb to noun)
21 regain (verb to iterative verb)
22 possibly (adjective to adverb)
23 discouraging (noun to negative adjective)
24 advisable (verb to adjective)

Part 4

25 what makes some cars (determiner + verb)
26 has been widely blamed (passive + adverbial collocation)
27 strength of the wind (noun + preposition + noun)
28 wishes (that) she could/was able to/were able to (wish for regrets)
29 expected to turn out for /up for/ up to /up at (passive + phrasal verb)
30 my complete/total dissatisfaction (adjective + noun)

Part 5: Take as much holiday time as you want

31 B: The main topic of the paragraph is how greatly the holiday policy at Netflix differs from what normally happens with regard to holidays in organisations and companies.

32 C: They said that the standard holiday policy was 'at odds with' (did not fit logically with, did not make sense with) 'how they really did their jobs' because sometimes they worked at home after work and sometimes they took time off during the working day.

33 D: The company decided: 'We should focus on what people get done, not how many hours or days are worked.'

34 A: Rules, policies, regulations and stipulations are 'innovation killers' and people do their best work when they are 'unencumbered' by such things – the rules, etc. stop them from doing their best work.

35 B: One 'regard' in which the situation is 'adult' according to the writer is that people who aren't excellent or whose performance is only 'adequate' lose their jobs at the company – they are 'shown the door' and given a 'generous severance package' (sacked but given money when they leave).

36 D: Nowadays, 'Results are what matter'. How long it takes to achieve the desired results and how these results are achieved are 'less relevant'.

Part 6: The Omnivorous Mind

37 B: 'But it begins rather slowly, and there are moments when the casual reader will want to skip some of the long-winded explanations to get to the point.' contrasts with A: 'Allen in his engaging book … takes us on a fast-paced tour.'

38 A: 'Allen's principle point is that the mind has always been central in determining people's eating habits, and it's a point he returns to regularly, whether in the context of the latest fads and fashions or deeply-seated cultural traditions' contrasts with B: 'Allen often strays far from his main contention.'

39 C: 'This book certainly challenges some of our preconceptions and attitudes towards eating.' matches D: 'there is still a great deal we don't know about our relationship with it. This book is going to help change that!'

40 D: 'Allen, however, is clearly writing for those of us living in places where food abundance is the norm rather than shortage, and this detracts from some of his broader claims about our species' relationship with what we eat. It is hard to know what people in less fortunate societies might make of them.' The other writers have a different view:
   A: 'Indeed, the main ideas in the book will strike a chord with people around the globe, even if the detailed examples are outside their experience.'
   B: 'Allen goes on to explore the reasons for this, and other conventions, in a way that will be accessible across cultures.'
   C: 'Even people from quite diverse cultural contexts will find familiar issues investigated along the way.'

Part 7: Fluttering down to Mexico

41 D: link between 'these creatures' and 'this mass of insects' in D, 'butterflies' and 'millions of them' before the gap and 'They' after the gap.

42 G: link between 'Their journey here' before the gap and the description of that journey in G.

43 C: link between the butterflies being 'in search of nectar' (for food) and drinking from pools of water before the gap and what they do after they have therefore 'Fed and watered' at the beginning of C.

44 F: link between beliefs for 'centuries' about the arrival of the butterflies and what was discovered about this more recently, in the 1970s.

45 A: link between 'this' at the beginning of A and the fact that the migration route is 'endangered'. The first sentence of A explains why the migration route is endangered and A gives the results of this. In 'This is why' after the gap, 'This' refers to the problems caused for the butterflies.

46 E: link between 'these' at the beginning of E and the four areas of the reserve that are open to the public mentioned before the gap.

Part 8: Seeing through the fakes

47 C: 'All became clear when art historians did further research'. The research explained why the painting used a pigment that was not available to artists until later.

48 F: 'the mistaken belief that museums have anything to gain by hiding the true status of the art they own.'

49 A: 'the study of any work of art begins with a question: is the work by the artist to whom it is attributed?'

50 E: The painting had 'under drawing in a hand comparable to Raphael's when he sketched on paper' and the 'pigments and painting technique exactly match those that the artist used in other works'.

51 B: 'how little was known about Melozzo 90 years ago, and how little could be done in the conservation lab to determine the date of pigments or wood panel'.

52 D: 'X-rayed the picture and tested paint samples, before concluding that it was a rare survival of a work by Uccello dating from the early 1470s.'

53 F: 'If they make a mistake, they acknowledge it'

54 A: 'museum professionals' and 'conservation scientists'

55 B: 'a costume historian pointed out the many anachronisms in the clothing.'

56 D: 'I well remember how distressing it was to read an article in which the former director of the Metropolitan Museum of Art, Thomas Hoving, declared that Uccello's lovely little canvas of *St George and the Dragon* was forged.'

Test 2, Writing (page 47)

Part 1

Question 1 (essay)

Style: Essay format, and formal or semi-formal language. Your paragraphs must be clearly divided by course with appropriate linking words and phrases; each paragraph should include an assessment of each of two types of book, its importance and whether it is really important to read.

Content: You can include or discuss the opinions expressed in the task, but don't take the words directly from the input quotes. You should:
- introduce the topic of reading different types of books.
- evaluate the importance of two types of book, starting a new paragraph for each. Give reasons for your opinions, e.g.:
  – fiction – it teaches you about other people's lives
  – history – you learn about the past so that you don't make the same mistakes/it gives you a sense of identity
  – science – it's important to understand developments in modern life

Remember to summarise your overall opinion in the conclusion.

Part 2

Question 2 (review)

Style: Either semi-formal or informal, but remember you are trying to interest the magazine readers, so use a range of colourful language and try to use features such as rhetorical questions to draw the reader in. Use clear paragraphs for each part of the review.

Content: You should:
- describe the music festival or concert.
- explain what you did there and what made it interesting or unusual.
- consider whether you think it is relevant today.
- give an interesting conclusion.

Question 3 (letter)
Style: Formal or semi-formal, avoiding colloquial expressions. You must use clear paragraphs, which could be one paragraph for each of the content points below.
Content: Think about the skills that might be needed for the job, especially dealing with people and using social skills. The job requires good communication skills, good organisation and someone who is a team player. You must include:
- your friend's relevant work experience.
- your friend's personal qualities.
- your reasons for recommending your friend for the job.

Remember to include details or examples to support your points, and conclude by summing up why you recommend the person for the job.

Question 4 (report)
Style: Semi-formal/formal as this is a report for your course organiser. You can either use paragraphs (one for each point) with or without headings, or bullet points. If you use bullet points, remember that you still have to show a range of language, so don't make them too simple and don't use them in every paragraph.
Content: Include information about:
- what you did, e.g. your responsibilities, daily routine.
- how you benefitted, e.g. gaining independence.
- any problems you had, e.g. settling in.
- recommendations for future students, e.g. research on the company before travel.

Remember to include details and reasons to support your ideas.

Test 2, Listening (page 50)

Part 1

1 B: M: 'It was the prospect of shopping for new stuff I couldn't face!
       F: 'Tell me about it!'
2 A: 'It's heavily linked to wanting to be the centre of attention, to clothes giving them a strong personal identity or whatever. It's basically a way of showing off'.
3 B: 'I had a cockiness, … I'd hear a hit record and think: "I could do that."'
4 A: 'If after my first hit I thought I'd made it, I was soon disabused of that notion'.
5 A: 'One time I danced in a culture show, and the dance director at my school, she asked: 'Are you interested in really training? Like, you seem to have talent.'
6 C: 'So much so, that I was on the point of rebellion on more than one occasion – though I'm happy to say that particular storm never actually broke.'

Part 2: Radio reporter

7   Communication Studies
8   marketing assistant
9   intimidated
10 Trainee Scheme
11 (live) interviews
12 journalism
13 news
14 flexibility

Part 3

15 C: 'It was pure chance that a friend asked me to design a set for a student musical he was directing'.
16 D: 'What you need to do is to put all the training in the background and get some hands-on experience – an apprenticeship's great for doing that, and I spent three years doing one.'
17 C: 'Having an affinity with a play is pretty vital. If you don't care about it, there's no point in doing it because you'll never come up with good ideas.'
18 A: 'Actually, it helps me to keep coming up with new ideas if I'm constantly changing my focus from one show to another.'
19 B: Neil: 'Unlike a lot of actors who claim not to pay attention to reviews, I keep up with what critics say about all productions, not just my own. That helps you keep any criticisms in perspective. Maybe a critic's been harsh on other productions or has fixed views about set design.'
       Vivienne: 'Well, I've never actually come across that.'
20 A: 'On stage, … requires the type of thinking I love best … I don't get that buzz working on a movie, I'm afraid.'

Part 4

21 E: 'My wife said I'd never make it, which only made me more determined actually.'
22 D: 'As a graduation gift, it was a lovely way of marking the achievement.'
23 B: 'My girlfriend wanted to go … I went along with the idea for her sake.'
24 G: 'Like me, they'd mostly seen that chap on TV at the site and decided to go too.'
25 C: 'I was looking to do a bit of serious walking to see what I was capable of.'
26 C: 'For me, the highpoint was how friendly the others were.'
27 A: 'What made it for me … was the actual design of the place.'
28 B: 'What blew me away … was looking out from the low walls of the site over the mountains.'
29 E: 'I hadn't expected the actual walk up to the site to be so impressive.'
30 G: 'I'll never forget the meal the night before the final ascent.'

Test 3, Reading and Use of English (page 58)

Part 1: Caving

1 C: Only the right answer creates the collocation.
2 B: The other words do not create the phrasal verb.
3 D: Only the right answer creates the collocation.
4 A: The other linkers aren't used in this type of sentence.
5 B: Only the correct answer creates the meaning in context.
6 D: Only the right answer creates the collocation.
7 B: Only the right answer is a verb used for water.
8 D: The other words don't create meaning in context.

Part 2: Why are sunglasses cool?

9   but (conjunction) fixed expression with 'anything'
10 whose (possessive pronoun) refers to 'eyes'
11 of (preposition) part of fixed expression with 'fame'
12 At (preposition) part of expression
13 came (phrasal verb)
14 as (adverb)
15 in (preposition) part of multi-word verb
16 was (verb) fixed phrase

Part 3: Customer Reviews

17 accompanied (noun to verb)
18 arguably (verb to adverb)
19 professional (noun to adjective)
20 unedited (verb to negative adjective)
21 analysis (verb to noun)
22 reliable (verb to adjective)
23 feedback (verb to compound noun)
24 recommendation (verb to noun)

Part 4

25 had no choice but to (fixed expression)
26 the race was about to (direct to indirect speech with 'about to')
27 led to the singer being ('led' + passive form)
28 sooner had Alex finished his homework (negative head inversion)
29 bored if I spend ('boring' to 'bored' + condition phrase)
30 doesn't approve of her (reporting verb)

Part 5

31 B: The last sentence of the paragraph means: There was nobody better than an American to 'document' (record, in this case with photographs) the way society in Ireland was changing and becoming more like American society. People in Ireland were happy to employ an American to take pictures that looked like the images in 'an expensive American advertising campaign'.

32 D: She had previously 'harboured higher aspirations' (aimed to do work that was more artistic and creative) but she 'didn't mind' doing wedding and portrait photography and compared her situation with that of Dutch painters who did similar kinds of work to make money in the past.

33 D: She preferred analogue cameras, which were 'the old-fashioned method'. It is implied that she spent a lot of time in the darkroom following this 'old-fashioned' method to produce the wedding photographs.

34 C: He asked her 'What's up?' (What's the problem?) and she decided that 'she would tell him' (= tell him what the problem was) 'eventually, but not yet'.

35 A: She describes feeling a connection with the past when she visited the cairns and he says 'You Americans and your history', meaning that she was talking in a way typical of Americans and their attitude to the history of places like that.

36 D: When she said 'I know it' she was agreeing with him that, because they were both photographers, they were only interested in things they could see, their area of interest was limited to 'surface' (only what is visible).

Part 6: Do computer games have educational value?

37 B: 'it seems perverse to suggest that such an individualistic pastime, that takes the player off into a world of complete fantasy, could ever promote interpersonal skills in the real world' contrasts with A: 'Gamers may not reflect on how the characters and scenarios they engage with could help them to interact with others in the real world, but recent research at the State University suggests that the games do perform such a function.'

38 D: 'the accusation frequently heard that gaming is both addictive and harmful has always smacked of prejudice' contrasts with B: 'The evidence that gaming can become compulsive behaviour … is quite convincing.'

39 D: 'The fact that only a small geographical area was studied detracts a little from the findings.' matches C: 'The current study would benefit from further work, however, as the researchers seem to be making quite sweeping claims on the basis of relatively thin evidence.'

40 B: 'this conclusion seems to be a step too far, and I can't see too many people taking it very seriously'. The others have a positive view:
A: 'this meticulous study adds more weight to the growing consensus that gaming may be good for us.'
C: 'the idea put forward here that social skills may develop as a result of gaming is an intriguing one, that's sure to spark some lively debate.'
D: 'it is sure to attract quite a bit of attention'

Part 7: The 'Britain in Bloom' competition

41 D: link between 'do a lot' and 'too much'. D contains an example of a place that did something to please him that in fact didn't please him.

42 G: link between what the competition was like 'In the early days' and what it is like now (it's now 'much more sophisticated' and 'much more competitive' than it was when it started).

43 E: link between the criticisms of the competition in E and 'such criticisms' after the gap.

44 A: link between the statement that the 'old tricks' no longer work and 'This' at the beginning of A; what people used to do in order to win doesn't enable them to win any more and A explains that this is because of changes to the judging criteria; link between 'these developments' after the gap and the changes described in A.

45 F: link between one place that regards the competition as important (Stockton-on-Tees) and a place that has won the competition (Aberdeen); link between 'With so much at stake' after the gap and the description of what is 'at stake' (the fact that winning gives a place a very good image) in F.

46 C: link between 'Some of this' at the beginning of C and the stories of 'dirty tricks' before the gap; Jim is saying in C that some of the stories about rivals doing damage to the flowers of other competitors are 'exaggerated' and not completely true.

Part 8: On the trail of Kit Man

47 B: 'discomfort, bad food and danger were seen as part of the authentic outdoor experience'.

48 D: 'this involves not only acquiring new clobber, but new jargon'.

49 C: 'The whole idea of going into the wild is to get away from the things that tie you in knots at home.'

50 A: 'Worried about getting lost? Relax with a handheld GPS unit, featuring 3D and aerial display, plus built-in compass and barometric altimeter.'

51 D: 'Many in the adventure business say gadgets have encouraged thousands who would otherwise not have ventured into the great outdoors.'

52 B: 'Kit Man and his kind stand accused by the old-schoolers of being interested only in reaching the summits of gadgetry.'

53 C: 'All this technology, I mean, it might look fantastic on paper, but when there's a real problem, it's almost certainly going to let you down.'

54 C: 'Who'd want to be stranded out in the wild with a gadget freak?'

55 A: 'At next month's Outdoors Show in Birmingham, all this kit and more will be on display for an audience which seemingly can't get enough of it.'
56 D: 'Evidence from the American market also suggests that technology has had a positive environmental impact'.

Test 3, Writing (page 70)

Part 1

Question 1 (essay)
Style: Essay format, and formal or semi-formal language. Your paragraphs must be clearly divided by course with appropriate linking words and phrases. Each paragraph should include an assessment of two of the courses, its importance and whether it deserves extra financial support from the government.
Content: You can include or discuss the opinions expressed in the task, but don't take the words directly from the input quotes. You should:
- introduce the topic of financial support for education.
- evaluate the importance of two of the courses, starting a new paragraph for each. Give reasons for your opinions, e.g.:
  – art – it teaches appreciation of beauty
  – sport – it teaches team spirit and co-operation
  – music – it is a life-long skill and pleasure

Remember to summarise your overall opinion in the conclusion.

Part 2

Question 2 (letter)
Style: Informal as you are writing to a friend. Use letter layout, with clear paragraphs and an appropriate greeting and ending.
Content: Include the following points:
- what type of accommodation is available, e.g. flat, house, cost of rent.
- opportunities for sport, e.g. football club.
- availability of part-time work, e.g. in a restaurant.
- how easy it is to find part-time work.

Question 3 (review)
Style: Semi-formal moving towards informal. The purpose of the review is to nominate what you think is the best TV series, giving your opinion of it with reasons. You need the language of description or narration, and evaluation. Use clear paragraphs: introduction, description/narrative, evaluation and conclusion with recommendations. You may like to use humour in your evaluation to make it more interesting and memorable.
Content: You need to:
- describe the TV series and what it's about.
- explain why it appeals to you.
- give reasons why it should be included in the top ten list.

Question 4 (proposal)
Style: Proposal format, with semi-formal/formal language. Your paragraphs must be very clearly divided, and you can use headings, numbering or bullet points, but remember to show a range of language.

Content: You should:
- state the purpose of the proposal.
- explain the current facilities and what is useful about them, e.g. study centre, which can be used 24 hours a day.
- describe any problems, e.g. not enough reference books.
- recommend ways of improving the current facilities with reasons, e.g. provide more books, computers, etc.

Test 3, Listening (page 72)

Part 1

1 C: F: 'I find that a tough one to answer, don't you?'
       M: 'It's hardly an easy thing to articulate.'
2 C: 'There's a difference between the actual experience and the sanitised reality printed on the page. And that's what I want to look into.'
3 B: 'It wasn't easy and I soon discovered that I wasn't really cut out to be an interviewer – so I wasn't comfortable in the role.'
4 C: M: 'But it really depends on the party and the crowd – you've got to give them what they want.'
       F: 'No two sets are ever the same in that respect and that's the beauty of it. I'm all for being flexible.'
5 B: 'I focussed on cake-making there because it's quite artistic, but also scientific. ... I like that idea.'
6 A: 'So I've learnt to follow my instincts, and fortunately we're beginning to see a firm customer base emerging as a result.'

Part 2: Computer game designer

7   developer
8   animation
9   book covers
10 user interfaces
11 Star City
12 narrative
13 difficulty level
14 dedication

Part 3

15 B: 'It was an exciting prospect for a teenager ... and I was full of questions.'
16 D: 'You have to make assumptions – interpretations based on the evidence you've got – and that often involves eliminating possibilities – ticking off the things it might be but clearly isn't.'
17 C: 'and the discoveries are mostly small and cumulative rather than dramatic, which is the point that the world at large really tends to miss.'
18 D: 'Basically, with a relatively modest budget, we can gather far more relevant data here than in many of the places that have been the typical focus of archaeological activity.'
19 C: 'you'll probably uncover data that'll reveal how people lived and the way different things influenced their way of life – be it political changes, climate change, disease or whatever.'
20 A: 'The project I'm involved in seeks to capture and preserve some of that rich fund of humour and anecdote – so that it can be preserved for future generations'

Part 4

21. G: 'I only really went along to the salsa group to keep my boyfriend company.'
22. E: 'acting skills … I thought if I joined, it'd be a chance to pick some up.'
23. H: 'We're doing golf this term; are you up for it or not?'
24. C: 'I thought a club would be a way of getting in touch with like-minded students on other courses.'
25. A: 'So when a doctor I met at the hospital said they did Tai Chi at lunchtimes there, why didn't I give it a try?'
26. H: 'I could've done with someone telling me how I was doing actually.'
27. F: 'I think everyone needs to be given something to get their teeth into.'
28. C: 'but I do find some of the people you meet there a bit superior.'
29. B: 'I feel kind of duty bound to be there to make sure there's always a match.'
30. D: 'I just wish they'd run a session at the university.'

Test 4, Reading and Use of English (page 78)

Part 1: Ceramics Fair

1. A: Only the right answer can follow 'as'.
2. B: The other words do not collocate with 'tradition'.
3. D: The other phrasal verbs do not mean 'established'.
4. A: Only the right answer can follow 'at'.
5. B: The other words cannot be followed by the infinitive.
6. C: Only the right answer can be followed by 'on'.
7. B: The other words are not things which could be 'on show'.
8. D: Only the right answer can be followed by 'at'.

Part 2: Cheating at Computer Games

9. out (phrasal verb)
10. few (quantifier)
11. as/like (adverb)
12. taken (verb indicating a period of time)
13. When(ever)/Once (linker)
14. which (relative pronoun) introduces a clause
15. makes (verb)
16. whom (relative pronoun) follows 'of' and refers to people

Part 3: Trolley Bags

17. useful (verb to adjective)
18. outward (preposition to adjective)
19. official (noun to adjective)
20. measurements (verb to plural noun)
21. eventual (noun to adjective)
22. restrictions (verb to plural noun)
23. uneven (adjective to negative adjective)
24. counterparts (noun to plural compound noun)

Part 4

25. matter how fast she runs: fixed phrase + inversion
26. not willing/unwilling to take the blame: lexical change + collocation
27. you do, you must not spend: fixed phrase + modal verb
28. was taken completely by surprise when: modified adjective to modified verb collocation
29. overall responsibility for keeping: adjective to noun phrase
30. by no means uncommon: fixed phrase negative adjective

Part 5: The impossible moment of delight

31. A: Some studies conclude that happiness comes from being wealthier than the people near you, but others say that happiness comes from having a 'good attitude' and not from 'comparison with the wealth of others'.
32. B: The survey found that the common idea of rich people not being happy is true and that it was not invented simply so that poor people would be 'happy with their lot' (to persuade the poor that their position is OK and that they shouldn't envy the rich).
33. C: Bloom thinks people are in 'a state of perfect pleasure' at the moment when they get something they want, but the writer believes that it's hard to 'pin down' (define, be certain about) the moment when people feel happiness most clearly. So he does not agree with Bloom that it's possible to say exactly when people are at their happiest.
34. C: These musical works fully illustrate his point that happiness is half expectation and half memory because half of them involves the music building up to a high point and half of them involves peaceful 'recall' after that high point.
35. A: The company's slogan stating that 'getting ready is half the fun' is 'honest and truthful'. Girls are happier getting ready for a party than when they are at the party, where they often do not have a good time (they may be 'standing around' or 'crying' at the party).
36. D: He believes they were at their happiest when they thought about completing their research and after completing it. This means that his main point about people being happiest before and after getting or doing something they want applies to the researchers and Bloom too.

Part 6: The Perfect Workspace

37. B: 'By encouraging workers to do things like choose the colour scheme or giving them the freedom to surround themselves with disorderly piles of papers if they so choose, firms can encourage them to do their best.' contrasts with A: 'Less convincing is the claim made in one study that productivity improves if each individual is given a measure of control over their own workspace.'
38. D: 'Some creative people need to experiment in real space and time, and there are still limits to what can be confined to a computer screen' matches C: 'I suspect that there are individuals engaged in both professions who would feel uncomfortable in such stereotypical surroundings. And why shouldn't they?'
39. B: 'Features such as low ceilings and small windows can have the opposite effect, and add to the impression of merely being a small cog in a big wheel.' matches D: 'Cramped offices with a lack of natural light aren't conducive to happy working relationships.'
40. C: 'Photographic evidence meanwhile reveals that Einstein had an incredibly messy desk, suggesting that disorder in the workplace doesn't obstruct the ability to come up with new ideas.' The other writers have a different view:
    A: 'clearly some people thrive on clutter, whilst others perform better if surrounded by order, and this is true across a range of occupations'
    B: 'it's a cliché to suggest that new ideas are more likely to emerge from chaos than from proscriptive order'
    D: 'a slick, minimalist environment, however fashionable, does not necessarily meet the needs of all groups of employees'

Part 7: Publishing's natural phenomenon

41 E: link between 'it' in 'Partly it was, and is' in E and 'its secret' before the gap ('it' = 'its secret').

42 B: B gives examples of covers that had the 'simplified forms that were symbolic' mentioned before the gap.

43 G: link between 'They' at the beginning of G and the two people who are the subject of the paragraph before the gap (Clifford and Rosemary Ellis); link between the 'original plan' described in G and what actually happened, described after the gap ('those' after the gap = 'photographic jackets' in G).

44 D: link between 'This' at the beginning of D and 'the common design' mentioned before the gap; link between 'They' after the gap and the covers described in D.

45 A: link between 'an even more demanding production method' and the production method described before the gap; link between 'Initially' and 'Later'.

46 C: link between 'In the process' and the writing of the book mentioned before the gap; Gillmor and the writer found the interesting things described in C while they were writing the book about the covers.

Part 8: The intern's tale

47 B: She was 'shocked' when she discovered how big the 'tracing patterns' were and how much fabric was used to make each dress.

48 D: Her 'seamstress skills came in handy' when working on the 'installation that's now on display in the gallery' – she contributed to the work of art by doing some sewing that appears in it.

49 D: She didn't know how to send something by courier and had to ask lots of questions in order to do this.

50 A: She 'didn't want to leave everyone', meaning that she liked all the people she worked with.

51 C: Her friends have money for houses, cars and holidays and she doesn't, but 'I never feel I've missed out because I'm doing what I've always wanted to do' – she is glad she chose this kind of work.

52 B: She says that if you are an intern, 'you have to work hard and for free, because that's what everyone else is willing to do'.

53 A: She knows that some of the scripts she works on 'are going to become films one day'.

54 C: 'If I was 35 and still working unpaid, I'd think 'What am I doing?''

55 D: She says that when she arrived in London, she 'didn't know how long it would take to get a job'.

56 A: 'Personally, I love anything that's been adapted from a book, especially if I've read it' – she prefers working on film scripts based on books.

Test 4, Writing (page 90)

Part 1

Question 1 (essay)

Style: Essay format, using formal or semi-formal language with clear paragraphs which should include an assessment of two of the points, its value and importance related to competitive sport and a conclusion highlighting the one with the greatest value. Remember to use appropriate linking words and phrases.

Content: You can include or discuss the opinions expressed in the task, but use only the ideas not the words. You should:
- introduce the topic of the value of competitive sport for young people.
- evaluate the importance of two of the benefits given in the task starting a new paragraph for each one. Give reasons for your opinions, e.g.:
  – developing a positive attitude
  – promoting a healthy lifestyle
  – teaching good use of time in training and preparing to play

Summarise your overall opinion about which is the greatest value of competitive sport in your conclusion.

Part 2

Question 2 (letter)

Style: Semi-formal, as it is to a magazine editor. Use letter layout, with clear paragraphs and an appropriate greeting and ending.

Content: You should:
- briefly describe your friend.
- explain what makes them special for you, with reasons.
- describe how you maintain the relationship.
- consider whether the relationship has changed over the years.

Question 3 (proposal)

Style: Proposal format and formal or semi-formal language as this proposal is for the college principal. Your paragraphs must be very clearly divided. You can use headings, numbering or bullet points. Remember that if you use bullet points in any section you must still show a range of language across the whole proposal.

Content: You should:
- state the purpose of the proposal.
- outline what students currently do to improve their communication skills, e.g. debating society.
- describe any problems they have, e.g. confidence.
- make recommendations for activities or improvements, with reasons, e.g. a 'buddy' system.

Question 4 (report)

Style: Report format and formal or semi-formal language. Your sections must be clearly divided, and you can use headings, numbering or bullet points. Remember to show a range of language across the whole report.

Content: You should:
- state the purpose of the report.
- outline the current activities of the music club.
- explain the future plans of the club.
- suggest ways of getting more people involved with the music club, giving reasons.

Test 4, Listening (page 92)

Part 1

1. B: F: 'It left half-an-hour late.'
M: 'Anyway, the pilot obviously made up time. I'd only just turned up and there you were.'
2. B: 'You could have flown into the little airport down the coast even with this airline.'
3. A: 'What they can't manage to do on their own is question it – have a critical view of its accuracy and usefulness. That's where the teacher comes in.'
4. C: 'We had a meeting last week to see how it was going and nobody wanted to change anything!'
5. B: 'What really blew me away was the fact that it's unaffected in a way you'd scarcely think possible.'
6. A: 'What makes them kind of unique is that they don't seem to be trying to sound like anyone but themselves.'

Part 2: The llama

7. face
8. light brown
9. mining
10. curious
11. threatened
12. (gentle) hum
13. grease
14. rugs

Part 3

15. A: 'I made some short films, and on the strength of that, some of the staff suggested I went in that direction.'
16. B: 'The fact that people I was at school with are now making their way in the film world is also testimony to its value.'
17. A: 'I knew I wasn't. I wasn't prepared to squander time and money doing something I hadn't yet got the experience and expertise to carry off.'
18. D: 'I've always wanted to create characters with a bit more to them than that: people with a depth that might allow an audience to see a different side to their characters.'
19. B: 'There's a lot of things I'd change if I were to make that film again.'
20. C: 'I have mixed feelings about the whole notion of being someone to look up to, of being a role model.'

Part 4

21. C: 'To keep within our tight budget.'
22. F: 'a foot massage. … then dozed off in the chair halfway through'.
23. B: 'We were so desperately tired that we got our heads down right there on deck for some sleep.'
24. D: 'I knew it'd be a long night of dancing … so I thought I'd better take a rest.'
25. G: 'The last bus had already left and we were some distance from the nearest town … we just all fell asleep right there.'
26. F: 'At least it made the night go quickly.'
27. B: 'I woke up with a stiff neck, and the pain lasted several days.'
28. H: 'A huge, smelly vessel moored up beside us.'
29. C: 'They were quite sniffy and a bit embarrassed.'
30. G: 'They told me people living there often did that at weekends, so I felt good.'

Test 5, Reading and Use of English (page 98)

Part 1: Book review – Galapagos

1. C: Only the right answer fits grammatically in this sentence.
2. B: The other words don't collocate with 'job'.
3. A: Only the right answer completes the fixed expression.
4. B: The other words don't create the fixed expression in context.
5. B: Only the right answer collocates with 'plus'.
6. B: The other words cannot be followed by the preposition 'in'.
7. C: The other words don't express the idea of 'just' in this context.
8. D: Only the right answer collocates with 'inspiration'.

Part 2: A history of table tennis

9. which/that (relative pronoun) introduces defining relative clause
10. made (verb) passive form
11. became (verb)
12. being (verb) present participle
13. By (preposition) time marker
14. (al)though (linker) introduces a concessive clause
15. rather (preposition) part of 'rather than'
16. against (preposition) collocates with 'warn'

Part 3: Dancing is good for you

17. behaviour (verb to noun)
18. significant (verb to adjective)
19. ridiculous (verb to adjective)
20. innumerable/numerous (noun to adjective)
21. effective (noun to adjective)
22. depression (verb to noun)
23. relationships (noun to plural noun)
24. enabling (adjective to verb)

Part 4

25. has taken over the management: passive to active + phrasal verb
26. no account must this door ever: negative head inversion
27. on the recommendation of: verb to noun phrase
28. occurred to us that: fixed phrase
29. it made no difference to Kevin: fixed phrase
30. I would/might be able to make: conditional sentence

Part 5: The new management gurus

31. C: When *Smart Swarm*'s author wrote an article on the same subject as his book some years ago, 30 million people read it and the writer predicts that it will 'become the most talked about in management circles'.
32. A: 'Miller believes his book is the first time anyone has laid out (demonstrated) the science behind a management theory.'
33. C: The writer draws a parallel between bees who have to make a decision – 'and fast' – and managers who 'need to be able to make the right decisions under huge amounts of pressure'.
34. C: They need to 'encourage debate' among a group of people and get them to vote on 'which idea is best'; they need to involve a variety of people in their team and get them to take part in the decision-making process.

200 ANSWER KEY

35 D: Ants do what they think is required in the circumstances, and 'the right number' of ants do each different task. This system works well and it can show managers that their own system of hierarchy and bureaucracy is stopping employees from being as effective as ants are ('is getting in the way of getting the work done').

36 C: they decided to keep their system of 'letting customers choose where they sit' because they discovered from studying ants that 'assigned seating would only be faster by a few minutes'.

Part 6: Worth its weight in gold?

37 D: 'Down through the centuries, people have bought and passed on to future generations, those works of art that seemed to embody the spirit of their age and would have lasting value.' contrasts with A: 'with hardly a thought as to what might endure to impress subsequent generations'.

38 A: 'Much harder is the business of predicting which of today's artists will be appreciated in years to come, as many disillusioned art collectors have learnt to their cost.' matches C: 'Critics and commentators find it hard enough to agree on what represents the finest in the artistic output of their own times, let alone predict the tastes of the future.'

39 D: 'the art helps form our view of both what life was like and how people thought at the time.' contrasts with B: 'a famous picture may come to be more memorable than the event it depicts, distorting our true understanding of the event itself'.

40 C: 'they risk heaping praise on work that is merely of transitory interest, and sadly this risk was never greater than in our present age, when mediocrity seems to be the norm'. The other writers have a different view:
A: 'What is not in doubt, however, is that some will end up being counted amongst the all-time greats.'
B: 'but also in the fullness of time quite rightly come to be regarded as definitive examples of a trend or period'.
D: 'This will be just as true of our own age, however eccentric the contemporary art scene might appear on the surface.'

Part 7: Is Kieron Britain's most exciting artist?

41 E: link between 'Each one' at the start of E and 'the sketches' that Kieron is doing.

42 G: link between the fact that Kieron correcting the writer about the use of certain terminology is not typical of seven-year-old boys and the fact that Kieron is not an 'average' boy; link between his 'precocious articulacy' (knowledge of and ability with words that would be expected of someone much older) in G and the fact he gives an adult a lesson in terminology (before the gap); link between 'Kieron actually can and does' after the gap and 'my seven-year-old could do better than that' at the end of G.

43 B: link between 'Standard seven-year-old boy stuff there' and Kieron's references to going to school and playing football, which are typical of seven-year-old boys.

44 D: link between the 'melee' (noisy mass of people and activity) in D and the scene described before the gap (a room containing a film crew making a film, family members and pets).

45 F: link between 'This' at the start of F and Kieron creating sketches based on those in the Seago book; link between 'it' in 'takes it back off me' and the 'sketchbook' he hands to the writer before the gap.

46 C: link between 'this' in 'aware of this' and the reaction if Kieron is still 'doing similar work when he's 28'; link between 'having none of it' (not accepting it) and the idea that he may stop doing art and take up other interests.

Part 8: The unstoppable spirit of inquiry

47 B: 'though it (the World Wide Web) impacts us all, scientists have benefited especially'

48 D: 'Whether it is the work of our Science Policy Centre, our journals, our discussion meetings, our work in education or our public events, we must be at the heart of helping policy makers and citizens make informed decisions.'

49 C: 'Within a day, 20,000 people had downloaded the work, which was the topic of hastily convened discussions in many centres of mathematical research around the world.'

50 C: 'The latter cries out for' (the blogosphere urgently requires) 'an informal system of quality control.'

51 A: 'Those who want to celebrate this glorious history' (of scientific research and discovery) 'should visit the Royal Society's archives via our 'Trailblazing' website.'

52 E: 'Scientists often bemoan' (complain about) 'the public's weak grasp of science – without some 'feel' for the issues, public debate can't get beyond sloganising' (lack of understanding of the issues causes public debate on them to be too simple).

53 A: 'The Society's journals pioneered what is still the accepted procedure whereby scientific ideas are subject to peer review.'

54 E: 'But science isn't dogma. Its assertions are sometimes tentative.'

55 E: 'there are other issues where public debate is, to an equally disquieting degree, inhibited by ignorance' (the public do not only lack knowledge of science; they lack knowledge of other things too).

56 D: 'we can be sure of one thing: the widening gulf between what science enables us to do and what it's prudent or ethical actually to do.'

Test 5, Writing (page 110)

Part 1

Question 1 (essay)

Style: Essay format, with formal or semi-formal language. Your ideas should be organised into paragraphs that reflect the argument. Try to use a variety of linking words and phrases so that your ideas are expressed coherently.

Content: You can include the opinions given in the task, but always rewrite them in your own words. You can use ideas of your own as well or instead of those given, but you must discuss suggestions about what individuals can do to solve environmental problems. You must discuss two of these ideas:
- recycling – whether it can make a difference, e.g. not many people do it.
- campaigning – how to get the message across, e.g. television.
- using energy – ways of saving it, e.g. solar panels, switching off lights.

Remember to write a conclusion that follows your argument, and suggests which idea makes the biggest difference to environmental problems.

Part 2

Question 2 (review)
Style: Should be relatively informal, but not too colloquial. Use language that will interest and engage the reader, and techniques such as rhetorical questions.
Content: You should:
- describe the memorable place.
- evaluate what was special about it.
- explain why it made a lasting impression on you.
- justify its inclusion in the magazine's list of memorable places.

Question 3 (report)
Style: Report format and formal or semi-formal language. Your sections must be clearly divided, and you can use headings, numbering or bullet points. If you do this, remember to show a range of language across the whole report.
Content: You should:
- state the purpose of the report.
- describe young people's shopping habits in your country.
- consider whether these habits are changing and why, e.g. shopping malls.
- suggest things that might change shopping habits in the future, e.g. online shopping.

Question 4 (proposal)
Style: Proposal format and formal or semi-formal language as this proposal is for the town council. Your paragraphs must be clearly divided. You can use headings, numbering or bullet points. Remember that if you use bullet points in any section you must still show a range of language across the whole proposal.
Content: You should:
- state the purpose of the proposal.
- outline any problems you have had with local transport, e.g. buses late, high prices.
- make recommendations for improvements, with reasons, e.g. more buses at night, special ticket prices for students, etc.

Test 5, Listening (page 112)

Part 1

1 C: 'I wasn't prepared for something written in the form of two first-person blogs.'
2 B: 'That was really quite a wake-up call for me, because I think I may have been guilty of doing that.'
3 A: 'I'd say the thing that sets it apart is its multi-functionality.'
4 B: 'It'd be a shame if she lost that edge. You know, if the commercial imperative began to dictate the flow of creativity. We've seen that so many times before with designers.'
5 A: 'Perhaps a CEO shouldn't be interfering in that stuff, but this company's my baby, so I guess it's inevitable.'
6 B: 'The real challenge is trusting yourself to pick the moment to go for it.'

Part 2: Ecocamp holiday

7 miserable
8 branches
9 (the) wind
10 privacy
11 (efficient) showers
12 boardwalk
13 medium
14 iceberg

Part 3

15 D: 'I look back and think: "Why wasn't I training? I just played games!" But that's how it was!'
16 A: 'After ice hockey, I ran cross-country with moderate success, and guys I met there put me onto rowing.'
17 B: 'It was just bad luck really; so near and yet so far.'
18 C: 'after about six months of arm-twisting, decided to make the leap'.
19 B: Greg: 'to put up with what I call the "full-on suffer".' Lina: 'and just go for it – no matter how much it hurts.'
20 C: 'You don't have a lot of protection if you come off and hit the ground. So I run and row as cross-training as much as I can.'

Part 4

21 C: 'looking at two drawings that were given to me as gifts.'
22 D: 'I can warm up with them, and they've taught me loads of stretches and things ... really makes you more supple and able to cope.'
23 F: 'I'll usually pop into dressing rooms putting little notes or candy on people's tables.'
24 H: 'I still find myself walking up to have a look (at the props) prior to curtain up.'
25 A: 'I go in the courtyard where I can just catch the breeze.'
26 A: 'On my last one, I came down with a sore throat.'
27 H: 'so I came out with a line I was supposed to say later.'
28 C: 'the press ... what they wrote initially wasn't that complimentary.'
29 E: 'I missed a step and stumbled on the way down.'
30 F: 'The actor looked around and saw a pigeon standing right behind him.'

Test 6, Reading and Use of English (page 118)

Part 1: Mr Espresso

1 B: Only the right answer collocates with 'credit'.
2 A: Only the right answer collocates with 'leading'.
3 B: The other words all need a preposition.
4 D: Only the right answer can be used for a country.
5 B: The other words do not collocate with 'seeds'.
6 B: Only the right answer can be followed by 'as'.
7 A: The other words do not collocate with 'companies'.
8 D: The other words do not indicate two things joined together.

Part 2: Drift Diving

9 so (pronoun) refers back to the content of the previous sentence
10 makes (verb) collocates with 'use'
11 on (preposition) follows 'depending'
12 or (conjunction) combines with 'either' to make a contrast
13 (al)though/but (linker) introduces concessive clause
14 no/little (determiner) to indicate absence in 'no need'
15 as (conjunction) part of 'as if'
16 more (adverb) part of the linking phrase 'what's more'

Part 3: The Limits of Technology

17 settlement (verb to noun)
18 breakthroughs (verb to plural compound noun)
19 isolation (verb to noun)
20 unexpected (verb to negative adjective)
21 disapproval (noun to negative noun)
22 annoying (verb to adjective)
23 regardless (noun to preposition)
24 unwelcome (adjective to negative adjective)

Part 4

25 remains to be seen (fixed phrase)
26 Patrick if he could borrow his (reported speech and verb change)
27 has every intention of writing (verb to noun + gerund)
28 unless there are/anyone has any (negative linker + verb + noun)
29 met with the disapproval (verb + noun)
30 to his/Philip's surprise he got (inversion)

Part 5: Cooking shouldn't be child's play

31 C: The writer says that if you 'take the fun out of cooking', your child might become 'a chef with a great future' – if cooking isn't simply fun for children when they are learning it, it's possible that they might develop into successful chefs.
32 B: Her mother noticed that she was very interested in cooking and gave her 'challenging tasks' to do; she gives an example of advice her mother gave her while she was doing a task to help her do it better.
33 A: The writer says that there is a belief that parents should praise their children all the time, telling them 'how clever and talented' they are, but there is evidence that this approach 'demotivates children' – it has the opposite effect from the one intended.
34 D: There are adult men who think that a piece of fish should be in the shape of a creature, in the same way that the food they ate when they were children was put into the shapes of certain things to amuse them. This is an example of the idea that all food is 'nothing but fun, fun and more fun'.
35 C: A 'chore' is a task that requires effort and is not fun; the writer says that because her mother made cooking a chore for her, she has eaten a lot less convenience food than she would have eaten if her mother had made cooking fun. Her point is that taking cooking seriously has an influence on the kind of food you eat.
36 B: Nigella thinks the way she was taught to cook in her family as a child was 'normal' but the writer thinks the 'culinary regime' (the cooking system) in her family was not 'ordinary' – it wasn't typical of most families. Nigella thinks it was fine but the writer thinks it should have involved more fun.

Part 6: Feedback in training: the issues

37 B: 'and this is the trainer's chance to address some of the individual needs of members of the group. Criticism that is softened by constructive comments may be beneficial' matches A: 'Each trainee needs feedback on how they're getting on as a course progresses and often need reassurance that they are meeting the targets set by trainers.'
38 B: 'Such verbal evaluation may be followed up in a written report to employers, but how much to include, and how it is worded, should be negotiated as part of the feedback discussion itself.' contrasts with C: 'The trainer needs to take notes against criteria agreed with companies, and make sure feedback on individuals doesn't become subjective – or open to manipulation by participants themselves.'
39 A: 'Some participants also seek to outdo their peers, which is not an atmosphere trainers will want to foster.' matches D: 'many companies ... mistakenly see training as a way of seeing which employee will perform best'.
40 C: 'Any feedback given to trainees, therefore, should take the form of a summing up and should be delivered after reports to employers have been completed.' The other writers have different views:
   A 'Each trainee needs feedback on how they're getting on as a course progresses'
   B: 'Each trainee needs to know how they are getting on at regular intervals during the course'
   D: 'which means good pre-course design and thorough ongoing and post-course evaluation'.

Part 7: The birth of *Coronation Street*

41 F: link between 'At that stage' at the beginning of F and when the writer was 21, mentioned at the beginning of the article; link between the work described in F and the work described before the gap.
42 D: link between 'the genius who created the show' before the gap and 'that person' in D.
43 A: link between 'this' at the beginning of A and the idea that the creation of the programme would be a good subject for a television drama, mentioned before the gap – the writer wasn't the only person who thought this was a good idea because someone commissioned him to write the drama.
44 G: link between the fact that there had never been a show about ordinary people and their lives and the fact that there had also never been an original show featuring regional actors – link between two things that had not happened before but which were both true of *Coronation Street*; link between the question 'so what was the point?' in G and 'It was that ...' after the gap.
45 E: link between the statement that 'It' (the idea of *Coronation Street*) should have ended there after the gap and the fact that the idea was rejected, as described in E; link between 'written and discarded' after the gap and the events described in E – Warren writing the script and the TV management rejecting it firmly ('in no uncertain terms').
46 C: link between 'that inauspicious beginning' in C and the problems just before the first episode was broadcast, described before the gap; 'inauspicious' = suggesting that something will go badly and not be successful; link between 'that event' in C and the broadcasting of the first episode, described before the gap.

Part 8: Activities for visitors to Norway

47 A: All riders are 'given a comprehensive safety briefing' (a talk about safety).
48 D: It 'is suitable for novices, though you should be reasonably fit' (it's appropriate for beginners but only appropriate for people who are reasonably fit).
49 A: The snowmobile is 'nothing less than a lifeline for those in more remote areas' – it is the everyday means of transport for people living in those areas and they depend on it. This is said to be true in the present (dog sledding was 'vital' in the past).
50 B: Some people from warmer countries 'think it is something that exists only in old footage' (film) 'of Eskimo living, but this isn't the case at all'.
51 D: 'whenever they realise an outing is imminent, they become as keyed up as domestic pets about to be taken for walkies – howling, leaping in the air and straining at their leashes' – this is how the dogs behave just before 'the signal to depart' and the activity begins.
52 D: 'Half- or full-day sled safaris are most popular, although overnight and longer tours are also available.'
53 C: 'Snowmobiling has high-octane attractions, but to appreciate fully the stillness and peace of the mountains, it's best to use your own feet to get around' – the contrast is between the energy and excitement of snowmobiling and the quiet and relaxation of skiing or snowshoeing.
54 B: 'you'll find out how the experts use the auger to drill through the ice, a skimming loop to keep the water from freezing over again and a familiar rod to catch the fish'.
55 C: 'gliding around the snowy terrain is not just a great way of getting close to nature, but also fantastic aerobic exercise'.
56 A: 'The only controls to worry about are a thumb-operated throttle and motorcycle-style brakes.'

Test 6, Writing (page 130)

Part 1

Question 1 (essay)
Style: Formal or semi-formal, and objective as you are presenting a point of view, with reasons and evidence. Use clear paragraphs, each one evaluating each of the two benefits you have chosen. Include an introduction that leads in to the topic and a conclusion that rounds off the argument and states your point of view.
Content: You should discuss two of the benefits of travelling to other countries given in the task and whether each one is actually a benefit or not. You should consider both the advantages and disadvantages of each one in order to present a coherent argument that leads logically to your conclusion about which is the greatest benefit. Remember to state your opinion clearly in the conclusion. You could consider:
- education – travellers learn a lot but can equally learn from books/the internet.
- experience – it provides a much wider range of experience than reading about places.
- convenience – this could be a disadvantage as it is expensive and takes time.

Your conclusion should state which one you consider to be the greatest benefit.

Part 2

Question 2 (report)
Style: Report format and formal or semi-formal language. Your sections must be clearly divided, and you can use headings, numbering or bullet points. If you do, remember to show a range of language across the whole report.
Content: You should:
- state the purpose of the report.
- describe current facilities available for older students, e.g. careers advice.
- describe facilities that you have found most useful.
- suggest improvements the college could make, e.g. set up connections with local businesses.

Question 3 (letter)
Style: Semi-formal to formal, as this is a letter to a company. Use clear paragraphs and include a conclusion repeating what you would like the company to do. You should use appropriate greetings and conclusions in your letter.
Content: You should:
- state the holiday you took and your reason for writing.
- outline the problems you had with:
  - arrangements, e.g. no representative on arrival
  - itinerary, e.g. not enough time at interesting places
  - accommodation, e.g. hotels dirty
- explain what you want the company to do about your complaints, e.g. provide compensation.

Question 4 (proposal)
Style: Proposal format, and formal language avoiding colloquial expressions. Paragraphs must be clearly divided, and should include reasons for why the previous year's activity could be improved. You can use headings, numbering or bullet points.
Content: You should:
- state the purpose of the proposal.
- describe the kind of drama and theatrical events that should be included in the festival.
- explain why these events would attract people of all ages.
- recommend extra facilities the town might need to provide.
- suggest ways of dealing with transport and accommodation issues.

Test 6, Listening (page 132)

Part 1

1 A: 'I went with high hopes of seeing something really spectacular from the headline band, and it just didn't happen.'
2 A: 'I think they should've been presenting us with something a bit more exciting.'
3 B: 'I sense that there may actually be little substance to stories that his job's on the line.'
4 C: 'If a top-flight football team isn't getting points, then something's got to change and that comes back to the manager because that's his responsibility – getting the results.'
5 C: 'But it really makes you think, you know, about more than just the art – about aspects of life itself.'
6 A: F: 'I'd have been happy to have seen some of his other stuff actually.'
M: 'Yeah, more of a range.'

Part 2: Learning the sport of surfing

7 national park
8 (the/a) period
9 tight
10 arm(s)
11 gloves
12 plastic
13 (their/the) knees
14 hair(-)dryer

Part 3

15 B: 'The upside was that I'd established that I was able to write.'
16 C: 'I wrote it as a kind of one-off book'
17 A: 'It was a chancy thing to do.'
18 B: 'I've had some hairy experiences.'
19 B: 'The sense of place in a crime novel is as crucial as the characters themselves.'
20 D: 'Whereas at the time I'd never even considered the police, I'd have more of an open mind now.'

Part 4

21 D: 'The thing I'd really recommend, is trying all the stuff that's grown in the region.'
22 F: 'Rolling up your clothes to put them in your bag can be your saving grace.'
23 B: 'You can often actually get much better deals elsewhere.'
24 H: 'My general rule is to take half the stuff I think I'll need, and twice the money.'
25 C: 'We got really into the local music … I'd recommend doing something like that.'
26 F: 'On the coach to the airport still trying to fit various clothes and papers into my luggage.'
27 E: 'I saw this locally-made rug I just knew would look fabulous at home. Sadly, no one pointed out that it wouldn't be easily transportable.'
28 G: 'I remember not joining a two-day trek with friends in South America for that reason.'
29 A: 'When I finally bothered to look, I found my ticket was actually for the previous day.'
30 C: 'I hadn't bothered researching the lie of the land.'

Test 7, Reading and Use of English (page 138)

Part 1: Renewable Energy Comes of Age

1 B: The other words cannot be followed by the infinitive + 'as'.
2 D: Only the correct word creates the idea of 'mirrors'.
3 A: Only the correct answer creates a phrasal verb that has meaning in context.
4 C: The other words do not collocate with 'behind'.
5 D: The other words do not collocate with 'rise'.
6 A: The correct answer is the correct term in this context.
7 D: The correct answer collocates with 'public'.
8 C: The other words would need a preposition.

Part 2: The Demise of the Motor Car

9 gave (verb) part of phrasal verb
10 up (preposition) part of phrasal verb
11 more (determiner) part of 'what's more'
12 For (preposition) part of set phrase
13 do (verb) refers to previous verb
14 others (pronoun) refers to people
15 such (intensifier) intensifies the adjective
16 what (determiner)

Part 3: Do Green Products Make us Better People?

17 supposedly (verb to adjective)
18 criminals (noun to plural noun)
19 behaviour (verb to noun)
20 satisfaction (verb to noun)
21 charming (noun to adjective)
22 complexity (adjective to noun)
23 undoubtedly / doubtlessly (noun to negative adverb)
24 invariably (adjective to adverb)

Part 4

25 completely lived up to Caroline's (intensifier + collocation)
26 in case it broke/should break ('in case' + past verb)
27 (should) happen to bump (set phrase + phrasal verb)
28 despite/in spite of her refusal (linker + noun phrase)
29 having had an argument (regret + '-ing' + noun)
30 has been a sharp increase in (collocation+ preposition)

Part 5

31 C: She had 'stacks of cassette recordings of herself reading the news in a cool, assured voice' and later she became a presenter on CNN television, so at this time she was practising for the career that she later had.
32 D: Lomba didn't know the answer and she gave him not only the answer but also 'a lecture' about the capital of Iceland (more information he didn't know).
33 A: He replied 'in the negative' (that he didn't know the answer) and her response to this was to jump up 'gleefully' (in a very happy way) and get her sketchbook – she was glad that he didn't know the answer because she wanted to show him what the jacket looked like.
34 D: At first he thought that the father's 'taciturnity' (he was quiet, he didn't speak much) was because of 'moodiness' (that he was often in a bad mood, often feeling angry) but then he realised that he had 'laughter kinks behind the eyes' (his eyes showed that he was amused), and that his lips were often moving, ready to open because he wanted to smile or laugh.
35 B: When she called him 'dear' and 'honey', he thought she was talking to someone else, one of her children, not to him, because he wasn't used to someone using those words for him.
36 A: She told Lomba that she wanted him to take care of Bola, because Bola was 'impulsive' and 'headstrong' (he acted without thinking, he did unwise things without considering the consequences) and Lomba was 'quiet' and 'level-headed' (sensible). In this way she wanted to follow the tradition of finding a friend of 'opposite temperament' for her child because that friend would be a good influence on the child.

Part 6: The winners and losers in mass migration

37 D: 'The existence of minimum wage legislation and other social initiatives, unimaginable in the nineteenth century, serve to distort the picture and make it difficult to say whether immigration is serving the needs of a growing economy effectively or not.' contrasts with A: 'Put simply, there's excess demand for labour in rich countries, and people from poorer countries arrive to plug the gap, thereby helping to keep the economies of the developed nations functioning smoothly.'

38 A: 'the wealth of developed nations is effectively invested in the economies of less-developed areas, and everyone benefits' contrasts with C: 'Meanwhile, poorer economies may be denied the contribution of some of their most able members.'

39 C: 'Migrants tend to come from less-developed parts of the world. Individuals are attracted by the opportunity to earn much more than they could back home, although this could be a false impression given the realities of living on a low income in a country with a high cost of living.' matches B: 'The potential benefits of migration can be overstated, however. Indeed, being by nature energetic and intelligent, some would-be migrants might actually be well advised to stay at home, where they are best placed to fuel economic growth and reap the benefits.'

40 D: 'I would question the assumption that the current level of economic migration across continents will be sustained'. The other writers have a different view:
   A: 'a trend that seems set to gather pace in years to come'
   B: 'Given that economic growth is the aim of most western governments, it is hard to see this changing anytime soon.'
   C: 'It seems an irreversible trend.'

Part 7: The sky's the limit for cloudwatchers

41 E: link between 'here' at the beginning of E and the Cloud Bar, where the writer is before the gap; link between 'this place' after the gap and 'here' in E.

42 G: link between 'Other beachgoers aren't as convinced' and the comments made by the person before the gap – other people don't think the place is 'fantastic' and 'inspiring' and don't think Britain has been 'crying out for' (really wanting) a place like this to be created; ('the society' mentioned in B has not been previously mentioned in the text at this point; B does not fit here because we would not know which society is being referred to).

43 B: link between 'Absolutely' at the start of B and the opinions expressed in the sentence before the gap; link between Ian Loxley's travels, the fact that his favourite place is local in B, and his view that 'you don't really need to travel at all to see interesting clouds' after the gap.

44 A: link between 'why this is' and the statement before the gap that for cloudwatchers, the most important factor is 'your philosophical disposition'; the way that clouds move and develop, mentioned in A, are the reasons why someone's philosophical disposition is the most important factor in watching clouds (their slowness suits people who want to think philosophically); link between 'That said' after the gap and what he says in A, to introduce a contrast between the two views of cloud watching (slow and exciting).

45 F: link between 'all such places' at the start of F and 'wilderness' just before the gap; the writer's point is that humans want to explore all wildernesses – 'them' in the first sentence of F = 'clouds' before the gap; link between 'similar experiences' after the gap and the experience described by the pilot in F.

46 C: link between 'such encounters' in C and the encounters with clouds described by Gavin Pretor-Pinney before the gap.

Part 8: What lies beneath

47 C: 'It is easy to be captivated by intelligent, seemingly friendly sea creatures such as dolphins, or even by the hunting prowess of the more sinister sharks.'

48 D: 'The Mediterranean has the largest number of invasive species – most of them having migrated through the Suez Canal from the Red Sea.'

49 D: 'As Mediterranean turtles lose their nesting sites to beach developments, or die in fishing nets, and the vanishing population of other large predators such as bluefish tuna are fished out, their prey is doing what nature does best; filling a void. Smaller, more numerous species like jellyfish are flourishing and plugging the gap left by animals higher up the food chain.' Predators are disappearing and being replaced by creatures they used to eat.

50 A: 'In total, the Census now estimates that there are more than 230,000 known marine species, but that this is probably less than a quarter of what lives in the sea.'

51 D: 'Hidden within the Marine Census results is a dark message. Maps showing the density of large fish populations in tropical waters reveal that numbers of many of the biggest open ocean species have declined.'

52 A: 'The truth is that, at present, much of what passes for scientific 'facts' about the sea and what lives in it are still based on guesswork.'

53 A: The Census contains the numbers of 'individual forms of life that can be scientifically classified as species'.

54 B: 'It is the creepy-crawlies that are out there in really big numbers. Almost 40 percent of identified marine species are crustaceans and molluscs' – 'creepy-crawlies' is used as an informal term for crustaceans and molluscs.

55 C: 'how would we begin to start naming the 20,000 types of bacteria found in just one litre of seawater trawled from around a Pacific seamount?'

56 A: The scientists involved in the Census 'hope that by creating the first catalogue of the world's oceans, we can begin to understand the great ecological questions about habitat loss, pollution, over fishing and all the other man-made plagues that are being visited upon the sea.'

Test 7, Writing (page 150)

Part 1

Question 1 (essay)

Style: Formal or semi-formal, and objective as you are presenting a point of view, with reasons and evidence. Use clear paragraphs, each one evaluating each of the two benefits you have chosen. Include an introduction that leads in to the topic and a conclusion that rounds off the argument and states your point of view.

Content: You should discuss two of the ways of encouraging people to lead healthier lifestyles before choosing the best. You should consider both the advantages and disadvantages of each one in order to present a coherent argument that leads logically to your conclusion about which is the greatest benefit. Remember to state your opinion clearly in the conclusion. You could consider:
- television advertising – many people see it, but may take no notice.
- government campaigns – seem official but many people don't like them.
- education in schools – good to reach children when they are young.

Your conclusion should choose the best way of encouraging people to lead healthier lifestyles.

Part 2
Question 2 (letter)

Style: Informal, as this is a letter to a younger friend. Use clear paragraphs, appropriate greetings and conclusions to your letter. You should write clearly, but you can use idioms.

Content: You should:
- explain your own experience of going to university.
- outline what you gained from it e.g. better work prospects, fun with friends.
- advise your friend on what you think he should do, with reasons.

Question 3 (review)

Style: Semi-formal moving towards informal. The purpose of the review is to describe a film you think is relevant to society today, giving your opinion of it with reasons. You need the language of description or narration, and evaluation. Use clear paragraphs: introduction, description/narrative, evaluation and conclusion with recommendations.

Content: You should:
- briefly describe the book or film.
- consider why you think it is important or relevant to society, with reasons.
- describe its message and what you learned from it.
- explain how it helped you to understand more about society in a useful way.

Question 4 (report)

Style: Report format and formal or semi-formal language. Your sections must be clearly divided, and you can use headings, numbering or bullet points. If you do, remember to show a range of language across the whole report.

Content: You should choose whether you want to write about a train or bus station. Then:
- state the purpose of the report.
- describe the bus or train station.
- outline its good or bad points and any problems you have had.
- suggest improvements that could be made to the bus or train station.

Test 7, Listening (page 152)

Part 1

1 A: M: 'But actually I've come round to thinking it's the real strength of the course, don't you agree?'
F: 'Undoubtedly. I mean, that's why I went for it in the first place.'
2 B: 'sophisticated software … I still think it's a shame we can't come in and use it out of class time.'
3 A: 'I'm still looking for the ideal rucksack or carry-on actually.'
4 B: 'I mean, without that – and a lot of people you meet don't have that – would I ever have had the courage to do half the things I've done?'
5 A: 'We got all these irate bloggers going overboard.'
6 C: 'We were misquoted in the first piece written about it. It said that I wanted to kill album artwork, which is just so far off the mark.'

Part 2: The swift

7 without feet
8 scream
9 new moon
10 (a) cliff/cliffs
11 paper
12 (a) thunderstorm/thunderstorms
13 silent
14 youngest/younger sons

Part 3

15 A: 'But what really appeals to me about kayaking is that it calls for several different skills to be used simultaneously.'
16 C: 'But most importantly, when you first start kayaking, just have fun.'
17 D: 'there aren't many competitions coming up, but (all the training's) worth it in the summer when the big ones come around.'
18 C: 'I'd weigh up the risks and only have a go once I felt up to the challenge.'
19 B: 'but it's tough doing the research yourself. As a beginner, I'd say get some insider tips from someone in the know.'
20 A: Glenda: 'my most valued are those when I'm on a great trip, getting to know new rivers and their surroundings in the company of fellow kayakers I trust and get on with.'
Declan: 'landing in Tasmania with my training partner Sam, to find that all the rivers were in flood, making each one flow. Over the space of a few weeks we paddled lots of them, some of which hadn't flowed in over twenty years.'

Part 4

21 F: 'But what made it perfect was all the ancient ruins in the area.'
22 A: 'I was about to take it up professionally but then injured my leg quite badly and had to drop the idea.'
23 D: 'It was my big chance as it would get me exactly where I'd always wanted to go.'
24 H: 'I'd lived in the city all my life and had plenty of friends there but we were all rushing around frantically as city-dwellers do.'
25 B: 'if I wanted to top up my qualifications, meant going abroad.'
26 F: 'Once there, I felt really driven to do well – there was just this new sense of optimism.'
27 D: 'Their recommendations opened a number of doors for me once my studies had finished.'
28 C: 'I'd never really seen myself as a movie buff before.'
29 H: 'We could go anywhere where I could set up by myself. It was exactly what we all needed.'
30 A: 'made me feel I really belonged in the place.'

Cambridge Advanced: Frequently Asked Questions

1. **Approximately how many marks are needed to pass the exam?**
▶ You need around 60% to pass the exam with a grade C.

2. **Do I have to pass each paper in order to pass the exam?**
▶ No. There is no pass or fail mark for each paper. The final grade is arrived at by adding the weighted marks from all the papers together.

3. **Are marks deducted for wrong answers?**
▶ No. If you're not sure, make a guess, you may be right.

4. **Am I allowed to use a dictionary?**
▶ No.

5. **In the Reading and Use of English paper, Part 4, do contractions count as one word or two?**
▶ Two, e.g. *don't* = two words, *do + not*.

6. **In the Reading and Use of English paper, Parts 2, 3 and 4, what happens if I misspell a word?**
▶ All spelling must be correct in this paper.

7. **In the Reading and Use of English paper, Parts 2, 3 and 4, can I give alternative answers if I am not sure?**
▶ If there are two answers, and one of them is wrong, no marks are given. So, it's better to decide which of your answers is best!

8. **In the Reading and Use of English paper, Part 4, what happens if I get the right answer, but make a small mistake in a key word transformation?**
▶ There are 2 marks for each answer, so you could still get 1 mark even if there was a small error.

9. **In the Reading and Use of English Paper, how long should I spend on each Reading question (Parts 5–8)?**
▶ That's up to you. You can do the tasks in any order, and knowing how to use your time well and the best reading skill to use is part of the test.

10. **In the Reading and Use of English paper, Part 8 has more questions, so is it more important?**
▶ No. All parts are equally weighted. Parts 1–3 and 8 carry 1 mark, and Parts 4–7 carry 2 marks.

11. **In the Writing paper, what happens if I write too many or too few words?**
▶ The word count is given as a guide only. Don't waste time counting; the examiners don't – they are more interested in your English! It is unlikely that answers under the lower limits will contain enough information/ideas to fulfil the task. Overlong answers are more likely to contain mistakes. Plan your time so that you write about the right amount and have time to check what you have written.

12. **In the Writing paper Part 1, should I use all the information given in the task?**
▶ You must cover two of the points given in the task. You can use the opinions given to help you with ideas for your essay if you like, but you should use your own words.

13. **In the Writing paper, how should I lay out the addresses?**
▶ Don't include the addresses. If you do include them, the examiners will ignore them, as this is not part of the task.

14. **In the Listening paper, how many times will I hear each recording?**
▶ Each recording is played twice.

15. **In the Listening paper, Part 2, do I have to use the words in the recording or can I use other words?**
▶ The word(s) you need to write are heard in the recording, but you won't hear them in the exact way you see the sentences on the page.

16. **In the Listening paper, Part 2, what happens if I misspell a word?**
▶ All answers need to be correctly spelt.

17. **In the Listening paper, Part 2, what happens if my answer is too long to fit on the answer sheet?**
▶ Most answers are single words, numbers or groups of 2–3 words. If you think the answer is longer, then it is probably incorrect.

18. **Do I have to take the Speaking test with another student? Can I choose my partner?**
▶ You can't take the test alone as your ability to discuss with another student is tested in Part 3. In Parts 1 and 2 you talk to the examiner, not to your partner, but in Part 4 you may discuss the examiner's questions with your partner. In some centres you can choose your partner, but not in others. You should check with the local organiser.

19. **In the Speaking test, Part 1, is it a good idea to prepare what I am going to say?**
▶ It's a good idea to practise, but not to prepare speeches. The examiners give marks for natural communication in English. If you give a prepared speech which doesn't answer the examiner's question, you will lose marks.

20. **In the Speaking test, Part 3, what happens if my partner makes lots of mistakes, or doesn't talk?**
▶ Don't worry. The examiners will help if necessary. You are not in competition with your partner and if you can help him or her, this will impress the examiners. Remember that Part 3 is about interaction, so you have to ask and answer questions as well as give your own opinion.